THE REMEMBERED I

The Remembered Dead explores the ways poets of the First World War – and later poets writing in the memory of that war – address the difficult question of how to remember, and commemorate, those killed in conflict. It looks closely at the way poets struggled to meaningfully represent dying, death and the trauma of witness, while responding to the pressing need for commemoration. The authors pay close attention to specific poems while maintaining a strong awareness of literary and philosophical contexts. The poems are discussed in relation to modernism and myth, other forms of commemoration (photographs, memorials), and theories of cultural memory. There is fresh analysis of canonical poets which, at the same time, challenges the confines of the canon by integrating discussion of lesser-known figures, including non-combatants and poets of later decades. The final chapter reaches beyond the war's centenary in a discussion of one remarkable commemoration of Wilfred Owen.

SALLY MINOGUE is a retired academic who is still writing. She has taught in both further and higher education. On retirement she was Principal Lecturer in English Literature at Canterbury Christ Church University. Her research interests have been eclectic, stretching from Philip Sidney's poetry to Alan Sillitoe's fiction. A common theme has been an interest in the demotic, as reflected both in colloquial language, and in the representation of working class life, in literature. This has informed her work with Andrew Palmer on First World War poetry.

ANDREW PALMER is Principal Lecturer in Modern Literature at Canterbury Christ Church University, where he has taught since 1996. He is a Senior Fellow of the Higher Education Academy. His teaching and research are focused on the literature of the twentieth century. With Sally Minogue, he has published, in addition to this book, articles on modern fiction and poetry. He has also published papers on Ray Davies's seminal Kinks album, *Arthur*, and the travel writing of Bruce Chatwin. He founded the MA in Creative Writing at Canterbury Christ Church University in 2003, and served as its Programme Director for eight years.

THE REMEMBERED DEAD

Poetry, Memory and the First World War

SALLY MINOGUE
ANDREW PALMER
Canterbury Christ Church University

CAMBRIDGE
UNIVERSITY PRESS

University Printing House, Cambridge CB2 8BS, United Kingdom

One Liberty Plaza, 20th Floor, New York, NY 10006, USA

477 Williamstown Road, Port Melbourne, VIC 3207, Australia

314-321, 3rd Floor, Plot 3, Splendor Forum, Jasola District Centre, New Delhi - 110025, India

79 Anson Road, #06-04/06, Singapore 079906

Cambridge University Press is part of the University of Cambridge.

It furthers the University's mission by disseminating knowledge in the pursuit of education, learning and research at the highest international levels of excellence.

www.cambridge.org
Information on this title: www.cambridge.org/9781108450874
DOI: 10.1017/9781108683838

© Sally Minogue and Andrew Palmer 2018

This publication is in copyright. Subject to statutory exception and to the provisions of relevant collective licensing agreements, no reproduction of any part may take place without the written permission of Cambridge University Press.

First published 2018
First paperback edition 2019

A catalogue record for this publication is available from the British Library

Library of Congress Cataloging in Publication data
Names: Minogue, Sally, author. | Palmer, Andrew, 1965– author.
Title: The remembered dead : poetry, memory and the First World War / Sally Minogue, Andrew Palmer.
Description: Cambridge; New York, NY: Cambridge University Press, 2018. | Includes bibliographical references and index.
Identifiers: LCCN 2018000610 | ISBN 9781108428675 (hardback)
Subjects: LCSH: English poetry – 20th century – History and criticism. | World War, 1914– 1918 – Great Britain – Literature and the war. | War poetry – History and criticism. | Death in literature. | Memory in literature. | Grief in literature. | Psychic trauma in literature. | Memorialization – Great Britain – History – 20th century. | War and literature – Great Britain – History – 20th century.
Classification: LCC PR605.W65M56 2018 | DDC 821/.91209358– dc23
LC record available at https://lccn.loc.gov/2018000610

ISBN 978-1-108-42867-5 Hardback
ISBN 978-1-108-45087-4 Paperback

Cambridge University Press has no responsibility for the persistence or accuracy of URLs for external or third-party internet websites referred to in this publication, and does not guarantee that any content on such websites is, or will remain, accurate or appropriate.

To the poets

that man's face will be / a mass of matter, horrid
slime – and little brittle bits –
Mary Borden

In that rich earth a richer dust concealed
Rupert Brooke

Carnage incomparable, and human squander
Wilfred Owen

There is a grave whose earth must hold too long,
too deep a stain
Charlotte Mew

Somewhere they must have gone
Isaac Rosenberg

What use / To have your body lying here?
Margaret Postgate Cole

these dead, who soon will have their dead
for burial clods heaped over
David Jones

We turned and crawled past the remembered dead
Arthur Graeme West

* * *

The songs I had are withered / Or vanished clean,
Yet there are bright tracks / Where I have been
Ivor Gurney

Contents

List of Figures		*page* viii
Acknowledgements		ix
	Introduction	1
1	'But You Are Dead!': Early Struggles over Representation	18
2	'The World's Worst Wound': Death, Consciousness and Modernism	53
3	'Fierce Imaginings': The Radical Myth-Making of David Jones and Isaac Rosenberg	81
4	Memorial Poems and the Poetics of Memorialising	110
5	'Disquieting Matter': The Unburied Corpse in War Poetry	136
6	'Horrors Here Smile': The Poem, the Photograph and the Punctum	168
7	Dulce et Decorum Est	187
Coda		213
Bibliography		217
Index		227

Figures

Cover: Image from the series *Aftermath I*. © K. J. Shepherdson. For this image of the Broadstairs War Memorial, Shepherdson took a Polaroid photograph, then lifted its fragile surface away from the backing and carefully transferred it onto watercolour paper. She describes the surface image as being 'like a small piece of fine silk or layer of skin' and the rough texture of the paper can be seen through its translucent film. This re-presentation of a public war memorial recalls the qualities of Charlotte Mew's poetic response to the Cenotaph (discussed on pages 119–22) and conjures many of the themes in this book.

1.1	Isaac Rosenberg's amendment to 'Dead Man's Dump', included in a letter to Gordon Bottomley, 20 June 1917. © The British Library Board, Loan 103/77 f31.	*page* 20
4.1	The Buttermarket War Memorial, Canterbury. Photograph © Nina Carrington.	112
4.2	Memorial tablet to the 16th Queen's Lancers, Canterbury Cathedral. Photograph © Nina Carrington.	113
5.1	'Dead Man'. Sketch by Keith Douglas. © The British Library Board, Add. 53775A No. 88.	158
7.1	'Ever Wilfred x', *La Maison Forestière Wilfred Owen* (under renovation). Photograph © Nina Carrington.	190
7.2	Shot-blasted letters, *La Maison Forestière Wilfred Owen* (under renovation). Photograph © Nina Carrington.	192
7.3	Transitioning stanzas of 'Exposure', over etched facsimile of 'Dulce et Decorum Est', *La Maison Forestière Wilfred Owen*. Photograph © Nina Carrington.	193
7.4	Reflective interior, *La Maison Forestière Wilfred Owen*. Photograph © Nina Carrington.	194

Acknowledgements

This book is the product of a long creative collaboration between its co-authors Andrew Palmer and Sally Minogue, inspired by the poets who are the subject of this work. Inevitably each of us has some personal acknowledgements to make; we'll begin with these before we go on to our joint ones. Sally first …

My first and greatest debt of gratitude is to Andrew, who restored my writing life to me. A collaboration is a balancing act, sometimes on the high wire; Andrew has always met me halfway, and kept me safe – as well as on my toes. Generous, rigorous, patient, funny, and above all gentle, writing partner and most dear friend – it has been a joy. My large, various and loving family is my bedrock, my refuge and my strength; my beloved brother and sister, Martin Minogue and Maureen Stanford, have been my constant stays, and before them our late mother and father who believed that any of us could do anything. Martin has read parts of this book with close critical attention and has given constant loving encouragement. My late partner Colin Radford is always at my elbow, cheering me on. My close friends have supported me not just in my writing – though they have done that endlessly and patiently – but more importantly in my life. Deep thanks go to Mandy Rose, Russell Jones, Trevor Gigg, Karen Shepherdson, Bill Hurley, Julie Hurley, Lesley Hardy, Will Hardy, Judy Radford, Tina Moss and Gay Mitchell; they have accepted me for what I am, and given of themselves unstintingly. Bits of this book have been spread across various kitchen tables whose owners fed and watered me and tolerated my moans – here I must thank particularly Sarah Pearson, and Daphne and Graham Day. A special thank you to my niece Emma Joussemet for our Owen pilgrimage in Ripon.

And Andrew …

I am deeply grateful to Sally for drawing me into a fruitful and rewarding writing partnership, now in its eighteenth year. In our shared endeavours, she has taught me how to work with curiosity, diligence and, above all, love for the text. I thank her also for being a friend among friends: always wise, always kind, and always there in times of difficulty and of celebration. I will always be grateful to my parents Monroe and Susette for shaping me, supporting me and allowing me to find my own path through life – and, most of all, for not steering me into the law. For many years of listening, encouragement and loving support, I thank my adored siblings, John and Fiona, and my life-long friends Gavin Shire, Darren Stewart, Murray Lohoar, Paula Fasht, Katya Jezzard-Puyraud and Amanda Smyth. I particularly thank Nathan Johnstone – old friend, fellow Cambridge author, hair-raising co-driver and musical mentor – for the long talks, the whiskies and the historical perspective. I have been fortunate indeed to find such friends, each wise in their own way and woven into my life and memories. Finally, with love and wonderment, I thank my wife, Nina Carrington – writer, photographer and escape artist – who has made this, and everything else, pointful.

Andrew also thanks Canterbury Christ Church University for supporting his work on this project by providing periods of study leave, support to attend and deliver papers at conferences at Cardiff, Oxford and Durham Universities, and funds which enabled our two trips to *La Maison Forestière Wilfred Owen*. Together, Sally and Andrew would like to thank Ray Ryan at Cambridge University Press for his patience and, most of all, for recognising our work. We also thank the two anonymous readers of the original manuscript for their kindness, positivity and constructive comments and our copy-editor, Anny Mortada, for her meticulous attention to detail. We are grateful to Hilary Fraser, Lyn Innes and Jan Montefiore for generous advice at proposal stage; and Hazel Stone for bringing us on board to co-curate the exhibition 'Remembering, We Forget: Poets, Artists and the First World War' at the Sidney Cooper Gallery, Canterbury. At a crucial stage of the book we benefitted from the facilities and quietude of Gladstone's Library.

We would both like to give special thanks to our dear friend Stefania Ciocia for her encouragement, her unfailing wit and her relentless faith in our work.

We owe a large debt of gratitude to the artist Simon Patterson, creator of *La Maison Forestière Wilfred Owen*, both for the work itself which inspired our final chapter and for his willingness to meet and talk about his work. His openness, enthusiasm and friendliness were a further inspiration. We warmly thank M. Jacky Duminy, the Mayor of Ors, for his helpful replies to our queries about the commissioning of *La Maison Forestière Wilfred Owen*, and for his tireless work in support of Wilfred Owen. We also thank the entire commune of Ors for their annual commemoration of Owen which we attended in November 2016 – the cortège, ceremony and reception were among the most moving and heartfelt commemorations we have encountered.

We are grateful to Douglas Dunn for permission to quote from 'Portrait Photograph, 1915', and for his kindly and helpful correspondence; we give warm thanks to Yusef Komunyakaa for permission to quote from 'Facing It'; and to Ian Venables and the Ivor Gurney Trust for permission to quote from Ivor Gurney's 'Swift and Slow' and 'The Songs I Had'. We particularly thank David Leighton for permission to quote from Roland Leighton's 'Violets', and for his gracious and friendly correspondence, including the sending of his pamphlet of Roland Leighton's poems (1984). We are grateful to Professor Desmond Graham and the British Library for permission to reproduce Keith Douglas's sketch, 'Dead Man'; the British Library for permission to reproduce Isaac Rosenberg's amendment to 'Dead Man's Dump'; K. J. Shepherdson for the image of Broadstairs War Memorial on our cover; and Nina Carrington for the photographs which appear in chapters 4 and 7.

A version of Chapter 4 has been published previously in the *Journal of Modern Literature* 29.3 (2006). A version of Chapter 6 has been published previously in *Word and Image* 29.2 (2013; Taylor & Francis, www.tandfonline.com).

Introduction

In Memoriam

As toilsome I wander'd Virginia's woods,
To the music of rustling leaves kick'd by my feet, (for 'twas autumn,)
I mark'd at the foot of a tree the grave of a soldier;
Mortally wounded he and buried on the retreat, (easily all could
    I understand,)
The halt of a mid-day hour, when up! no time to lose – yet this sign left,
On a tablet scrawl'd and nail'd on the tree by the grave,
Bold, cautious, true, and my loving comrade.

The impulse to mark a life that has just been lost is constitutive of being human. Here Walt Whitman catches the dash, the hurry and risk, of retreat in battle ('when up! no time to lose – '), but also in its midst that same impulse, not just to bury and so to protect and dignify the body, but to leave a trace of what the dead man meant to his living friend.[1] The personal element of this is evident; while the past participles ('scrawl'd', 'nail'd') embody the past moment, they carry also a sense of the present, the moment of scrawling and nailing – the pressing need for speed. The speaking voice embodied in the elisions contributes to this effect. And the italics, signifying the inscription, act also to emphasise to the reader what the dead man was to his friend: '*Bold, cautious, true, and my loving comrade*'.

Whitman takes us into the moment when he comes upon a marker of a life cut short. But he further takes us into the moment when the companion of the dead man decided to mark that life, with words that are both deeply personal and publicly commemorative. Two levels of time are recorded, both caught in the one inscription. Whitman shows us the

---

[1] Walt Whitman, 'As Toilsome I Wander'd Virginia's Woods', *Leaves of Grass: Comprehensive Reader's Edition*, ed. Harold W. Blodgett and Sculley Bradley (New York: New York University Press, 1965), 307.

impulse to remember and the impulse to memorialise. Remembering needs no inscription; memorialising needs an audience. Crucial to the memorial is that others will read it, others who never knew the dead man. Furthermore, the memorial marker can be read when the once living rememberer, the person who made the inscription, is also long gone.

In this way, Whitman's poem becomes a further memorial to the dead man, as the reader too stumbles upon the inscription in the act of reading the poem. For a twenty-first-century reader, the historical moment is so long gone that there could be a quaintness in that constructed encounter. But it is the peculiar quality of poetry, especially that which speaks directly and intimately to the reader, that it can carry her imaginatively into the drama of the moment. Whitman propels us into the past moment so that it seems like our present. And, as he performs this act of imaginative recreation which we call *remembering*, he also reflects on the business of remembering itself.

In his second, final stanza, Whitman redoubles the act of memory by recording the way that the inscription comes back to him:

> ... at times through changeful season and scene,
>   abrupt, alone, or in the crowded street,
> Comes before me the unknown soldier's grave, comes
>   the inscription rude in Virginia's woods,
> *Bold, cautious, true, and my loving comrade.*

This is the moment of real drama in the poem, as the inscription of a man's past life – the marker of his deadness – rears into the present consciousness. We move from the past tense of the first stanza, where the memorialising of the dead man is recorded, to the present tense of the second, where the memory of the dead man's memorial erupts into the lived life of the poet. The inscription of a man's past life becomes more present than the minutiae of the current, lived life, and thus brings thoughts about extinction into the living consciousness. As we see this death, through Whitman's poetic reflection on its commemoration, we have the fleeting understanding that we too will die.

This existential understanding (as distinct from an awareness of the brute fact of death) is a highly modern preoccupation, so it is no surprise that Whitman, for all his historical distance, struck a chord with the poets of the First World War. Ivor Gurney, Harold Monro, Isaac Rosenberg, Siegfried Sassoon and Edward Thomas were all overt admirers.[2] 'Drum Taps' in

---

[2] For a fuller account of Whitman's influence on First World War poets see Andrew Palmer and Sally Minogue, 'Modernism and First World War Poetry: Alternative Lines', *A History of Modernist Poetry*,

particular made an impression on these poets, being a sequence of poems about the current of battle; Rosenberg called it 'unique as War Poetry in my mind'.³ To grasp the ineluctability of our own extinction is one thing; it is deferrable, not necessarily immediate. But for those encountering deaths in the midst of battle, this understanding is a fearful thing, for not only is death the ultimate fate, it is imminent. The business of remembering those who died, and the dependent business of memorialising them, is in the First World War made acute by the suddenness of their deaths and the cutting-short of their lives. These factors bring into sharp focus standard features of death: that it comes to us all; that its exact moment is unknown.

In the First World War, death was intensely anticipated and while its particular moment was unknown, its likelihood in a given sector could be judged.⁴ This did not make the sudden apprehension of a particular death any less vivid or unsettling. Henri Barbusse, writing in the midst of the war, catches this exactly when he recounts crossing the battlefield with his fellow soldiers, and coming across a head, separated from its body, 'planted in the ground, a wet and bloodless head, with a heavy beard'. At first the sight is grotesque, no more – then they realise that they know the person to whom the head belongs:

> 'Ah!' we all cried together, it's Cocon!'
> When you hear of or see the death of one of those who fought by your side and lived exactly the same life, you receive a direct blow in the flesh before even understanding. It is truly as if you heard of your own destruction. It is only later that you begin to mourn.⁵

The moment of understanding another person's death is, then, full of complexity. It is a point where common humanity comes to the fore, as one person sees and knows the one thing that links all human beings, that they are mortal. There is a sense of loss, whether individual if the person is known to you, or generalised if not – Whitman catches both. There is the sudden knowledge and understanding of one's own future extinction. And at the moment when we know ourselves to be most fully, selflessly human, as we feel for a fellow human being's extinction, we selfishly fear for our own. Perhaps from all of this comes the desire to put into language

---

ed. Alex Davis and Lee M. Jenkins (Cambridge: Cambridge University Press, 2015), especially 234.
³ Isaac Rosenberg to Joseph Leftwich, 8 December 1917; *Isaac Rosenberg*, ed. Vivien Noakes (Oxford: Oxford University Press, 2008), 355.
⁴ As Denis Winter clarifies, losses were very much greater at particular times and in particular battles. See Winter, *Death's Men: Soldiers of the Great War* (London: Penguin, 1979) for useful chapters on the actuality of death and injury at the Front, and the psychological effect of that on combatants.
⁵ Henri Barbusse, *Under Fire*, trans. W. Fitzwater Wray (1917; London: Dent, 1965), 265.

something about the life lost. As is also evident from both Whitman and Barbusse, these feelings are brought into sharp focus by death in battle. Whatever our feelings about war, whether we see the death as heroic or futile, or both, the sudden cutting down of life in battle seizes us, perhaps partly because that life is often young, and death comes well before the usual allotted time. Because of this, the impulse to memorialise can ally itself powerfully with the deeply conservative desire to keep the dead person alive or, at least, to keep open the possibility that the dead person can, in some sense, return to us. Both forces, as we shall see, permeate the poetry of the First World War.

All these elements are further intensified where the writer – the one doing the scrawling – is himself in imminent danger of suffering the same fate. As Santanu Das reminds us: 'The trench experience was one of the most sustained and systematic shattering of the human sensorium: it stripped man of the protective layers of civilization and thrust his naked, fragile body between the ravages of industrial modernity, on the one hand, and the chaos of formless matter, on the other.'[6] In this situation, where 'Death could drop from the dark / As easily as song',[7] soldier-poets such as Wilfred Owen, Isaac Rosenberg, Ivor Gurney and David Jones – and non-combatants like Mary Borden, Harold Monro and Wilfrid Gibson who were close enough and/or imaginative enough – seek to commemorate dead soldiers in ways which evade comfortable pieties and reach for those complexities. If the cataclysmic nature of the war was experienced most directly by combatants, or by those close to the action as were many medical workers, its effect was also powerful on those at home who held particular soldiers dear or, if a male non-combatant, felt the strains of his position. A different dimension of the experience of remembering dead soldiers is expressed in poems by those who could experience the war only through fear of loss, and loss itself. The imaginative effect of the war on poets at the time cut across barriers of experience.

Starting with these poets of the war years, and moving beyond to poetry written in the succeeding century, this study is concerned primarily and specifically with the ways those who died in the First World War have been commemorated in poetry. The poem written by a First World War combatant poet about the loss of a friend in the thick of battle is the

---

[6] Santanu Das, 'War Poetry and the Realm of the Senses: Owen and Rosenberg', *The Oxford Handbook of British and Irish War Poetry*, ed. Tim Kendall (Oxford: Oxford University Press, 2007), 74.
[7] 'Returning, we hear the larks' in Rosenberg, *Isaac Rosenberg*, 113.

equivalent of Whitman's discovered '*Bold, cautious, true, and my loving comrade*'. This may be a specific memorial to a specific man, such as Alan Mackintosh's 'In Memoriam Private D. Sutherland' or Siegfried Sassoon's 'The Last Meeting'.[8] Such a poem is the ur-text of our discussions. But as we have suggested above, there is far more to the memorial poem, the poem that gives some sort of account of someone who has (or those many who have) just died.

The memorial poem, being a reflection in language, is a deeply self-conscious act, often set in a formal and thematic tradition. Many of the First World War poets were steeped in the classical tradition, with its set pieces of heroic action, and its often formulaic responses to death in battle.[9] The broader elegiac tradition, with classical roots but developed in a particular way in English poetry from Milton through to the Romantic poets, was also a profound influence. Faced with the grotesque reminders of what happens to the body in sudden, violent death, First World War poets grappled with a poetic inheritance which didn't seem to fit their current experience. Sometimes they took refuge in the simplicities of that inheritance; the more interesting examples are those where we can see poets asking questions of the traditions, disrupting formal certainties, and struggling to find new forms and languages to fit new modes of consciousness.

Our title, *The Remembered Dead*, is indicative of that struggle. The phrase is taken from Arthur Graeme West's poem 'The Night Patrol', and he uses it in a way that deliberately unsettles our understanding of remembrance. West is an interesting figure. He is little known as a poet, and is probably best known for his posthumous *The Diary of a Dead Officer* (1919), in which he expresses constant uncertainty about the rightness of the war and whether he should be fighting in it, as well as voicing his deep dislike of the condition of soldiery. He enlisted as a private soldier, but was recommended for officer training, and it was during that training that he conceived a deep disbelief in the rightness of the war.[10] Nonetheless, and

---

[8] Ewart Alan Mackintosh, 'In Memoriam Private D. Sutherland killed in Action in the German Trench, May 16, 1916, and the Others who Died' in George Walter (ed.), *The Penguin Book of First World War Poetry* (London: Penguin Books, 2006), 95–6. (While Mackintosh refers in both the full title and the body of the poem to the others who died alongside Sutherland, the initial address of the poem to the dead man's father, and the repeated use of his forename, David, makes it *ad hominem*.) Siegfried Sassoon, 'The Last Meeting', *Collected Poems 1908–1956* (London: Faber & Faber, 1961), 35–40.

[9] By 'First World War poets' we refer to all poets of the period.

[10] See his account of his agonised thought process in August 1916: Arthur Graeme West, *The Diary of a Dead Officer* (London: George Allen & Unwin, 1919), 50–5.

in spite of deciding at key points that he would register his dissent, he returned to the Front as an officer, and was killed in 1917.

In September 1916, he was in the front line and writing about the effect on his men of seeing their comrades killed under heavy shelling. For the most part, he describes their traumatised state while representing himself as the calm officer walking among them with words of comfort. One survivor 'mutter[s] away on the firing-step like a nervous rabbit and making vague gestures with his hands and head', others 'cowered and trembled'; West meanwhile 'talked to them and did [his] best to comfort them' and later sits smoking a cigarette in order to 'soothe the men simply by being quiet'.[11] But he begins to touch on his own trauma when he describes the process of trying to dig out buried men:

> you dig and scratch and uncover a grey, dirty face, pitifully drab and ugly, the eyes closed, the whole thing limp and mean-looking. This is the devil of it, that a man is not only killed, but made to look so vile and filthy in death, so futile and meaningless that you hate the sight of him.[12]

In 'The Night Patrol', West considers the corpses around him in a different way.[13] The poem begins in the thick of night-time reconnaissance. The first words of the poem – 'Over the top!' – carry the sense of fear and excitement of a daytime attack, but this is one of several reversals of expectation that operate in the poem. Written in blank verse, the poem nonetheless carries both the immediate speech of the officer's instructions to the night patrol, and the interior narrative of those on patrol, deliberately gathered in the pronoun 'we', though the controlling consciousness is that of the individual poet/narrator. The importance of the 'we', however, is to suggest both the communality of the patrol and of the experience; this is no singular, heightened consciousness at work – this is what men saw and felt. By line 12 the 'we' has disappeared and instead a general observation and consciousness are depicted:

> Packs, rifles, bayonets, belts, and haversacks,
> Shell fragments, and the huge whole forms of shells
> Shot fruitlessly – and everywhere the dead.

But the dead are not objects of pity or distress, or even reminders of imminent extinction as in Barbusse. What West fixes on is their 'vile

---

[11] Ibid., 66–7.
[12] Ibid., 67.
[13] Ibid., 81–3.

sickly smell of rottenness'; he devotes eight lines to their smell. Just as 'everywhere the dead', so 'the dead men stank through all, / Pungent and sharp'. He even describes the fading of their smell as his patrol passes further away from them. There is something discomfiting about the tone of the description; the intent emphasis on the smell reminds us that there is little awareness of these bodies as dead human beings – they are dead matter. Even Barbusse, with his attempt to describe the alienating feeling given by meeting the dead body of someone he has known, retains in doing so a sense of common humanity – that is what disturbs him when he recognises, not just a dead head, but the dead head of Cocon. But the narrator of 'The Night Patrol' has abandoned any sense of the bodies as humans. We think briefly that there is compassion in the lines 'They lay, all clothed, / Each in some new and piteous attitude'. But the run-on line that follows puts us right: 'That we well marked to guide us back'. The bodies are 'marked' only as landmarks, the best signposts to be had in a landscape stripped of distinguishing natural features. The narrator identifies in scrupulous detail different dead individuals or groups, but only and specifically to act as guide points back to the home trench.

There is a certain knowingness in the alienated consciousness West voices; he wants the reader to know what war has done to its soldiers, reading the trench landscape in terms of the geography created by different kinds of dead bodies. But this is also a poem about survival:

> We lay in shelter of the last dead man,
> Ourselves as dead, and heard their shovels ring.

The shovels belong to the Germans; playing dead, under cover of 'the last dead man', means that the men on the night patrol might survive. The consciousness which sees dead men simply as useful way-markers and sources of cover is pragmatic; the dead can be used to help the living survive. And the night patrol does survive:

> We turned and crawled past the remembered dead:
> Past him and him, and them and him, until
> For he lay some way apart, we caught the scent
> Of the Crusader and slid past his legs,
> And through the wire and home, and got our rum.

The flatness of tone and emotion is almost comical. Yet underlying the whole is a sense of irony, an understanding that this is not how it should be. 'The remembered dead' are not honoured as individuals, they are turned into useful objects. But as readers we would not feel the shock of this without the other, honouring and honourable sense of 'the remembered dead' underlying it.

'The Night Patrol' is the converse of Whitman's 'As Toilsome I Wander'd Virginia's Woods'. But, for all that, the Whitman sentiment underlies West's poem – for what West highlights is the way the extremes of battle and the constant currency of death in the First World War sapped men of even the most natural of feelings, compassion for the death of a fellow man and the desire to remember the dead. This is all the more clear if we set 'The Night Patrol' alongside a similar poem, Max Plowman's 'The Dead Soldiers'. Plowman also describes the corpses strewn across No Man's Land as a series of markers – 'A crescent moon of men who showed the way' – and movingly creates an image of a whole group of men killed at one time, almost carelessly:

> Just as the scythe had caught them, there they lay,
> A sheaf for Death, ungarnered and untied.[14]

Plowman describes, in words similar to West's, the dead men's 'Fantastic forms, in postured attitudes, / twisted and bent'. The images are powerful, and yet Plowman is unable to pull himself fully away from the consolations of the elegiac tradition. Where West's image of 'an archipelago of corrupt fragments' emphasises both the navigational utility and the inert non-humanity of the corporeal remains, Plowman's lunar image – 'a crescent moon of men' – seems to romanticise and beautify the dead, and reiterates their humanity. West's speaker notices the dead cornstalks beneath his body which 'No man had reaped', but pointedly resists the metaphorical connection with the uncollected bodies; Plowman succumbs with the biblical image of dead men as mown grass 'ungarnered'. Where West's speaker has forgotten the humanity of the objects by which he steers, Plowman struggles to remember it: 'Their individual hopes my thought eludes / But each man had a hope to call his own'. West emphasises the stink while Plowman limits himself to the less visceral sense of sight and, in the closing lines, shifts into argumentation:

> God in every one of you was slain;
> For killing men is always killing God,
> Though life destroyed shall come to life again
> And loveliness rise from the sodden sod.

---

[14] 'The Dead Soldiers' in Max Plowman, *A Lap Full of Seed*, (Orford: Blackwell, 1917), 75–6.

Plowman here makes use of a Shelleyan trope which appears in a number of poems from this period, that of the corpse rising up as flora, which has its origins in 'Adonais', Shelley's elegy on the death of John Keats. Shelley consoles himself and the reader with the idea that 'The leprous corpse ... / Exhales itself with flowers of gentle breath', which, as the poem later confirms, embodies spiritual as well as physical regeneration.[15] However, for Plowman the consolations of elegy are eclipsed by his pacifist convictions.[16] For all its power to move us, 'The Dead Soldiers' retains familiar poetic tropes which search for meaning in soldiers' deaths. West's deadpan conclusion, with its unspoken irony indicating that all is changed utterly, is the more radical. Like both Plowman and West, the poets discussed in this book reconsider and re-engage with the poetic tools they have inherited, often struggling to reshape them, and sometimes refusing them, in order to commemorate meaningfully those who have been killed.

Cultural Memory

If, in this book, we are often focused on the ways individual poets have worked within and pushed against their poetic traditions, we remain strongly aware of wider cultural forces which shape our experience and understanding of 'First World War poetry' as a body of work and, by extension, the commemoration that goes on within it. For 'First World War poetry' is a key element in the socio-cultural memory of the war and its dead. In using the term 'socio-cultural memory', we refer to a body of ideas originating in the 1920s, whose principal exponent was Maurice Halbwachs, and to developments of his theory in the latter part of the twentieth century. Common to this work is an emphasis on the social and collective nature of memory, and the way it is shaped by ideological forces, even when it appears to be individual and personal. Halbwachs argues that, 'The succession of our remembrances, of even our most personal ones, is always explained by changes occurring in our relationships to various collective milieus – in short, by the transformations these milieus undergo separately and as a whole.'[17] For Halbwachs then, memory is

---

[15] 'Adonais' in *Selected Poems of Percy Bysshe Shelley* (London: Oxford University Press, 1960), 314–31; see especially stanza 20 (321–2) and stanza 42 (328).
[16] This poem is an early expression of Plowman's dissent, which led to a courageous refusal to serve in 1918. See the biographical note in Dominic Hibberd and John Onions (eds), *The Winter of the World: Poems of the Great War* (London: Constable, 2008), 323.
[17] Maurice Halbwachs, *The Collective Memory*, trans. F. I. and V. Y. Ditter (1950; New York: Harper and Row, 1980), 49.

always socially determined, even where it appears to be individual and personal, and this determination inheres foremost in the influence of social frameworks to which the individual belongs, the most important of which are the social groups to which she belongs: 'No memory is possible outside frameworks used by people living in society to determine and retrieve their recollections.'[18] Halbwachs's concept of collective memory includes both the formation of memory and its transmission, and one distinction he makes between memory and history is that of the span of time: memory (as defined within a group) has a limit, at most, of a hundred years: the utmost span of a life. History, conversely, stands as a sort of sentinel separate from the mobility and interactivity of social memory. Building on these ideas, Aleida and Jan Assmann accept Halbwachs's concept of collective memory but make a distinction within it between *communicative* and *cultural* memory: the former allows for the structures of the personal, individual and everyday in the formation and expression of memory; it is the means by which groups 'conceive their unity and peculiarity through a common image of their past'.[19] As with Halbwachs's notion of collective memory, communicative memory has a 'limited temporal horizon ... [that] does not extend more than eighty to (at the very most) one hundred years into the past'. Cultural memory, conversely, is not time-limited. It refers to 'fixed points ... fateful events of the past, whose memory is maintained through cultural formation (texts, rites, monuments)'.[20] The Assmanns ascribe to 'cultural memory' the performative attributes of communal, ceremonial memory and its transmission.[21] They further define cultural memory as comprising 'that body of reusable texts, images, and rituals specific to each society in each epoch, whose "cultivation" serves to stabilize and convey that society's self-image'.[22] One might almost call this state-sponsored memory. It is

---

[18] Halbwachs, *On Collective Memory*, ed. and trans. Lewis A. Coser (Chicago: University of Chicago Press, 1992), 43. Note that, though this title is similar to *The Collective Memory*, Coser's edition is actually largely a translation of Halbwachs's earlier works, *Les cadres sociaux de la mémoire* (Paris: Presses Universitaires de France, 1952), originally published in *Les Travaux de L'Année Sociologique* (Paris: F. Alcan, 1925), and *La topographie légendaire des évangiles en terre Saint: Étude de mémoire collective* (Paris: Presses Universitaires de France, 1941).
[19] Jan Assmann, 'Collective Memory and Cultural Identity', trans. John Czaplicka, *New German Critique*, 65 (1995), 127. Although he is the sole author of this article, Jan Assmann uses the pronoun 'we' throughout, explaining in a footnote that these ideas about communicative and cultural memory were formed jointly with Aleida Assmann.
[20] Ibid., 129.
[21] Ibid., 126–9.
[22] Ibid., 132.

in this sense that we use the term 'cultural memory', which is in turn underpinned by Halbwachs's theories of collective memory.

The First World War is, perhaps, the supreme 'fixed point' or 'fateful event' of our modern age. Our understanding of its significance is shaped in on-going processes by 'texts, rites, monuments' and, at the heart of these interventions lies our commemoration of the dead. As we move beyond the war's centenary – and so beyond the living testimony crucial to communicative memory – it is freshly important to be alert to its formation as a cultural memory and, in particular, to the ways in which the dead are represented and commemorated.

Amidst forms of commemoration organised by governments, town councils or other civic organisations, *writing* appears to have the potential for more independent expression and, for this, we value it highly. Roland Barthes makes this distinction in his *Mourning Diary*. On a journey to bring his mother's body, three days after her death, from Paris to Urt in France's south-west corner, he stops for lunch at Sorigny. In his diary, he notes: 'I walk a few steps with Jean-Louis on one side of the square (with its hideous monument to the dead), bare ground, the smell of rain, the sticks. And yet, something like a savour of life (because of the sweet smell of the rain), the very first discharge, like a momentary palpitation.'[23] Suffering the first stages of a very present and painful grief, Barthes is repelled by the monument in the town square. He experiences a brief glimpse of a life beyond grief *in spite* of its presence.[24] Barthes does not explain why he finds the monument hideous but we can see some of its problems. The French historian Antoine Prost has written that 'war memorials embody an intricate system of signs' including their location, design and inscriptions.[25] Prost notes that: 'The most common type of monument ... was the naked stele, erected in a space symbolically dominated by the town hall, listing the names of the dead together with a time-honored inscription: "The commune of ... [or simply the name of the town] to its children, dead for France".'[26]

---

[23] Roland Barthes, *Mourning Diary*, text established and annotated by Nathalie Léger, trans. Richard Howard (2010; London: Notting Hill Editions, 2011), 13.
[24] Some five and a half months after passing through Sorigny, Barthes writes of the 'Necessity of the "Monument"', but he has in mind the idea that his own writing is a kind of monument (ibid., 113).
[25] Antoine Prost, 'Monuments to the Dead', *Realms of Memory: The Construction of the French Past*, vol. 2: *Traditions*, under the direction of Pierre Nora, English language edition ed. Lawrence D. Kritzman and trans. Arthur Goldhammer (New York: Columbia University Press, 1997), 309–10.
[26] Ibid., 311. The second ellipsis and the square brackets are Prost's.

The monument at Sorigny, in its location and inscriptions, matches these commonest features. In addition, on the 'naked stele' (or block), there is a statue of a muscular angel bearing on his left shoulder the body of a dead soldier. The monument has a civic function which does not seem to speak to real, personal grief. Its familiar inscription – '*A ses enfants morts pour la France*' – is ideologically loaded in almost every word: the pronoun *ses* sees parenthood appropriated by the town hall, suggesting that these men were the town's to sacrifice and that the loss is borne by the town; the word *enfants* infantilises the dead, as if their deaths were a tragic accident rather than the outcome of incompetent politics; and *morts pour la France* challenges the patriotism of anyone who demurs. The angel, with its powerful limbs and enormous wings, suggests the dead are borne up in death rather than mulched down.[27]

The shortcomings of the monument at Sorigny are all too evident when we remember Whitman's poem. Its retrospective, public nature and the ubiquity of its design mean that it lacks the moving specificity of 'a tablet scrawl'd and nail'd on the tree by the grave'. Its location in the town square introduces at least an element of propaganda whereas the hasty memorial lost in Virginia's woods speaks of a real, searing grief and a personal need to commemorate. As Whitman's writing seeks to share with readers the powerful effect of the genuine memorial, so Barthes's writings about loss seek to fill the gap left by the formulaic memorial.[28]

For those who place a high value on literary writing, then, the temptation is to see poetry as the opposite of the civic memorial: a genuine expression of remembrance and grief as opposed to an attempt to create cultural memory by committee. And yet, for each poet we discuss, there is an internal tug of war between the broad forces of cultural memory and their personal understanding – which is also, of course, shaped by collective memory. Furthermore, poems reach readers through a process of canon formation which is subject to the agency of publishers, newspapers and politicians directing policy in education. Perhaps more than any other body of literary writing, the poetry of the First World War comes to us through anthologies, each of which makes a claim about which poems are significant, effective and worth preserving. Several critics have traced the development of this canon through anthologies from 1914 onwards.[29] One

---

[27] We discuss the relationship between war memorials and war poems in more detail in Chapter 5.
[28] Barthes writes about his grief in both *Mourning Diary* and *Camera Lucida* (1981). We return to the latter in Chapter 6.
[29] See Hugh Haughton, 'Anthologizing War', *Oxford Handbook*, ed. Kendall, 421–44.

of the most influential interventions remains Brian Gardner's anthology *Up the Line to Death* (1964), which can serve as an example of the workings of cultural memory. This collection of poems has been a set text in British school curricula for many years and, as such, has had a powerful influence in the creation of cultural memory about the war. Tim Kendall, in an excoriating blog entry of 2010, denounced this anthology because, in pursuing its goal of demonstrating 'the wickedness and futility of all wars' it excludes great poems which do not fit, while including second-rate work that does.

> The possibility that soldiers experienced the War in a multitude of ways is quickly disallowed: 'the lice, cold, hunger, fear, wet, and misery were the same', Gardner assures us. And what Gardner calls the 'journey' from the 'idealism' of 1914 to bitterness and anger after the Somme is mapped sketchily but unquestioningly. Gardner selects and regiments his poems so that they will make that particular route-march without the slightest risk of ever straying from the path.[30]

Kendall is incensed by the inclusion of some poor poetry to support a reductive narrative while the less easily herded Ivor Gurney is excluded: 'the thought that the poet of "Pain" and "To His Love" has been ignored in favour of slop by Edward Shanks and Robert Nichols is almost unbearable'.[31]

Kendall's anger about this one anthology is a symptom of a wider point: that First World War poetry is a key element in British cultural memory of the war which is both constructed and contested. In this respect, it can be understood as a *lieu de mémoire*. This term, coined in the 1980s by the historian Pierre Nora, indicates 'sites' that function symbolically to represent or codify a national sense of memory. He defines the term thus: 'A *lieu de mémoire* is any significant entity, whether material or non-material in nature, which by dint of human will or the work of time has become a symbolic element of the memorial heritage of any community.'[32] Such *lieux* may be monuments, national symbols and

---

[30] Tim Kendall, 'Brian Gardner: Up the Line to Death', *War Poetry* blog, 9 October 2010, http://war-poets.blogspot.co.uk/2010/10/brian-gardner-up-line-to-death.html.

[31] Kendall's own *Poetry of the First World War: An Anthology* (Oxford: Oxford University Press, 2013) is a valuable contribution supported by excellent scholarly apparatus. That said, some of Kendall's choices are also contentious; for example, the heavy weighting towards Kipling.

[32] Pierre Nora, *Realms of Memory: The Construction of the French Past*, vol. 1: *Conflicts and Divisions*, English language edition ed. Lawrence D. Kritzman and trans. Arthur Goldhammer (New York: Columbia University Press, 1992), xvii. See especially Nora's introductory chapter, 'Between Memory and History'.

colours, ritual events, concepts – and certain literary texts.³³ Such texts are *lieux de mémoire* because:

> the effects of time and the vicissitudes of history have enlarged our understanding of memory in such a way as to bring out new meanings in the selected works. It is this perpetual sedimentation of new meanings, this permanent metamorphosis, that turns a book already invested with a certain form of memory into a veritable *lieu de mémoire*.³⁴

Nora gives the example of Ernest Lavisse's *Histoire de France*, the textbook 'from which, between 1880 and 1914, fifteen million French children learned what they were supposed to know about the history of France'.³⁵ In the same volume, Antoine Compagnon uses the same concept to characterise Marcel Proust's *Remembrance of Things Past*: 'We turn certain books, like … *A la recherche du temps perdu* into very special *lieux de mémoire*, and they become essential to us because they help, because literature helps, us to think of memory in terms other than historical.'³⁶ For those of us who have used *Up the Line to Death* as pupils or teachers, it may seem something like Lavisse's *Histoire* – a ubiquitous and influential element in the cultural memory of the war. The body of anthologised First World War poetry has functioned like Proust's multi-volume work, complementing the historical account to construct cultural memory.

Thus, when a poet's work appears in an anthology like *Up the Line to Death*, the poet gets co-opted into the *lieu de mémoire*. We can see this happening most clearly with Wilfred Owen. Mark Rawlinson has argued of Owen that: 'his normative status threatens to reduce his poems to convergent paraphrases and memorable epigrams … his work is misremembered or misrecognised as a kind of attenuated and graphic combat story; and his lines are widely valued, in defiance of the evidence, for their refusal or transcendence of the merely poetic.'³⁷

---

[33] Nora says that the term *lieu de mémoire* has, in French, 'profound connotations' and, in a note to its first appearance in an English-language journal, he thanked the editors and his translator 'for conserving the term in French, while occasionally using *site* as an English equivalent' (Nora, 'Note', *Representations*, 26 (1989), 25). The translation of *lieu(x) de mémoire* must have been much discussed. In Nora's Preface and General Introduction to the English Language edition, he sticks with the untranslated phrase *lieu(x) de mémoire* when talking about the concept, reserving *Realms of Memory* for the title of the whole work. The English 'realms' is more appropriate in the plural; the singular 'realm' doesn't quite answer to the particularity, yet allusiveness, of '*lieu*'.

[34] Nora, *Realms of Memory*, vol. 2, xi.

[35] Ibid., xi.

[36] Antoine Compagnon, 'Marcel Proust's *Remembrance of Things Past*', in ibid., 246.

[37] Mark Rawlinson, 'Wilfred Owen', *Oxford Handbook*, ed. Kendall, 114–15.

He quotes Desmond Graham's complaint that ' "we tend to read Owen slackly, assuming that we already know what he's saying" ', and describes how Owen's poetry is taught in schools to a utilitarian agenda.[38] This is the effect on poetry of cultural memory formation. The sharp edges are blurred, the useful bits gain prominence, complexity and contradiction are quietly set aside. Individual poems, once part of the *lieu de mémoire* called 'First World War poetry', come closer to the memorial at Sorigny. Conversely, however, the process of expansion and transformation in social, cultural and literary critical attitudes over the past century has led to a broadening of the First World War canon to include non-combatant poets, women poets, poets from the then Empire and poetry in popular forms such as the trench songs that Kendall includes in his anthology. Alongside this extension of the body of work available to us under the general heading 'First World War poetry', changes of understanding have allowed us to see elements in the central canon which might previously have been ignored. Most notable here is our far greater awareness of the homosocial and homoerotic dimensions of certain poems.[39] Whether the process of cultural formation has narrowed our response in certain cases or broadened it in others, individual poems remain just that – poems; by careful reading we can reclaim their complexity, nuance and resistance to overarching cultural narratives. This understanding informs all the discussions which follow.

In this book, then, we are closely concerned with the way that soldiers who were killed (principally but not exclusively in the First World War) are remembered in poetry. The theories of memory provided by Halbwachs, Jan and Aleida Assmann, and Nora remain in our discussions, secondary to the poetry itself. Sometimes individual poems subvert monolithic theories; where they do, it is the poems that interest us. Nonetheless, these significant ideas are central to our intellectual understanding of the function of memory in the twentieth century and beyond. In our first chapter, we show how some poetry of the First World War was key to the early formation of dominant ideas about that conflict, and so to ways of thinking about those killed and their commemoration. We move on to consider a range of poems which subvert the dominant collective memory of the war, offering challenging representations of those killed to create

---

[38] Quoted in ibid., 115. Original source: Desmond Graham, *The Truth of War: Owen, Blunden, Rosenberg* (Manchester: Carcanet, 1984), 24.

[39] See, for example, Adrian Caesar's *Taking it Like a Man: Suffering, Sexuality and the War Poets* (Manchester, Manchester University Press, 1993), and Martin Taylor's anthology, *Lads: Love Poetry of the Trenches* (London: Constable, 1989).

alternative forms of remembering. Our second chapter continues to focus on poetry emerging directly from the First World War, and considers its relation to the dominant literary movement of that period, modernism – a relation which has consistently been downplayed. Here our close concern is with the ways in which the omnipresence of death and the difficulty of writing commemorative poetry in a climate of human obliteration led to poets finding new forms and languages to answer to what were effectively new states of consciousness. We argue that this poetry is on a continuum with modernism rather than in opposition to it.

In Chapter 3 we move from wide angle to close-up, focusing on two major poets, David Jones and Isaac Rosenberg, who in certain ways stand at odds to even the expanded canon of First World War poetry. These poets look hard at the dying and the dead body, and they each in their own way reinterpret the use of myth in responding to death, whilst resisting false consolation. In Chapter 4, our pivotal chapter, we expand from the particularity of the historical moment of the First World War to consider broader poetic responses to the issue of how to remember those killed in battle, which use the war memorial as their initial subject. We also pan out from the specifics of English culture to include American poems about memorials, in order to set poetry about First World War memorialisation in a wider cultural context. The way we remember those who die in battle remains central, but the chapter, like the poems it discusses, stands at one remove from the dead themselves, reflecting on the whole business of memorialisation from a historical distance. An inherent inflexibility in the memorial monument is here contrasted with the greater flexibility and complicatedness available to the poet writing in the twentieth century, but looking back at war rather than writing from its midst.

In Chapter 5, we consider the difficulty poets faced in representing the battlefield's unburied corpse, drawing on Julia Kristeva's notion of the abject. We trace a series of strategies through some of the wartime anthologies, and then in the work of Owen, Blunden and Rosenberg before focusing closely on Keith Douglas, the pre-eminent English poet of the Second World War, and his poetic relationship with his First World War predecessors, Rosenberg in particular. We argue that Douglas's originality lies in recognising the abjection of the corpse whilst retaining Rosenberg's attention to its actuality. If Rosenberg looks hard at the dead body, Douglas observes it with a colder eye, without submitting to the despair of the abject.

In Chapter 6, those who died in the First World War again become our central subject. However, all the (later twentieth-century) poems we discuss have as their initial subject a photograph relating to those who fought and died in the conflict. Like the poets in Chapter 4, these poets use another form of commemoration as the lens through which to see those who died, and to reflect on how we remember them. We look at the ekphrastic poem as a mode for reflecting on death, and on the particular relation to memory that the photograph provides. Roland Barthes's reflections on death, memory and photography in *Camera Lucida* are significant in this chapter.

The centenary period 2014–18 has brought the issues we consider in this book to the fore of people's everyday lives, at the very point when we move beyond communicative memory. In Chapter 7, we look in detail at one twenty-first century work, Simon Patterson's *La Maison Forestière Wilfred Owen*, which commemorates Owen by opening his poetry to new generations. This chapter closes with a fresh look at 'Dulce et Decorum Est', a poem about remembering the dying, the dead and those who witnessed their deaths, and considers the way the poem is revivified by new ways of seeing a hundred years on.

This book has at its heart individual poems which offer challenging representations of those killed in a conflict now a hundred years distant, to create alternative forms of remembering. How we remember those who died in the First World War is, in this centenary period, a vital, current issue, when young soldiers are still dying on behalf of their countries or ideologies. We believe that the poetry that came from the First World War, and the subsequent poetry which reflects upon it or upon the way we remember the dead, is similarly vital and current, and in giving it our close attention we seek to honour 'the remembered dead' in as honest a way as possible.

CHAPTER I

'But You Are Dead!'
Early Struggles over Representation

> – These are men whose minds the Dead have ravished.
> Memory fingers in their hair of murders,
> Multitudinous murders they once witnessed.
> Wading sloughs of flesh these helpless wander,
> Treading blood from lungs that had loved laughter.
> Always they must see these things and hear them,
> Batter of guns and shatter of flying muscles,
> Carnage incomparable, and human squander
> Rucked too thick for these men's extrication.[1]

In 'Mental Cases', Wilfred Owen gives us an unflinching account of the indelible images of violent death which continued to haunt some men's minds even when they were removed from the actualities of the war. In depicting the particular hell of these 'mental cases', he also presents us with the close, detailed observation of death which most combatants experienced. 'Wading sloughs of flesh' and 'treading blood from lungs' remind us that soldiers might be literally knee-deep in the bodies of others; 'shatter of flying muscles' catches the way flesh could be blown to fragments, spattering the still-living. 'Carnage incomparable, and human squander / Rucked too thick' emphasises the sheer quantity of the butchery. Here, Owen sees soldiers' deaths uncompromisingly as 'multitudinous murders' but, in other poems, he variously focuses on the dead body with an angry distress born of tenderness ('Futility'), treats the ubiquity of death with bitter irony in the voice of the ordinary soldier ('A Terre'), catches the moment of death in furious battle ('Spring Offensive') and imagines the dead of both armies conversing in the caverns of hell ('Strange Meeting'). And that is only one poet. In this first chapter we foreground the central subject of our book – the way we remember through

---

[1] 'Mental Cases' in Wilfred Owen, *The Complete Poems and Fragments*, 2 vols, ed. Jon Stallworthy (London: Chatto & Windus, 2013), 169.

poetry the soldiers killed in the First World War – by looking at a range of poetic representations, written during the war and just afterwards.

All poets living through the First World War, whether combatant or not, were faced with the task of representing experiences which were so far from normality that they must have sometimes seemed to defy representation. In 'Mental Cases' Owen reaches for a grotesquerie of language, resonating with a deliberately Shakespearean timbre, to answer to the excesses of tragic horror he depicts. We see poets of this era continually seeking different forms and voices, sometimes stumbling, sometimes erring towards bathos or sentimentality, as they try to give expression to what might seem inexpressible.

As the memory theorist Jan Assmann suggests: 'The rupture between yesterday and today, in which the choice to obliterate or preserve must be considered, is experienced in its most basic and ... primal form in death.'[2] This imperative was intensified on the front line, where death was ever-present and often both sudden and obliterating. To witness such deaths at close quarters must have been traumatic enough in itself; to this was added the imminent likelihood of one's own death. As Edmund Blunden writes, 'The more monstrous fate / Shadows our own, the mind swoons doubly burdened', reflecting the fact that, when a poet wrote about the death of a fellow soldier, he was also imagining his own extinction.[3] The existential vertigo this could produce was a challenge to capture, and it is not surprising that poets sometimes chose to veil or elide it. At the same time, combatant poets – indeed all combatants – had little time or space in which to reflect properly, as is evident sometimes in the content of the poems, but more notably in the materiality of surviving texts. While some poetry was written on leave or in training camps, or behind the lines, much was also written in the front line, on scraps of paper, backs of envelopes, with stubs of pencils (see Figure 1.1).

So the poet was faced with the large questions of life and death, made inescapable by the present actuality of the corpse – 'the lawn green flies upon the red flesh madding' – yet he might barely have had time to put pencil to paper, if indeed he had pencil and paper.[4]

There was the further problem that the poetic tradition on which these writers characteristically drew often failed when they tried to use it to

---

[2] Jan Assmann, *Cultural Memory and Early Civilisation: Writing, Remembrance and Political Imagination* (Cambridge: Cambridge University Press, 2011), 19.
[3] 'Third Ypres' in Edmund Blunden, *Poems 1914–30* (London: Cobden-Sanderson, 1930), 156.
[4] Ibid.

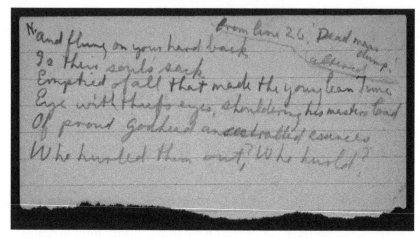

Figure 1.1   Isaac Rosenberg's amendment to 'Dead Man's Dump', included in a letter to Gordon Bottomley, 20 June 1917.
© The British Library Board, Loan 103/77 f31.

express their current experiences and reflections. The classical and epic repertoire was enmeshed with deeply heroic values which the mechanical slaughter of the First World War undermined; the Romantic poets' pastoral redemption was swamped by the muddy wasteland of the Front. Edgell Rickword comments on the gulf between the literary tradition and the actuality of death on the line in 'Trench Poets', where the speaker attempts to cheer a corpse with various poems from the Metaphysical tradition:

> I tried the Elegies one day,
> but he, because he heard me say:
> 'What needst thou have more covering than a man?'
> grinned nastily, so then I knew
> the worms had got his brains at last.[5]

The issue of representation was then both a human and an artistic problem for the poets of the First World War. It was compounded by the demands of public representation at home which remained true to the ideal of honour and noble sacrifice (even when, as sometimes with press reportage, those writing were privy to the more complex underlying picture). Such representation often issued in government-led propaganda, with a number

---

[5] Edgell Rickword, 'Trench Poets' in Tim Kendall (ed.), *Poetry of the First World War: An Anthology* (Oxford University Press: Oxford, 2013), 219.

of prominent poets enlisted in its service.⁶ The misrepresentations of propaganda, combined with the censorship and self-censorship at the Front, made it difficult for those at home to have any idea of the realities of trench warfare. The bursting apart of values along with bodies did not penetrate the Home Front except in rare cases, and the private representations of non-combatants struggled with the realities of a world entirely other than that experienced at home. This struggle presented itself in an acute form to those who were writing poetry in response to the war. And this in part revolved also round competing ideas of poetic representation – what a poem should be at this time, and how to represent war and the experience of war in a poetry that would be seen as good.

In looking at the way these poets represented dying, death and those killed, we also begin to consider the developing processes of remembrance and commemoration. The poets writing out of the heat of the First World War were forming the first literary expressions of a shared grief. The nature of remembering and remembrance was an inherent concern for any poet in the front line: these were poets acutely aware of posterity, not so much in relation to their own poetic reputation, but in terms of constructing a memory. This memory might have been specific, personal, individually commemorative, or it might have been more overtly political and historical, seeking to represent a particular view of what death meant in this war. In the event, the memories these poets constructed helped to create a particular understanding of their historical moment: their poetry contributed to the formation of collective memory.

We look first at the very nomenclature poets used for those who died, since this linguistic choice was part of the first formation of memory about this historical moment, as well as the first commemoration of those who died. The versions of address to, and description of, the dead that were passed down affect current formations of memory and the choice of commemorative languages used to mark the First World War's centenary.

---

⁶ Prime Minister Herbert Asquith gave Charles Masterman the task of establishing an organisation to place 'before the peoples of neutral countries and of the Dominions the British case for entering the war and for justifying wartime policy decisions' (M. L. Sanders and Philip M. Taylor, *British Propaganda during the First World War, 1914–18* (Macmillan: London, 1982), 39). Masterman held a conference on 2 September 1914 recruiting prominent literary figures to this cause (ibid., 39–41). For a fuller account of the literary dimension of Masterman's propaganda effort, see Gary S. Messinger, *British Propaganda and the State in the First World War* (Manchester: Manchester University Press, 1992), 24–52. For a discussion of Hardy's ambiguous contribution, the poem 'Men Who March Away', see Andrew Palmer, ' "Friend with the Musing Eye": Persuasion and Dissonance in "Call to Arms" Poems of the First World War', *Writings of Persuasion and Dissonance in the Great War: That Better Whiles May Follow Worse*, ed. David Owen and Cristina Pividori (Leiden: Brill Rodopi, 2016), 138–51.

For even to talk of 'the dead' is to make a choice about how we remember, since it generalises and removes us from the specific individuals who were killed. At the same time many of the early poems make another sort of choice, bringing the dead back to life, contradicting the actuality occasioning the poem. The most common form of resurrection is to speak to those who have died as though they were present. Thus Ivor Gurney, in his retrospective 'Farewell', can't help addressing his dead comrades as '*you dead ones*', as if they might still hear him, unable quite to grasp even now – 'But you are dead!'[7] Sassoon similarly addresses his great friend Robert Graves in 'To His Dead Body': 'Safe quit of wars, I speed you on your way' (Graves had been mistakenly listed as 'Died of Wounds' and when the poem was written Sassoon believed him dead).[8] May Wedderburn Cannan expresses the particular impotence of women left behind to mourn, speaking to her dead lover in 'Lamplight' ('You took the road we never spoke of').[9] Only Gurney amongst these meticulously speaks of 'you dead *ones*', and addresses some of them by name, in one of his many breaches of poetic convention. But it is clear too in both Sassoon's and Wedderburn Cannan's poems that a particular, known person is being addressed and, in that address, he is being thought of as in some sense still able to hear what the poet is saying.

Elsewhere, poets make the dead men themselves speak to us, in a kind of prosopopoeia, as in John McCrae's 'In Flanders Fields'.[10] Here, however, they have again become a mass, a generalised not an individual body, the capitalised 'Dead':

> We are the Dead. Short days ago
> We lived, felt dawn, saw sunset glow,
> Loved and were loved, and now we lie
> In Flanders fields.[11]

These ways of imagining dead soldiers refuse to accept the very fact that occasions the poem: their lives are over. The dead are not *entirely* dead, these poems say; they can hear us, see us, admonish us. This idea

---

[7] 'Farewell' in Ivor Gurney, *Collected Poems*, ed. P. J. Kavanagh (Manchester: Fyfield Books/Carcanet, 2004), 266.
[8] 'To His Dead Body' in Sassoon, *Collected Poems*, 22.
[9] May Wedderburn Cannan, 'Lamplight' in Kendall, *Poetry of the First World War*, 182.
[10] Prosopopoeia: 'A figure by which an imaginary or absent person is represented as speaking or acting' (*Oxford English Dictionary*); 'whereby we speak of the absent, the dead or the inanimate as if they were alive, as if they were possessed of human consciousness and intent' (J. Hillis Miller, *Tropes, Parables and Performatives: Essays on Twentieth Century Literature* (Hemel Hempstead: Harvester Wheatsheaf, 1991), 163). The term, literally, means making a face or mask.
[11] John McCrae, 'In Flanders Fields' in Hibberd and Onions (eds), *Winter of the World*, 56.

of the dead persisting in the living world may sometimes spring from a specific religious conviction about the survival of the soul after death; but more frequently the dead are imagined as embodied, sentient and either speaking or hearing. In terms of the response of collective memory to the death of our fellow humans, this is perhaps a particularly striking cultural expression of what Jan Assmann calls 'an act of resuscitation performed by the desire of the group not to allow the dead to disappear but, with the aid of memory, to keep them as members of their community and to take them with them into their progressive present'.[12]

These hallucinatory re-appearances of the dead to the living have become a standard phenomenon in the fiction which reimagines the First World War, starting with Virginia Woolf's depiction of the dead Evans appearing to Septimus Warren Smith.[13] Whether such disruptions of 'normal' reality are the product of the extreme psychological pressures of combat, or of the stress of personal loss, the sense and even the material apprehension of the dead person existing after death is likewise a familiar epiphenomenon of bereavement. The pathological nature of hallucinatory reappearances of the dead to the living reminds us that the idea of a dead man somehow continuing to live is not necessarily benign. Far from being a comfort, there is a horror in the irrepressible irruption of the dead into the minds of men who want only to forget them, as Owen's 'Mental Cases' vividly depicts. This disjunction enters the poetic discourse of the First World War. On the one hand, there is a fear of seeing the dead rise up again, because that means the memory of all that death can never be extinguished – hence 'Memory fingers in their hair of murders'. On the other, if the dead man can be imagined as sentient enough to enjoy the peace of death, to still be able to hear the poet address him, or indeed to speak himself, then death becomes less fearful to those still living, as well as offering consolation about how the dead themselves 'feel'.

The desire to keep the dead alive was perhaps more acute and more sustained in the First World War precisely because of the numbers of dead.[14] Those who wrote poetry might naturally, then, take it a step

---

[12] Assmann, *Cultural Memory and Early Civilisation*, 19–20.
[13] Virginia Woolf, *Mrs Dalloway* (1925; London: Penguin, 1992). See also Pat Barker, *Regeneration* (London: Viking, 1991); Helen Dunmore, *The Lie* (London: Hutchinson, 2014).
[14] Denis Winter comments interestingly on the complexity of the statistics about the number of dead in the First World War, with very large numbers of men dying in particular battles and even on particular days, while these were balanced by lighter casualties at other times. His conservative estimate is that 10 per cent of soldiers died in the First World War in comparison with 5 per cent in the Boer War, and 4½ per cent in the Second World War (Winter, *Death's Men: Soldiers of the Great War* (London: Penguin, 1979), 203–4). These high numbers were also a cause in the well-documented rise in belief in the occult and in the possibility of contacting individuals after death.

further and give voice to or address those who had died. But perhaps the more powerful influence was poetic convention, notably that of the elegy, which simultaneously weeps for the dead person and addresses him as shining through all eternity. The acme of this poetic expression of an ever-persisting life for those who are dead can be found in Rupert Brooke's five sonnets, published originally in *New Numbers* in early March 1915, and then republished in *1914 and Other Poems*, hastily assembled by Edward Marsh after Brooke's death in April, and published posthumously in June 1915.[15] This was an immensely powerful text in its historical moment, and that moment has reverberated to the present day. Brooke's sonnets are undoubtedly an example of both the formation and the transmission of cultural memory. Here we'll look at those five sonnets as the expression, early in the war, of a particular sort of feeling about death in battle, and as the epitome of one sort of poetic remembrance which contributes powerfully to cultural memory. These poems were deeply resonant and highly influential, and became for a time a touchstone against which both other poetry and soldierly and masculine behaviour and values were measured. The extent to which Brooke's poetic contemporaries either conformed to or departed from his poetic world view is thus a useful starting point to look at the range of poetic responses to death in the First World War, and at the complex problem of how best to remember 'you dead ones' in poetry.

In using Brooke's sonnets as both index of and point of contrast to the ways other poets represented and commemorated those who died, we will refer to the theories of memory touched on above. We will also draw, in this chapter and elsewhere, on two recent commentaries on the way the rhetoric of mourning in First World War poems is rooted in traditional forms but at the same time departs from those conventions in response to the particularity of the experience of death, loss, mourning and remembrance in the First World War. In the first, Jahan Ramazani argues that, while elegy as a genre remains significant in the twentieth century, it must be an altered elegy to represent an altered world; one of his examples of this altered elegy is the poetry of Wilfred Owen.[16] In the

---

See Jay Winter, *Sites of Memory, Sites of Mourning: The Great War in European Cultural History* (Cambridge: Cambridge University Press, 1995), 54–77.

[15] Rupert Brooke, *1914 and Other Poems*, ed. Edward Marsh (London: Sidgwick & Jackson, 1915). Rupert Brooke, *The Collected Poems*, with a memoir by Edward Marsh (1918; London: Sidgwick & Jackson, 1989) followed in July 1918.

[16] Jahan Ramazani, *Poetry of Mourning: The Modern Elegy from Hardy to Heaney* (Chicago: University of Chicago Press, 1994).

second, Elizabeth Vandiver reaches even further back to the representations of death in battle in classical epic, showing the deep influence of classical tropes on First World War poets, especially those who were steeped in that tradition through their public school education.[17] There is an inherent link between Ramazani's and Vandiver's work in that the elegy of the seventeenth, eighteenth and nineteenth centuries itself draws on classical models, often ossified into literary conventions in the formal elegy. In Brooke's sonnets we see both influences at work – the atavistic appeal of the unaltered formal elegy, decorated with the spiritual paraphernalia of death in battle as represented in classical epic. From elegy come the tropes of the dead body being at one with nature and thereby still having life, providing consolation and redemption both through that and through the act of commemoration in the elegy itself. From martial epic comes the idea that only through battle can a man's qualities be tested, and that the normal values of the peaceful world are mean and, in the end, meaningless – 'all the little emptiness of love!'[18]

Brooke completed a draft of the sonnets towards the end of December 1914, while at training camp, and by mid-January they were in proof stage ready for *New Numbers*.[19] He had volunteered only a few weeks after the outbreak of war and, in October 1914, after minimal training, his company was sent to Antwerp to reinforce Belgian troops; this turned almost immediately into a retreat. Brooke describes his relief, 'to find I was incredibly brave!', revealing, rather touchingly, in the next sentence that his bravery hadn't yet been much tested: 'I don't know how I'd behave if shrapnel were bursting over me and knocking the men round me to pieces.'[20] So he didn't see combat of the sort that Owen, Sassoon, Gurney, Rosenberg and others would see at the Front, though not for want of trying. The sonnets are, then, written out of only a very brief experience of a soldier's life. But as the poetry of Harold Monro and Wilfrid Gibson – both non-combatants writing early in the war – shows, lack of experience is no barrier in itself to an imaginative understanding of what death in battle might be like.[21] And it's not as if Brooke lacked the necessary imagination;

---

[17] Elizabeth Vandiver, *Stand in the Trench, Achilles: Classical Receptions in British Poetry of the Great War* (Oxford: Oxford University Press, 2010).
[18] 'Peace' in Brooke, *Collected Poems*, 312.
[19] Christopher Hassall suggests he had begun them as early as October but does not give documentary evidence (Hassall, *Rupert Brooke: A Biography* (London: Faber & Faber, 1964), 467–78).
[20] Letter to Cathleen Nesbitt, 17 October 1914; *The Letters of Rupert Brooke*, ed. G. Keynes (London: Faber & Faber, 1968), 624.
[21] See Harold Monro, *Children of Love* (London: Poetry Bookshop, 1914) and Wilfrid Gibson, *Battle* (London: Elkin Mathews, 1915). Monro is discussed later in this chapter, Gibson in the next.

in the same letter describing his reaction to active service, he mentions writing final letters before action:

> I felt very elderly and sombre, and full of thought of how human life was a flash between darknesses, and that *x* per cent of those who cheered would be blown into another world within a few months ... it did bring home to me how very futile and unfinished life was... There was nothing except a vague gesture of good-bye to you and my mother and a friend or two. I seemed so remote and barren and stupid. I seemed to have missed everything.[22]

This is the note of futility and existential absurdity that we find in some of the most interesting poetry of the war: note that Brooke says not *It* but *I* seemed 'remote and barren and stupid', transferring the sense of alienation to his very self. There is a similar note of the understood void that future death represents in 'Fragment' (entitled posthumously by Marsh), written in April 1915 just before his death, where he foresees, as he wanders on the ship's deck at night, that 'This gay machine of splendour' would 'soon be broken, / Thought little of, pashed, scattered'. Seeing the live bodies of his shipmates through the saloon's lamplit window while he remains unseen outside, he understands that they are already 'coloured shadows, thinner than filmy glass, slight bubbles ... Perishing things and strange ghosts – soon to die'.[23]

Yet there is not an iota of that existential anxiety in the sonnets; their tenor owes more to the literary traditions in which he was steeped than to the force of his experience. 'Fragment' was not included in *1914 and Other Poems* (1915), but it was published in the subsequent, highly popular *Collected Poems* of 1918, which ran to sixteen impressions before a revised edition appeared in 1928. However, as a small but significant counter-voice to the tone of the sonnets, it went unnoticed, and remains so now.[24] The sonnets, conversely, were widely promulgated and embody a number of standard values which were broadly shared at the beginning of the war, at least by the officer class, since many of them derived from the classical models in which the officers were educated. Central was the idea that 'God ... has matched us with His hour', which underwrites the belief that war provided a unique challenge to manhood to prove its finest qualities, and so men should be grateful for this chance that history has given them.[25]

---

[22] Letter to Cathleen Nesbitt, 17 October 1914; Brooke, *Letters*, 623.
[23] Brooke, *Collected Poems*, 318.
[24] 'Fragment' does appear on the Rupert Brooke Society website as the last of only nine selected representative poems, and the text notes that it 'suggests a style more like that of later WW1 poets, one which Brooke might have developed had he lived' (www.rupertbrooke.com/poems/).
[25] 'Peace', sonnet 1, in Brooke, *Collected Poems*, 312. Subsequent references to Brooke's sonnets in this chapter, all *Collected Poems*, 312–16.

Inevitably, therefore, death became a necessary – *the* necessary – risk, and had to be depicted as part of the general good. In the first of two sonnets entitled 'The Dead' (sonnet III), indeed, death becomes a positive gain since, if one makes the ultimate sacrifice in a challenge set by God and country, death becomes the best prize. Vandiver goes so far as to say that Brooke sees such a death as the *sine qua non* of a happy life, and that, in sonnet III, he 'appropriates classical tropes to delineate the requirements for human happiness'.[26] In his opening sonnet, 'Peace', Brooke couches that sacrifice in terms of a Christian God, but when reflecting on being sent to the Dardanelles it is of the Trojan War and the classical gods, not God, that he thinks. Vandiver notes 'the complexity with which classical, medieval and Christian imagery intertwined in the minds of public-school graduates to support the insistence that the deaths of … young men … were not only necessary but glorifying'.[27] Thus for Brooke the 'Dead' are 'rich' and in dying they offer 'rarer gifts than gold', 'Honour has come back, as a king, to earth' and 'we' (men who fight) 'have come into our heritage' ('The Dead', sonnet III).

There is no room in this set of values for either the grisliness or the existential absurdity of death. Rather the imagery of cleanness, beauty and wholesomeness accompanies any reference to the body – 'swimmers into cleanness leaping' ('Peace'), 'Washed by the rivers, blest by suns of home' ('The Soldier', sonnet V), 'pouring out', not blood, but 'the red Sweet wine of youth' ('The Dead', sonnet III). Even when the body is buried, 'There shall be / In that rich earth a richer dust concealed' ('The Soldier'). Perhaps most powerful in Brooke's vision is the idea, written into the very grammar and syntax of the lines, that the dead body will somehow *know* the peace that spells the end of life. Certainly, this is a common conception for anyone trying to grapple with the idea of death, since it is difficult for us, alive, to think of the state of non-being. Being faced with bodies suddenly, regularly and randomly annihilated would make it difficult to accept this consoling fiction, that the dead can feel the peace that comes with the loss of sentience. Yet this is precisely what Brooke envisages: 'a body of England's, breathing English air, / Washed by the rivers, blest by the suns of home' ('The Soldier'). The strength of Brooke's sonnets, and what perhaps led them to be so influential initially, is the fact that his poetic values are of a piece with his moral values. There is no room for questioning or doubt,

---

[26] Vandiver, *Stand in the Trench, Achilles*, 285. She notes that in the classical context 'human' here means male.
[27] Ibid., 71.

as he forges a complete and consistent set of images in which the reality of an actual body torn apart cannot possibly insert itself. Instead, richness, cleanliness, safety, beauty, comfort and peace are all stitched in not just to the vocabulary but to the tight form of the sonnet.

Jan Assmann, specifying the characterising features of cultural memory (in the context of Egyptology), suggests that it is defined in part by its 'specialised tradition bearers', those figures who represent what, in a different conceptual framework, we might call the dominant ideology.[28] If Brooke was a bearer of that ideology – born and brought up first in the environs of and then, from the age of three, within Rugby School when his father became housemaster of the School Field House; educated in his father's House; classical scholar at King's College Cambridge, where his uncle was Dean; a member of the Cambridge Apostles as an undergraduate, then appointed to a Fellowship at King's; highly literate and literary, well-travelled and extremely well-connected – he was also a victim of it. When Brooke was looking for a way into the war, Edward Marsh, his great friend, admirer and literary promoter and also Winston Churchill's Private Secretary, eased the way for him to join the Royal Naval Division, one of Churchill's pet projects. That led to Brooke's brief skirmish in Belgium, after which he drafted the 1914 sonnets. Then he was off to the Dardanelles, another of Churchill's ventures, this to prove disastrous. For Brooke and his fellow officers, steeped in Greek poetry, to fight in Gallipoli was tantamount to refighting the Trojan War. While Brooke's letters on the subject are infused with self-reflexive irony, there's no doubt about his excitement at this coincidence of geography and value. He writes to Violet Asquith, 'Oh Violet it's too wonderful for belief … I'm filled with confident and glorious hopes … Will Hero's Tower crumble under the 15 in. guns? Will the sea be polyphloisbic [roaring loudly] and wine dark and unvintageable?'[29]

Brooke, at this early stage of the war, and with no actual experience of 'shrapnel … bursting over me and knocking the men round me to pieces', clearly reaches back to both his classical and his English literary antecedents, in a way one might almost describe as innocent. Brooke's sonnets then would, in Halbwachs's and the Assmanns's terms, be seen as culturally determined, by his class, his education and his literary understanding. Astrid Erll notes, in discussing the Assmanns's concept of cultural texts: 'In uncommon, difficult, or dangerous circumstances it is especially traditional and strongly conventionalised genres which

[28] Assmann, *Cultural Memory and Early Civilisation*, 41.
[29] Letter to Violet Asquith, February 1915; Brooke, *Letters*, 662.

writers draw upon in order to provide familiar and meaningful patterns of representation for experiences that would otherwise be hard to interpret.'[30]

We can see then the way that Brooke, at this time of personal and national danger, naturally reached for the comforting genres of epic and elegy, and the values they embody, and went to the familiar and canonical form of the sonnet as a means of expression of those values. Epic is a founding cultural text and repository of cultural memory, but also a key generic carrier of ideas about war; elegy is founded on certain classical values and tropes, embodying an inherently consolatory and redemptive attitude to death and mourning; and the sonnet is the axiomatic English lyric form, contained and controlled but expressive of deep personal emotion. Thus Brooke reached back, against the pull of modernity, to a deeply conservative understanding of death in battle. Brooke answered perhaps to a precise ideological moment, just before he could be exposed to the bleak failure and human cost of the Gallipoli campaign.

The responses to Brooke's death were equally closely entwined with ideology, but less innocently so. Even before Brooke's death, 'The Soldier' had been picked out by the Dean of St Paul's to feature in his Easter sermon. Immediately after his death, the man and his poems were conflated as a prime example and expression of patriotic masculine sacrifice. In Churchill's encomium for Brooke as lost hero, published in *The Times* of 26 April 1915 (Brooke had died three days earlier), we can see the turning of the man and his writings into a combined *lieu de mémoire*, which would go on to be endlessly re-sacralised.[31] This secondary movement, which turned Brooke and his sonnets into a myth, rendered his poetry even further regressive, un-individualised and ultimately in the service of state memory. Canonised, in both senses, by a premier politician, and a premier churchman, Brooke and his poetry had little chance to be anything other:

> Rupert Brooke is dead… A voice had become audible, a note had been struck, more true, more thrilling, more able to do justice to the nobility of our youth in arms engaged in this present war, than any other …
>
> During the last few months of his life, months of preparation in gallant comradeship and open air, the poet-soldier told with all the simple force of genius the sorrow of youth about to die, and the sure triumphant consolations of a sincere and valiant spirit. He expected to die; he was willing to die for the dear England whose beauty and majesty he knew; and he advanced towards the brink in perfect serenity …

---

[30] Astrid Erll, *Memory in Culture*, trans. Sara B. Young (Basingstoke: Palgrave Macmillan, 2011), 148–9.
[31] For our use of the term *lieu de mémoire*, see pp. 13–15 above.

> The thoughts to which he gave expression in the very few incomparable war sonnets which he has left behind will be shared by many thousands of young men moving resolutely and blithely forward into this, the hardest, the cruellest, and the least-rewarded of all the wars that men have fought. They are a whole history and revelation of Rupert Brooke himself. Joyous, fearless, versatile, deeply instructed, with classic symmetry of mind and body, he was all that one would wish England's noblest sons to be in days when no sacrifice but the most precious is acceptable, and the most precious is that which is most freely offered.[32]

Max Egremont notes, in passing, that Marsh was in fact the author of this eulogy, which would explain its note of hectic dolour.[33] But Churchill certainly knew what he was doing, hitching his own wobbling reputation to a star which he was himself helping to create. As a politician he was taking power from a dead soldier-poet by iconising him at the moment when the cultural memory of this occasion was in the process of being formed.

The absences in this passage are as interesting as the presences. Churchill had initiated the two engagements that Brooke had been involved with, Antwerp and Gallipoli, both of which were strategic failures. This is turned on its head into the paradigm of noble sacrifice which Brooke's sonnets encapsulated. And no mention is made of the cause of Brooke's death – weakness brought about by sunstroke, followed by septicaemia caused by an unnoticed insect bite. The lacuna leaves the reader to imagine a glorious death in battle. Brooke's sonnets are marked by the same lacunae; the physical nature of death is displaced into absence by the idiom and ideology that marked the start of the war, themselves underwritten by Homeric values, and promulgated in the public and private schools which produced most junior officers.

In the months and years after his death, versions of Brooke were constructed as both communicative and cultural memory simultaneously. We can see this process at work in Virginia Woolf's contemporary responses. In a *Times Literary Supplement* review (27 December 1917) of John Drinkwater's *Prose Papers*, she commends his piece 'Rupert Brooke' because it does not simply assent to the poet's 'canonisation'. She ends the review with an exhortation: 'If the legend of Rupert Brooke is not to pass altogether beyond recognition, we must hope that some of those who knew him … will put their view on record and relieve his ghost of an

---

[32] Quoted in Hassall, *Rupert Brooke*, 515.
[33] Max Egremont, *Some Desperate Glory: The First World War the Poets Knew* (London: Picador, 2014), 68–9.

unmerited and undesired burden of adulation'.[34] When Edward Marsh's *The Collected Poems of Rupert Brooke* was given to Woolf to review by the *Times Literary Supplement*, she had the perfect opportunity to fulfil the duty she had outlined, to put her more complicated view of Brooke 'on record'. Indeed, she described Marsh's memoir as 'a disgraceful sloppy sentimental rhapsody' – but only in her private diary.[35] In her review of 8 August 1918, in spite of the protection of anonymity, she was much more cautious, repeating only that 'those who knew him' (implying that Marsh didn't) would be left 'to reflect rather sadly upon the incomplete version which must in future represent Rupert Brooke to those who never knew him'.[36] She thus did not take the opportunity to deconstruct the myth she knew was being made. An explanation of sorts is given in a letter to Katherine Cox, Brooke's former lover, admitting that she is the author of the review: 'when it came to do it I felt that to say out loud what even I knew of Rupert was utterly repulsive, so I merely trod out my 2 columns as decorously as possible'.[37] The reluctance which even Woolf (in a position at that time of some cultural influence) felt to speak 'out loud' shows the power of cultural pressure on the individual – though rarely are its workings so clearly revealed.

Had Brooke survived to experience more fully the horrors of war, his poetic representations might have been different, and the cultural representation of him and his work would have changed accordingly. His merging Gallipoli with Troy, and seeing the waters he crossed towards his death as 'wine dark', may have been collectively and culturally formed, but they remain an aspect of his individual consciousness, which consciousness might have been changed by different experiences. Charles Sorley was raised 'upon the self-same hill' of classical literature as Brooke.[38] However, Sorley's response seems to have been to see not the richness but the blankness of death, at least in his most famous poem, 'When you see millions of the mouthless dead'. His emphasis is on that 'mouthless': they cannot speak and perhaps, too, they are literally mouthless. Indeed all the

---

[34] 'The New Crusade' in *The Essays of Virginia Woolf*, vol. II, ed. Andrew McNeillie (San Diego: Harcourt Brace Jovanovich, 1990), 203.
[35] 23 July 1918; *The Diary of Virginia Woolf*, 5 vols, ed. Anne Olivier Bell (Orlando: Harcourt, 1977), vol. I, 171.
[36] 'Rupert Brooke' in Woolf, *Essays*, vol. II, 278.
[37] 13 August 1918; *The Letters of Virginia Woolf*, 6 vols, ed. Nigel Nicolson (London: Hogarth Press, 1975–80), vol. II, no. 959.
[38] 'Lycidas' in *The Poems of John Milton*, ed. John Carey and Alastair Fowler (London: Longmans, 1968), 241.

senses are missing; he warns the reader not to imagine that the dead can hear our praise:

> When you see millions of the mouthless dead
> Across your dreams in pale battalions go,
> Say not soft things as other men have said,
> That you'll remember. For you need not so.
> Give them not praise. For, deaf, how should they know
> It is not curses heaped on each gashed head?[39]

He tells us not to cry for them ('Their blind eyes see not your tears flow'), nor to honour them, because:

> It is easy to be dead.
> Say only this, 'They are dead.' Then add thereto,
> 'Yet many a better one has died before.'

Vandiver notes that Sorley refers directly here to the passage in the *Iliad* where Lycaon, the son of Priam, begs Achilles for mercy, and Achilles responds by reminding him that 'Patroclus too has died, who was far better than you.'[40] The import is that all come to death; being good, being powerful in battle, being Patroclus himself, makes no difference. But Sorley is not reminding us here of the truism that all are equal in death, in the manner of Thomas Gray's 'Elegy Written in a Country Churchyard', but rather that, if even such a great one as Patroclus must die, then all deaths are equally meaningless. Sorley set great store by this passage, asserting in one of his letters to his old headmaster at Marlborough that it 'should be read at the grave of every corpse in addition to the burial service'.[41] Echoes of his bleak view are already there in his 1914 poem, 'All the hills and vales along':

> Earth that blossomed and was glad
> 'Neath the cross that Christ had,
> Shall rejoice and blossom too
> When the bullet reaches you.
> ...
> Earth will echo still, when foot
> Lies numb and voice mute.[42]

---

[39] Charles Hamilton Sorley, *The Collected Poems*, ed. Jean Moorcroft Wilson (London: Cecil Woolf, 1985), 91. First published in January 1916.
[40] Vandiver, *Stand in the Trench, Achilles*, 293; Vandiver's translation.
[41] Letter to St. J. B. Wynne Wilson, 28 November 1914; *The Letters of Charles Sorley*, ed. W. R. Sorley (Cambridge: Cambridge University Press, 1919), 245.
[42] Sorley, *Collected Poems*, 68–9. This poem, first published January 1916, is thought to have been written in August 1914, though not sent home until April 1915, see John Press, *Charles Hamilton Sorley* (London: Cecil Woolf, 2006), 14.

This, however, is a poem of a very different tone, fostered by the sing-song rhythm and rhyme which puts the serious and non-serious on the same level to reflect nature's indifference. In 'When you see millions of the mouthless dead', Sorley, like Brooke, calls on the sonnet form to give his vision a greater gravitas but, in doing so, he shows us that this form can also be framed to cut against tradition. Customarily, a sonnet will have some kind of 'turn' or change in direction in its final section, and Sorley seems about to make such a turn, though later than usual, in the last quatrain, offering the possibility of hope, of contact beyond the grave:

> Then, scanning all the o'ercrowded mass, should you
> Perceive one face that you loved heretofore,

But he quickly withdraws this in the next line, by completing the sentence with these four words: 'It is a spook', and adding: 'None wears the face you knew.' The dead are dead, and all we can say about it is: 'They are dead.' To say otherwise is a falsehood. For all its being so closely informed by Sorley's classicism, this sonnet is a great negation of the very values the *Iliad* upholds.

If Brooke's sonnets are prime examples of hegemonic texts embodying the dominant ideology, Sorley's last sonnet is a triumphantly individualistic counter-example to the power of that hegemony. Using a traditional verse form, and drawing on his own deep classical learning, he deliberately rejects the language, iconography and values of Brooke's sonnets. His considered response to those sonnets (made only a few days after Brooke's death) was that the poet was 'far too obsessed with his own sacrifice, regarding the going to war ... as a highly intense, remarkable and sacrificial exploit'. His summary judgement was that 'he has taken the sentimental attitude' (an interestingly ambivalent phrase since it can apply to both moral and poetic values).[43] 'When you see millions of the mouthless dead' may be a deliberate riposte to that attitude.[44] Certainly it subverts elegy in the way Ramazani suggests a properly modern elegy should, to the point of being an anti-elegy: 'In becoming anti-elegiac, the modern elegy more radically violates previous generic norms than did earlier phases of elegy: it becomes anti-consolatory and anti-encomiastic, anti-Romantic and anti-Victorian, anti-conventional and sometimes even anti-literary.'[45] Such a

---

[43] Sorley, *Letters*, 263.
[44] Kendall suggests, in a note to the line 'Say not soft things as other men have said' that the 'other men' 'probably include Rupert Brooke' (Kendall, *Poetry of the First World War*, 284).
[45] Ramazani, *Poetry of Mourning*, 2.

literary poem can't really be said to be anti-literary, but it does use its poetic reference points to undermine the standard tropes of elegy, and in so doing is one of the few First World War lyrics to cast the authentically cold eye of modernity on the predicament of remembering the dead. Even the apparent generalisation and reification of the 'millions of the mouthless dead' is there to remind us that death nullifies the individual, not by rendering him a part of a greater whole ('the dead'), but by making him anonymous. 'None wears the face you knew'. No *one* is left.

While those at the Front saw 'the mouthless dead' on a regular basis, those at home were given false constructions of such deaths. The disjunction between the reality of life and death at the Front and the way that was represented at home is well documented and contributed further to the difficulty that serving soldiers had in making sense of their experiences on active service, so utterly at odds with the banalities of home life but also at odds with the way their experiences were being reported at home, and being received. This is poignantly evident in the correspondence about Brooke between Vera Brittain and Roland Leighton. Indeed Brittain herself comments in her memoir *Testament of Youth* on that gulf of experience, made worse by the delay between letters sent and those received, speaking of 'that terrible barrier of knowledge by which War cut off the men who possessed it from the women who, in spite of the love that they gave and received, remained in ignorance'.[46] Roland Leighton, known best now as Brittain's fiancé, was, like Brooke, deeply versed in classical literature and its ethos. In July 1914, as he left Uppingham School, he was laden with prizes for Greek and Latin, and had won a Classical Postmastership to Merton College, Oxford.[47] He left school with the words of his headmaster in his Speech Day address ringing in his ears: 'If a man cannot be useful to his country, he is better dead.'[48] By October 1914 he had enlisted as a second lieutenant, and was continuing to write promising poetry. In March 1915, his regiment was sent to the Front. In all these ways his path mirrored Brooke's, though his family was more bohemian. In August 1915 Vera sent Leighton a copy of the recently dead Brooke's newly published *Poems 1914*, expecting, not unnaturally, that he would share the ideals expressed

---

[46] Vera Brittain, *Testament of Youth* (1933; London: Virago, 2004), 190.
[47] Paul Berry and Mark Bostridge, *Vera Brittain: A Life* (London: Chatto & Windus, 1995), 49, 57–8. Berry and Bostridge record a contemporary of Leighton's saying that his prize books were so many that he 'trundled them back to his dormitory in a wheelbarrow' (ibid., 58).
[48] Recalled in Brittain, *Testament of Youth*, 70.

there. Leighton's initial response was frustration that he himself had not achieved as he had wished. At the same time, he issued a muted challenge to Brooke's ideas: 'it is only War in the abstract that is beautiful'.[49] His more deeply felt response came, however, in September, a few weeks after the leave in which he and Vera had become officially engaged. In this letter to her, he describes the dead bodies he has seen, making bitter reference to Brooke's sonnet III and to the values of the five sonnets in general:

> ... in among the chaos of twisted iron and splintered timber and shapeless earth are the fleshless, blackened bones of simple men who poured out their red, sweet wine of youth unknowing, for nothing more tangible than Honour or their Country's Glory or another's Lust of Power. Let him who thinks War is a glorious, golden thing, who loves to roll forth stirring words of exhortation, invoking Honour and Praise and Valour and Love of Country ... let him but look at a little pile of sodden grey rags that cover half a skull and a shin bone and what might have been Its ribs, or at this skeleton lying on its side ... perfect but that it is headless, and let him realise how grand and glorious a thing it is to have distilled all Youth and Joy and Life into a foetid heap of hideous putrescence. Who is there who has known and seen who can say that Victory is worth the death of even one of these?[50]

This passage is the more remarkable in that Leighton is responding to seeing the dead bodies of German soldiers.[51] He had been at the Front for seven months; he was twenty; it was relatively early in the war. Leighton is angry with himself, and with the entire ethos of his youth – embodied in his school, his many prizes and his classical learning – which he had embraced so willingly. He is angry with Brooke for so powerfully voicing that ethos in his sonnets. And he is, implicitly, angry with his beloved Vera for sharing those values – though she went on praising Brooke to Roland in her letters, apparently oblivious to the source of his bitterness.[52]

Leighton had, a few months earlier in April 1915, written 'Violets', addressed to Vera but not sent at the time of writing, though he sent her some of the actual violets which it describes.[53] The poem has a softness and tenderness missing from his angry letter – it is a love poem, and it is

---

[49] Ibid., 149–50.
[50] Quoted in ibid., 174.
[51] Berry and Bostridge, *Vera Brittain*, 89.
[52] Ibid., 89. Brittain's biographers are hard on her about this, but it is the result of the very thing Brittain herself fearfully identifies: the 'barrier of knowledge' between home and the Front.
[53] Brittain, *Testament of Youth*, 122. He sent her the poem some weeks later. The poem is quoted in full by Brittain, ibid., 114, under the title 'Villanelle'. ('Violets' is the title Leighton gives in manuscript.)

written only a couple of weeks after Leighton's arrival at the Front – but the contrast it draws is the same:

> Violets from Plug Street Wood,
> Sweet, I send you oversea.
> (It is strange they should be blue,
> Blue, when his soaked blood was red,
> For they grew around his head;
> It is strange they should be blue.
> ...
> (And you did not see them grow
> Where his mangled body lay
> Hiding horror from the day;
> Sweetest, it was better so.)

The simple oppositions of this poem derive from Leighton's address to his loved one at home, but they perhaps also reflect his own struggle to reconcile the beauty of the violets with the 'soaked blood' in which they grew. Beside the fierce, almost brutal, and precocious detachment of Sorley, and indeed beside the immense confidence of Brooke, Leighton's poem betrays his poetic inexperience. But there is a poignant quality to his attempt to bring together the incompatible poles of his experience. This is a very young man trying to come to terms with the immediate experience of battlefield death.

These poets were struggling with how to represent rightly those who were being killed. Sorley's depiction of 'the dead' as 'mouthless' and 'millions' is highly unusual. In First World War poetry 'the dead' (especially when capitalised as 'the Dead') often suggests a community of like-minded beings. Moreover, it turns an adjective into a noun so that we don't have to say out loud what it is that's dead; it deprives dead men of their bodies, makes them ethereal, insubstantial, spiritual. And that makes it easier to use abstract nouns like immortality, holiness, honour and nobleness, all of which appear in Brooke's sonnet III, 'The Dead'. Clearly there is a difference between the non-capitalised and the capitalised 'dead'. But in general the poets who think in a more complex way about death invoke particular dead bodies rather than either 'the dead' or 'the Dead'.

The most powerful of such poems are those which try to make sense of, or attend to the detail of, the act and moment of dying, rather than a generalised death, or the dead. If we step back here from the way the already-dead are depicted to look at the way First World War poets depicted the actual moment of dying, we see also a progression to some extent from the traditional mode of remembrance, with its attendant traditional forms and tropes, to a more obviously modernist enterprise. The ubiquity of death at the Front prompted (especially combatant) poets to dwell on the moment when the living consciousness ceased. This is perhaps the most mysterious moment but the most pregnant with meaning for those concerned with the existential. In its high modernist forms this issued in an acute interest in the nature of consciousness and ways of representing that accurately in language. In First World War poems which try to capture this moment, we see these conceptual and philosophical concerns worked out in the human landscape of those about to die, those dying and those just dead.

Isaac Rosenberg – who was also critical of Brooke's 'begloried sonnets', telling one friend: 'they remind me too much of flag days' – brings his keen poetic eye to the detail of death in exactly this way in 'Dead Man's Dump'.[54]

> The wheels lurched over sprawled dead
> But pained them not, though their bones crunched,
> Their shut mouths made no moan[55]

Here we see the acute difference between Brooke's 'the rich Dead' and Rosenberg's 'sprawled dead', the latter not dignified even by the definite article (though we will argue they are dignified in a different way). 'Shut mouths' is maybe not as strong a protest as Sorley's 'mouthless', but it reminds us that someone else's actions have actively shut these mouths. And the oxymoron of 'pained them not, though their bones crunched' captures the vertiginous existential ambivalence of the dead body. We are glad it feels no pain. But it feels no pain because it is dead. This is all the comfort we have; worse, this is all the comfort the dead body *can't* have. He describes the stretcher-bearers leaving a just-dead man with the older dead bodies on the dump:

> Burnt black by strange decay
> Their sinister faces lie
> The lid over each eye,
> The grass and coloured clay
> More motion have than they

---

[54] The first phrase is from a letter to Mrs Herbert Cohen, undated, 1916, the second from a letter to Mr Sydney Schiff, August 1916. Both are in *The Collected Works of Isaac Rosenberg*, ed. Ian Parsons (London: Chatto & Windus, 1979), 237, 240.
[55] Rosenberg, *Collected Works*, 109–11.

These lines recall Wordsworth's exploration of this paradox:

> No motion has she now, no force,
> She neither hears nor sees,
> Rolled round in earth's diurnal course,
> With rocks and stones and trees.[56]

Wordsworth's Lucy is on a continuum with the 'sprawled dead'; do we take comfort from Lucy's neither hearing nor seeing, or do we shiver at the coldness of this rough universe? Rosenberg poses the same question, yet perhaps even more feelingly since we imagine the dead body at the same time both feeling and not feeling pain. Lucy is literally dead to the world; Rosenberg, in a modernist way, creates at once the sensation and the lack of sensation, allowing the two worlds to collide.

While Rosenberg begins uncompromisingly with the fact of being dead, and the numbers of the dead, his real interest is in that one brief moment between life and death. He tries to apprehend what lies beyond the body, if anything does, questioning that moment when the body dies:

> Earth! Have they gone into you?
> Somewhere they must have gone ...
> Who hurled them? Who hurled?

He is 'hurled' – to where, and by what or whom, lies unanswered, unanswerable. Rosenberg doesn't even allow us to rest there, bleak moment that it is. He pursues the feelings of the living:

> What of us, who flung on the shrieking pyre,
> Walk, our usual thoughts untouched,
> Our lucky limbs as on ichor fed,
> Immortal seeming ever?

He recognises here something difficult to admit, that the living are lucky – and they feel lucky; for all that someone else is dead, they are still alive, and in that moment they feel immortal as though the ichor that ran through the veins of the gods runs also through theirs. But this poem is a drama, moving us from stage to stage of the lived consciousness of death. No sooner than we have shared the understanding of the survivor's sense of immortality, than dread strikes;

---

[56] 'A slumber did my spirit seal' in William Wordsworth, *The Poetical Works*, ed. Thomas Hutchinson, rev. Ernest de Selincourt (London: Oxford University Press, 1961), 149.

> The air is loud with death,
> The dark air spurts with fire
> The explosions ceaseless are.
>
> Timelessly now, some minutes past,
> Those dead strode time with vigorous life,
> Till the shrapnel called 'an end'!

The existential drama of being glad to have survived (which must have carried a sort of elation as the odds were made visible by the surrounding dead) is immediately undercut by the terror of anticipating that 'end'. In this way, Rosenberg constantly cuts against the imagined reality he himself has created. Drawn into thinking about the soul, or at least into thinking hopelessly that something must exist beyond the body ('Somewhere they must have gone'), we are yanked back to the body:

> A man's brains splattered on
> A stretcher-bearer's face

Rosenberg can't stray far, though, from that question of whether anything lies beyond; it is tied relentlessly to the barbarism of the crunching apart of the dead – or worse, the dying – body.

There is, too, a constant exchange between the dying and the living. Rosenberg echoes the human response in the muscular one; the stretcher-bearer slips his load when caught by the horror of a man's brains splattering over him, but the shoulders bend again to pick up the stretcher, to take on the human weight though it is hopeless. By which time,

> The drowning soul was sunk too deep
> For human tenderness.

This might seem a natural ending to the poem, but Rosenberg pushes further, always trying to find the moment of death. He distinguishes between 'this dead' ('the drowning soul … sunk too deep / For human tenderness') and 'the older dead', lighting finally on 'one not long dead'. He imagines this man's last moments:

> His dark hearing caught our far wheels,
> And the choked soul stretched weak hands
> To reach the living word the far wheels said

This is an anguished understanding. We feel the supplication of the dying man, but also his foresight; he knows he is about to die. In the drama of the poem, this is the moment where Rosenberg unites the initial 'the wheels lurched over sprawled dead' with this final, and particular, 'the rushing wheels all mixed / With his tortured upturned sight'. It is here that we realise that the poem is returning to the poem's beginning. The wheels that 'lurched over sprawled dead / But pained them not' are only now approaching the body of 'one not long dead'. As 'the choked soul' reaches for 'the living word', so Rosenberg is reaching, like the dying man, for the moment between living and dying. In the end, he can only catch the moment of death as observed from outside, by the living:

> We heard his weak scream,
> We heard his very last sound,
> And our wheels grazed his dead face.

As we are ejected from the poem by this image of apparent indifference, we may feel, like the soldiers and the observant poet, complicit in this death. But the care Rosenberg has taken throughout the poem, standing back from this moment while also giving it the full weight of his poet's close gaze, makes that complicity also a compassionate one. We feel with and for the dying man whilst not softening the brutality of such a death in war. Rosenberg makes this a sort of recovery of the dead, but not the dishonest one proposed by Brooke; it recovers by paying proper heed.

At an earlier point in the poem, Rosenberg has toyed with a more conventional idea of the moment of death, that of the soul leaving the body in some almost-palpable form:

> None saw their spirits' shadow shake the grass,
> Or stood aside for the half used life to pass
> Out of the doomed nostrils and the doomed mouth

He envisages the spirit as a kind of a shadow (recalling the old idea of a shade, a ghost), and an exhalation, a wind. Vandiver connects Rosenberg's passage beautifully with its Homeric antecedents, noting that for Homer the word *psyche* could mean breath (when passing from the dead body), soul (which survives in the underworld after death) and life (as in the Greek phrase for fighting for one's life); she exemplifies these nuances of the word in Homer's descriptions of the death of Patroclus and of Hector, and adds: 'Rosenberg's lines reflect these nuances, referring to spirits that leave the body at the moment of death ... and also to "life" including the sense "breath", when "the half used life" passes from "doomed nostrils and the doomed mouth".'[57] What Vandiver misses, however, is that Rosenberg evokes the idea of the *psyche* rushing from the body, only to remove it: 'None

---

[57] Vandiver, *Stand in the Trench, Achilles*, 299.

saw' it leave the body. Here, as throughout the poem, Rosenberg eschews all standard forms of representing the dying. His is a unique gaze, which combines the depth of understanding of Homeric and elegiac tropes with a hard-eyed look at what actually happens. The mystery doesn't disappear – the poem is littered with questions – nor are attempts to account for the mystery dismissed. But they are carefully displaced by reminding us of what he has *seen*.[58]

It may be that Rosenberg's marginality as an East End Jewish poet allowed him to remake a poetic tradition in which he was not fully steeped. In a world of increasingly mobile and disparate communities, the memory theorists' notion of a coherent and determining collectivity loses some of its force. A further example is Mary Borden, an American émigré in London literary circles, who was able to incorporate the Whitmanesque in radical ways that transform the traditions of poetic commemoration. Her position as an incomer who set up her own hospital at the Somme, seeing at close quarters the damaged, dying and dead bodies of the *poilu*, was unique, and her poetry is unlike anything else written during this war. It is a Whitmanesque free verse, long, open and allusive. In one poem she writes of the mud as a character and a will with its own voice ('Song of the Mud'); in 'Unidentified' she turns her relentless gaze – and so ours – on the ordinary man in the trenches, about to die and lose his identity at any moment.[59] Her poetic task is to identify him, by making us, as readers, look at him, look at him properly. Like Rosenberg, she pays due heed, but in a different mode. Hers is a philosophical look, and while it accommodates the fearful conditions of the trenches where 'Death … suddenly explodes out of the dreadful bowels of the earth', she really wants us to see man as a poor, bare, forked animal. He is also 'Your giant – your brute – your ordinary man'; nothing about him is heroic, except that he stands up, and stays upright, even though

> One blow – one moment more – and that man's face will be
> a mass of matter – horrid slime – and little brittle bits –

---

[58] Vandiver also notes that the language of the sixth stanza – *pyre, ichor, immortal* – draws on Homeric diction and moreover 'strongly suggests the classical trope of apotheosis through fire, in which a mortal becomes immortal by burning'. However, she adds that Rosenberg alludes to apotheosis only 'to underline the illusory nature of such a hope' (ibid., 300). The irony is intensified with an awareness that *ichor*, as well as being the fluid in the veins of the gods, is an archaic word for the fluid discharged from an open wound.

[59] Mary Borden, 'Unidentified' in Kendall, *Poetry of the First World War*, 81–4. For more on this poem, see Palmer and Minogue, 'Modernism and First World War Poetry'.

Borden's is an extraordinary vision of the man who is about to die. She learnt this from working in 'that confused goods yard filled with bundles of broken human flesh. The place by one o'clock in the morning was a shambles. The air was thick with steaming sweat, with the effluvia of mud, dirt, blood.'[60] Her reference to 'a shambles' echoes the view of many soldiers that the trenches most closely resembled an abattoir.

Despite the very wide differences in their cultural experiences, and despite their very different relations to the broad forces of cultural memory, Rosenberg and Borden show the same determination to hold an unflinching gaze on the dying or about-to-die man, in circumstances which threaten to render that man *only* an animal, in the sense of a beast without consciousness. Their humane insistence on seeing the *man* – the man containing the animal – derives surely from their common experience of the mutilated body, which unites them more than their differences separate them.

Poets affected by different social and cultural factors, such as those that framed Rosenberg's and Borden's view, might then be united by something beyond their differences, such as their outsiderishness. Conversely, poets with very similar cultural formations in terms of class, education and social situation, such as Brooke and Sorley, might represent death in battle in ways that were diametrically opposed. Cutting across all such differences there seems to have been the possibility of apprehending something human *tout court* – perhaps especially in relation to death and the business of dying. First World War texts are no more transparent than any other texts; but they are tied powerfully to a historical and material reality which may at times eclipse socio-cultural differences which we have learnt to be alert to. The differences are there; but let us be aware also of the similarities in experience in the making of memory during a searingly intensive passage of history expressed, in this poetry, through individual consciousnesses. Such variability of attitude to, and expression of, the contingencies of individual experience, which nonetheless remains at some level a common experience, offer a caveat to the constructivist, collectivist framework posited by Halbwachs and his followers. Santanu Das has set a powerful example in his insistence on the importance of *both* the cultural conditions which shaped literary expression (and its reception at the time and subsequently) *and* 'the material conditions which produced the literature'.[61] We acknowledge gratefully the influence of that example;

---

[60] Borden, *The Forbidden Zone* (1929; London: Hesperus, 2008), 98.
[61] Santanu Das, *Touch and Intimacy in First World War Literature* (Cambridge: Cambridge University Press, 2005), 6.

and we share his central concern with 'men and women for whom the material conditions of everyday life – the immediate, sensory world – were altered radically by the war and often came to define their subjectivities'.[62] While taking into account the cultural mediations which existed at the time, and those which have affected us since, we must beware of allowing the material experience that underlies the poetic texts to be over-mediated by cultural accretions. We must tread carefully amongst the complicated interweavings of the individual, the social and the cultural, and always be alert to the way the 'subjectivities' of ordinary men and women were responding to what they experienced.

If, within this flexible framework, Brooke and Sorley nonetheless represent an insider's view, and Rosenberg and Borden, in some sense, an outsider's view, Wilfred Owen was both insider and outsider. His lack of public school, or even grammar school, education placed him outside the establishment, but his own aspirations were to enter that world as he pursued a classical education through his own efforts.[63] Owen's poetic considerations of dying are often troubled or marred by aureate diction; beside Rosenberg's unflinching eye, Owen's sometimes seems clouded by romanticism. He also often elides or obscures the moment of death itself. 'Spring Offensive' provides a rare description in his work of soldiers being killed, but the moment takes place in a subordinate clause of a sentence which comments ironically on the ways in which those deaths will later be spoken of:

> Of them who running on that last high place
> Breasted the surf of bullets, or went up
> On the hot blast and fury of hell's upsurge,
> Or plunged and fell away past this world's verge,
> Some say God caught them even before they fell.[64]

'Some *say*'. This reminds us of Rosenberg's raising the idea of the *psyche* being seen to leave the body, only to refuse it. Owen tells us that, unlike those who say such things, surviving soldiers 'speak not … of comrades that went under'. Apart from the soldierly euphemism 'went under' (which itself indicates the difficulty of confronting that moment), 'Spring Offensive' is written in high rhetorical style, with a vocabulary sometimes Keatsian, sometimes epic, sometimes frankly archaic. In using that mode

---

[62] Ibid., 11.
[63] Vandiver gives a detailed scholarly account of the extent of Owen's classical education and knowledge; Vandiver, *Stand in the Trench, Achilles*, 113–35.
[64] Owen, *Complete Poems and Fragments*, 192–3.

it tries to catch the moment of high excitement and terror of 'going over the top':

> So, soon they topped the hill, and raced together
> Over an open stretch of herb and heather
> Exposed. And instantly the whole sky burned
> With fury against them; earth set sudden cups
> In thousands for their blood; and the green slope
> Chasmed and deepened sheer to infinite space.

This is one way of representing the moment of death in battle which identifies its connections with athletic prowess and heroic combat. But it is far away from the philosophically scrupulous attention of Rosenberg and Borden. Owen does, however, give us an account closer to theirs in spirit, but different again in its insight into the prospect of death, in 'A Terre'. But he can do this only in a voice other than his own, the voice and vocabulary of a crippled soldier. If this man had his way, he would be speaking from the grave ('I tried to peg out soldierly') and he is very nearly dead ('Less live than specks that in the sun-shafts turn') but, living, he contemplates the conundrum of what awaits him:

> Your guns may crash around me. I'll not hear;
> Or, if I wince, I shall not know I wince.[65]

This is like Sorley's cold reminder, as perceived internally by the ordinary soldier – albeit one who has read Shelley, though only to ironise him:

> 'I shall be one with nature, herb, and stone,'
> Shelley would tell me. Shelley would be stunned:
> The dullest Tommy hugs that fancy now.
> 'Pushing up daisies' is their creed, you know.

Shelley's pantheistic vision is reduced to the soldier's wry notion of death, where the consolation of oneness with nature has been leached from the language.[66] Owen signifies that new understanding with his mixture of languages, 'stunning' the Shelleyan poetic with the clear-eyed vernacular of the common soldier (just as Rosenberg called up the Wordsworthian consolation only to reject it). All that remains of that unified vision of the world in Owen's poem is a kind of anticipatory prosopopoeia, whereby the good-as-dead man (he is 'three-parts shell', with a bandage that 'feels

---

[65] Owen, 'A Terre', ibid., 179.
[66] Owen (like Max Plowman; see our Introduction, pp. 8–9) draws on Shelley's 'Adonais', putting a paraphrase of stanza 42 into his soldier's mouth, but in order to challenge rather than endorse the offered consolation. See 'Adonais' in Shelley, *Selected Poems*, 328.

like pennies on my eyes') is given a voice. At times, he speaks of himself as already dead ('To grain, then, go my fat, to buds my sap') and finally speaks to the living as if from the grave:

> My soul's a little grief, grappling your chest,
> To climb your throat on sobs; easily chased
> On other sighs and wiped by fresher winds.

Here, he inhabits his future dead self, but he sees that he will have already become only the grief another person can utter for him – and so recognises that he will have no voice himself. This is a prosopopoeia of the modern universe, recognising that the voice of 'the dead' will not be heard.

In 'Strange Meeting' Owen takes a further step along this road, dramatising a meeting between two dead soldiers from opposite sides; both dead men are given direct speech, and they speak both to each other and to us. Unlike Brooke's imagined dead, gambolling in an eternal pastoral idyll, these men are doomed to haunt 'some profound dull tunnel', a cross between the underground caverns of the battlefield and a mythic underworld, surrounded by other dead. But in being given a voice, not only are they reanimated, but they can seek redress each from the other. When one of the dead springs up, the 'I' of the poem sees where he is:

> I knew that sullen hall, –
> By his dead smile I knew we stood in Hell[67]

While the poem recognises the actual hell of the battlefield which has led to these men's deaths, the foray into the underworld, and the reconciling of the unreconciled, place it firmly in a classical line running back through Dante to Homer and Virgil. Apostrophe and prosopopoeia themselves derive from that classical tradition, one grounded in the epic account of battle, but one too where the dead can be reimagined and re-encountered without entailing the Christian belief in resurrection. Vandiver thus places this encounter in the tradition of katabasis, in which the living visit the dead of the underworld and then return to the land of the living (as exemplified in the *Odyssey* and the *Aeneid*). But this is to miss a central tenet of Owen's poem: *both* those figured here are dead, and neither will return to the world above. This is a meeting of the equal dead, and the oxymoron of addressing 'the enemy you killed, my friend' makes sense only in the imagined state of after-death: Owen's is an imaginative reanimation of the dead within a powerful poetic tradition, one which enables him to

---

[67] Owen, *Complete Poems and Fragments*, 148.

give voice, *per impossibile*, to what the dead might think if they had the power to reflect on their own fate. But it is not consolatory, except in so far as those who died are at least represented in a continuing poetic tradition. For these poets, addressing the dead, and giving voice to the dead, are part of the powerful tradition of being a poet: to speak to and to speak for. And for a combatant seeing men dying all around him, what is more important than to speak to and for the dead body itself? But Owen, Rosenberg and Borden do this by creating a new framework for that speaking, one that refuses the comfort of a continued aliveness-in-death.

Owen's vision is not modernist in the way that Rosenberg's and Borden's are; his poetry is soaked with traditional forms and language. But he brings the dead to life in a different way, one that is emphatically not Brookeian even though it may use similar modes. 'Greater Love', for all its Brooke-like diction, is nonetheless a riposte to Brooke too, recalling the 'red sweet wine of youth' in 'Red lips are not so red / As the stained stones kissed by the English dead'.[68] It is also an ironic retort to the biblical quotation – 'Greater love hath no man than this, that a man lay down his life for his friends' – often inscribed on war memorials.[69] For what Owen explores in the poem is the interplay between love for a man when alive ('red lips', 'slender attitude', 'dear voice') and the actuality of death, where the lips can kiss only the 'stained stones', the mouth is 'stopped', and the body 'trembles not exquisite' but is 'rolling and rolling there / Where God seems not to care' (echoes of Wordsworth's 'Lucy' again). In what is a daring poem in its open declaration of male beauty, Owen expresses the paradox that drove many like him to return to be with their fellow soldiers even when they began to doubt the point of the war. That 'greater love' prevailed, but it entailed the endless loss of the men that inspired it.

Harold Monro had a quite different imaginative landscape, created in part by his constant interchange with, immeasurable encouragement to, and financial and cultural support of, the poets who passed through his seminal Poetry Bookshop (including Owen).[70] As the war started, many of these were heading to battle, his friend Brooke at that time the most significant amongst them. Monro was too old to fight. But like Owen he recognises the power of the young male body as he contemplates death in war. His poignant sequence 'Youth in Arms' traces a brief narrative starting

---

[68] Ibid., 166.
[69] John 15:13.
[70] Monro's Poetry Bookshop was a pivotal influence as an actual meeting point for poets and as a publisher of key texts, with Monro himself as the presiding spirit.

with the uniformed young man preparing for war, and ending with his dead body. The last of the four poems, 'Carrion', encapsulates the best qualities of the previous three. The poet imagines the dead young body as a still-alive, to-be-desired, body:

> It is plain now what you are. Your head has dropped
> Into a furrow. And the lovely curve
> Of your strong leg has wasted and is propped
> Against a ridge of the ploughed land's watery swerve.[71]

'Lovely curve' and its answering 'watery swerve' marry the man's body with the landscape. This is a return to the unified Romantic, as he imagines 'The crop that will rise from your bones is healthy bread'. We don't quite believe that determinedly optimistic note though; and there is also something of the Brookeian misting over, as the poet imagines that the earth will not fall on the body

> from the spade with a slam,
> But will fold and enclose you slowly, you living dead.

It all seems wishful thinking, but we can forgive the writer given his honesty about the beauty of the dead body in that first stanza. 'The lovely curve / Of your strong leg' is what he really grieves for.

Poets left behind to wait, to fret, to write hopeful, cheerful letters to those fighting, to re-meet and then as soon bid goodbye to lovers, friends or sons, then begin the whole business of waiting again – this is what marks the writing of both men and women put at a distance from the place of death, yet always imagining it. Often these poets remain stuck in an old-fashioned rhetoric – as sometimes even combatant poets do – but it is more difficult for the home poets to break out of it as they are stuck, too, in a place of longing and fear for the loved person in battle. There is little or no agency in such a role, unless, like Borden, you have work. Women left to fret or grieve, but also give support, are in a particularly cramped position as poets.

Eleanor Farjeon, circumscribed even more by her loving the married Edward Thomas while (probably) not being his lover, writes the perfect poem of a distanced, delayed understanding of the loved one's death. 'Easter Monday' catches the particular agony inflicted by the time delay in getting news of the loss of a loved one.[72] She has written and sent three

---

[71] Harold Monro, 'Carrion' in Hibberd and Onions (eds), *Winter of the World*, 21.
[72] Eleanor Farjeon, 'Easter Monday' in Catherine Reilly (ed.), *Scars upon My Heart: Women's Poetry and Verse of the First World War* (London: Virago, 1981), 36.

letters to Thomas, only to discover later that he was dead all that time; the structure of the poem holds this dramatic irony within its form. Taking a line from his own letter to her in the first half of the poem – ' "It was such a lovely morning" ' – she repeats it in the second half to reflect her own experience of that Easter Monday, when she was still ignorant of his death. The multiplying ironies are reflected in the simplicity of the last line: 'There are three letters that you will not get.' It is heartbreaking that, even now, she cannot stop herself from continuing to address him in the present. Farjeon wrote her poem in the knowledge that Thomas was dead; Vera Brittain inscribed her poem 'To My Brother' on the flyleaf of a poetry anthology, *The Muse in Arms*, which she sent to her brother Edward on the Italian Front, thinking him still alive.[73] But Edward was killed four days after she sent it, and before he could read her poem of tribute. Reading it now, we can't escape that irony; our hindsight embeds it in the poem.

Many of the poems written by those outside the battle are necessarily valedictory, and here we come back to memorialisation. The remembrance uttered by combatant poets, speaking from the thick of battle, even if a poem was written on leave or behind the lines, is imbued with the here and now of death. But, with some exceptions such as Gurney with his named comrades, they mourn a whole group of people even when it is one death that they fix on. The poems of those left to grieve at a distance are characteristically personal, and they address *that* person lost. This is different from the general address to the dead we discussed earlier, and different too from the gaze of either Rosenberg or Borden on the impersonal dead body. When Brittain wrote to her brother, she did not know he would be dead when her poem arrived; but Farjeon writes to Edward Thomas, whom she knows to be dead, in exactly the same intimate tones. Margaret Postgate Cole's 'Afterwards' is likewise addressed to 'my beloved'.[74] These poems escape the charge of a dishonest bringing to life of the dead. These women poets know full well the men they address are dead; these are elegies on an ordinary scale, with the scale of grief reined in. Postgate Cole touchingly invokes the future she and her lover might have imagined for themselves:

> eating strawberries and cream and cakes –
> O cakes, O cakes, O cakes, from Fuller's!

---

[73] Berry and Bostridge, *Vera Brittain*, 135–6; Brittain, 'To My Brother' in Reilly, *Scars upon My Heart*, 15.
[74] Margaret Postgate Cole, 'Afterwards' in Reilly, *Scars upon My Heart*, 21–2.

They might, too, have returned to 'the larches up in Sheer', and this she does in the 'afterwards' landscape of the poem, but now alone:

> And lying in Sheer
> I look round at the corpses of the larches
> Whom they slew to make pit-props
> For mining the coal for the great armies.

Nature has been laid waste to feed the mechanised demands of battle; the larches are corpses as her dead lover is a corpse:

> And think, a pit-prop cannot move in the wind …
> Though you planted it out on the hill again it would be dead.

The Wordsworthian/Shelleyan pact between man and nature has been felled by this war; not only are the larches dead, the pit-props are dead, and the man is dead:

> What use is it to you? What use
> To have your body lying here
> In Sheer, underneath the larches?

From the depth of personal grief and loss, Postgate Cole raises the same existential questions that Borden does, that Rosenberg does, that Sorley and Owen and Monro do, and that so many First World War poets do. The non-combatant poets joined the combatant poets in the task of remembrance and memorialisation – keeping the dead in the imagination of the living.

If Brooke was the earliest manifestation of 'cultural memory' about the First World War, Owen's poetry has become an alternative accredited 'cultural memory' of a different kind. The Assmanns's theory of the role of reception in the formation of memory makes these two competing strands possible. Owen's work certainly became the late-twentieth-century popular site for our understanding of First World War deaths, mourning and remembrance – and to an extent remains so. But a feature of this centenary moment, at which we reconsider all the issues outlined in this chapter, is the far greater diversity of representation now available to us. Poems and poets of all ilks have been revived and reverberate in the public memory. Among the most notable of these is Ivor Gurney, who has emerged as a major voice only in the last twenty years. Gurney addresses like no other both the particulars of death in battle and the far larger sense of desperate loss as it turns into existential terror.

In 'To His Love', Gurney creates the poetic correlative of what Roland Barthes calls the Irremediable. Barthes, analysing, only days after his mother's death, his own intense and lacerating feelings of loss asks, 'In the sentence "She's no longer suffering", to what, to whom does "she" refer? What does that present tense mean?'[75] Barthes notes the contradiction in our tendency to think or speak of the dead as still alive, yet claim consolation for them in their *not* being alive, as though they can experience the lack of suffering. In fact, of course, they experience nothing. That they experience nothing is itself a consolation, but one that can't be known by them precisely because they experience nothing. And for those of us left behind, it is not a consolation either because the horror is precisely *that* they can experience nothing.[76] That is the existential void, the 'Irremediable' of death.[77] Gurney, in 'To His Love', expresses the void, as well as reflecting on memory itself. The poem is at heart the commemoration of a particular man. Gurney had been in the front line since June 1916; in August of that year he heard that his much loved friend from Gloucestershire days, Will Harvey, was missing, presumed dead. Gurney's deep sense of loss at that time is recorded in several letters. The received view of 'To His Love' is that it was finished *after* Gurney learned that Harvey was not in fact dead, but was in a prisoner of war camp. But the poem doesn't read like that. Rather it has the feel of an ungoverned grief and despair, a cry of loss. 'He's gone' – in that small phrase Gurney leaps straight into the modern voice.[78] The colloquial elision of 'He's' is inexorably in the present, while the dependent 'gone' is ineluctably in the past. The voice is colloquial, yet all the pain of the poem is contracted into that brief clause. Everything that comes after is predicated on the loss it expresses: 'all our plans are useless indeed'.

The tenses of the poem play backward and forward so that we are not sure where we are in time. 'We'll walk no more on Cotswold' conjures up a future and cancels it at the same time, just as the present of 'he's' is cancelled by the past participle 'gone'. Yet the sheep remain steadily in the historic present, feeding and taking no heed. The same interplay of tenses can be seen in the second stanza:

> His body that was so quick
> Is not as you
> Knew it, on Severn river
>   Under the blue
>   Driving our small boat through.

---

[75] Barthes, *Mourning Diary*, 15.
[76] Unless their suffering is so great that we *prefer* that they experience nothing.
[77] Barthes, *Mourning Diary*, 90.
[78] 'To His Love' in Gurney, *Collected Poems*, 21.

We move though 'was' (past), 'Is' (present), 'not' (cancelling the present 'is'), 'Knew' (past again) and 'Driving' (continuous present). The subject of the poem is still alive in memory, yet unimaginably dead; the play of tenses against each other tries to make sense of that.

Here we have a poet, in the midst of fighting, hearing, as he thought, of the death of a man he loved. But the poem goes beyond those specifics, catching the existential vertigo that comes with understanding that a man alive one minute can be dead the next, cancelling his future, and making a mockery of his past. At the Front, sudden death was everywhere; but the death of this one man brings the poet up against the problem of making some meaning of it. If the first three stanzas of the poem with their grazing sheep, Severn river and violets call up the comfort of pastoral, in the final stanza we see the flash of horror which cannot be concealed by any amount of flowers, and which links back to the modernity of the opening, 'He's gone':

> Cover him, cover him soon!
>   And with thick-set
> Masses of memoried flowers –
>   Hide that red wet
>   Thing I must somehow forget.

'Red wet' in a First World War context can only mean one thing; but then Gurney uses the actual word 'Thing' which, in its very lack of specificity, adds to the line's power after the particularity of place and flower names. It is these which are now made silly by what is unimaginable in any specific terms. The loved 'body that was so quick' has been reduced to a 'thing', its quickness spilled out in the 'red wet', and that memory is now caught forever, making the earlier innocent memories impossible. Being the one thing to forget, it is forever remembered. Tim Kendall suggests that 'Gurney attempts to observe the rites of official remembrance while withstanding a panicked reaction to the wounded corpse'.[79] But Gurney is signalling a lacuna rather than a contradiction – an existential panic. He allows no comfort into the poem; the lure of pastoral redemption is floated before us only to be refused. Rather he wants to reflect that moment of utter hopelessness when the past is made barren and the future hopeless, that moment of laceration, the irremediable. The sudden horror of the last two lines ends the poem on a void, ejecting the reader into the real world

---

[79] Tim Kendall, *Modern English War Poetry* (Oxford: Oxford University Press, 2006), 86.

beyond the poem and to a fresh understanding of her own mortality. It is a long poetic journey from Brooke's *red sweet wine* to Gurney's *red wet thing*.

The grief we feel for soldiers killed in war is so sharp because their lives have been brutally cut short. The grief for those killed in the First World War is sharper still because so many were amateur soldiers – carpenters, teachers, bakers, mechanics – who had no clear idea of the realities ahead. When Owen reminds us of the 'Carnage incomparable, and human squander / Rucked too thick for these men's extrication', he is lamenting a double tragedy, the scale of death itself, and the inability of men's minds to comprehend it. The poets we consider in this book did somehow manage the act of imaginative extrication from 'carnage incomparable, and human squander', bringing to us – at the distance of a hundred years – some understanding and engagement with a moment in history whose horrors sometimes seem to defeat representation. More than that, they bring us face to face with our human, mortal selves and the fact of our own extinction. Out of their own grief for the loss of comrades, from the feared loss of their own lives, and from the grief of those at home who suffered the loss of loved ones, came poems, each one an attempt to move beyond the howl of despair, to give it shape and meaning. These poets look hard at death – though their eyes are sometimes cloaked – and they bring us missives from that Front, in the form of poems. It is the intention of this book to look as closely as the poets do.

CHAPTER 2

'The World's Worst Wound'
Death, Consciousness and Modernism

The words we use to describe the modernist revolution are metaphors: fragmentation, dissolution, dissonance, rupture – and wound. If we draw our attention back to the literal meanings of those words, and the realities to which they refer, we find ourselves at the Front. Siegfried Sassoon, looking back in 1928, said simply: 'here was the world's worst wound'.[1] D. H. Lawrence wrote, also in 1928, in *Lady Chatterley's Lover*:

> Slowly, slowly the wound to the soul begins to make itself felt like a bruise, which only slowly deepens its terrible ache, till it fills all the psyche. And when we think we have recovered and forgotten, it is then that the terrible after-effects have to be encountered at their worst ... The bruise was deep, deep, deep ... the bruise of the false, inhuman war.[2]

In later cultural criticism, the characterisation became more fixed; Malcolm Bradbury, writing in 1976, notes that: 'of the great transition into the modern place, modern time, modern indifference, modern hardness, the war was the ultimate symbol. It expressed itself, again and again, as violation, intrusion, wound, the source of psychic anxiety.'[3] These metaphorical uses, we must remember, depend for their resonance on the actual wounds which were inflicted on those who experienced the war. Fatal damage to the flesh, both actual and imminent, is testified to in many prose accounts; rotting corpses and gaping skeletons were part of the everyday landscape, even part of the revetments of the trenches themselves.[4] At the centre of our discussion is the way in which the

---

[1] 'On Passing the New Menin Gate' in Sassoon, *Collected Poems*, 188.
[2] D. H. Lawrence, *Lady Chatterley's Lover* (1928; Harmondsworth: Penguin, 1960), 51. Lawrence is writing initially about Clifford Chatterley's maiming, then alluding more generally to the effect of the war.
[3] Malcolm Bradbury, 'The Denuded Place: War and Form in *Parade's End* and *USA*', *The First World War in Fiction: A Collection of Critical Essays*, ed. Holger Klein (London: Macmillan, 1976), 193–4.
[4] See Barbusse, *Under Fire*, 268–70, 275–6; Blunden, *Undertones of War* (1928; Harmondsworth: Penguin, 1982), especially 124–5, 130; Siegfried Sassoon, *Diaries 1915–1918*, ed. Rupert Hart-Davis (London: Faber & Faber, 1983), 144–5.

ubiquity and suddenness of death, and the continuing presence of dead bodies, affected the consciousness of the poet in a new way. The desire to comfort or mourn must have vied with the impulse to recoil in disgust, not just from the sensory experience of rotting bodies, but from the existential abyss which opened to the living.

Eric Leed, in a seminal study, suggests: 'The front is a place that dissolved the clear distinction between life and death. Death, customarily the "slash" between life/not-life, became for many in the war a "dash", a continuum of experience the end of which was the cessation of any possibility of experience.'[5] Thus the combatant was faced with dead bodies both as an ever-present reminder of mortality and a continuing presence in the world of the living, threatening the individual's very sense of self, since he might at any moment be swallowed up either by an element which combined mud and rotting flesh, or by sudden extinction. For the poet this threatened dissolution of both flesh and self also issued as a contradiction: how to express these things in the specificity of experience that is almost unsayable. Sometimes the poet's gaze is directed inward, to his own consciousness, sometimes outward to the particular grisliness of a landscape populated by corpses. In some cases, these two sorts of horror, the existential and the grossly physical, exist in counterpoint, sometimes they merge; either way, they put pressure on standard modes of expression. If the modernist enterprise is to reflect in language the specificities of shifting consciousness and perception in response to the pressures of modernity on the sense of self, this takes us directly to modernism. Kurtz's cry of ' "The horror! The horror!" '[6] as he looks into the heart of his own existential darkness is so resonant because it expresses just enough of that darkness whilst recognising that anything more specific would falsify both the enormity and the essential privacy of the experience – perhaps the reason it was taken up by T. S. Eliot as the original epigraph to that constitutively modernist poem, *The Waste Land*.[7] Here, however, we shall argue that the most profound expression of the 'horror', existential and actual, is to be found in the poetry of the war

---

[5] Eric Leed, *No Man's Land: Combat and Identity in World War I* (Cambridge: Cambridge University Press, 1979), 21.
[6] Joseph Conrad, *Heart of Darkness* (1902; Harmondsworth: Penguin, 1973), 111.
[7] Eliot removed the epigraph after a negative comment by Pound, thus taking the poem further from historical specificity. See the title page of the original draft of the poem in T. S. Eliot, *The Waste Land: A Facsimile and Transcript of the Original Drafts Including the Annotations of Ezra Pound*, ed. Valerie Eliot (London: Faber & Faber, 1971), and editorial note 1, 125.

itself; in its struggle to find the new forms of expression required, it is also a modernist poetry.

It is a particular irony that, while the First World War itself is both an iconic site of change, fracture and dislocation, and one, if not *the*, definitive historical marker for the birth of modernism, the poetry of that war has largely been left out of the modernist fold.[8] The work of the canonical poets, even where that canon has been widened, is still placed, culturally and formally, as a poetry of witness, while poets such as Herbert Read and David Jones, whose poetry is, in technique anyway, more obviously modernist, remain even now marginal figures both in the canon of First World War poetry and in accounts of literary modernism. And this is in spite of multiple, rich re-readings of this body of poetry particularly over the last thirty years. We want to redress that balance, arguing that in recognising the modernist dimensions of some First World War poetry we will also understand modernism more fully. The poems we consider remind us forcibly of the realist dimension of modernism, and not just at the level of consciousness, but with the recognition that the First World War was a material, historical event, the experience of which, whether at first hand or at a remove, issued in certain poems which would not have been written in that form without it. The materiality of individual experience, as well as the consciousness through which that experience was mediated, were in that sense referents of the language used in such poetry.

Astradur Eysteinsson points out that, for a number of its adherents, modernism, 'far from rejecting the "real world" … is seeking reality at a different level of human existence, reality as it is processed by the human consciousness'.[9] One problem about such high modernist 'realism' is that the emphasis on subjectivity leads to a constant questioning of the existence or even of the possibility of a shared common reality; the *reductio* of high modernism is solipsism. Michael Levenson sees this as resulting finally in a separation of language from the need to represent reality:

> On the one side … the real collapsed into the perceived, and the artist began to usurp the place of the world … The second threat to mimesis came from

---

[8] The prose of the war has been seen much more readily as allied with modernism. See Allyson Booth, *Postcards from the Trenches: Negotiating the Space between Modernism and the First World War* (Oxford: Oxford University Press, 1996), especially 50–63, 67–87, 104–21; Randall Stevenson, *Literature and the Great War 1914–1918* (Oxford: Oxford University Press, 2013), 47–61, 114–20; Trudi Tate, *Modernism, History and the First World War* (Manchester: Manchester University Press, 1998), especially 1–6, 64–95; Alan Warren Friedman, *Fictional Death and the Modernist Enterprise* (Cambridge: Cambridge University Press, 1995), especially 207–29.
[9] Astradur Eysteinsson, *The Concept of Modernism* (Ithaca: Cornell University Press, 1990), 184.

the word itself, the word freed from the need to signify at all ... In short, from the perspective of either the autonomous poet ... or the autonomous word ... the obligation to depict the world loses its hold.[10]

The contradiction inherent in the work of the canonical modernist writers is, then, that while they seek to give expression to an anti-materialist, anti-historicist understanding of the world – they do so in language, in the permanent forms of art. In this sense they *are* in fact arch-realists since they seek to bring even the ineffable into the grasp of language. No matter how plural, multi-vocal and structurally fragmented a text may be, it remains and sustains as a text, and thus as part of the world; and in so far as it is constructed in language, it also refers to the world, however that world may be refracted into different realities by individual consciousnesses.

This paradox is at the heart of modernism. Critics and theorists have allowed the potential contradiction here as itself part of the pluralistic nature of modernism and, in doing this, have relied on the use of metaphor. Thus the title *The Waste Land* seems to express perfectly the inherent emptiness and desolation of a world in which fragments of consciousness are all that is left, with no stabilising reality for them to cohere in. But the words 'waste land' depend for their metaphorical meaning on a literal meaning which precedes that: a land which is barren, cannot produce, is desert. Similarly, the fragments of consciousness in Eliot's poem originate from identities, those identities differentiated for us in the poem by means of different uses of language, different voices.[11] Both waste land and voices originate, then, in the real world, and the artistic representation of a dissolution of that reality is only that, a representation, a metaphor, which depends for its meaning on a pre-existent reality.

The modernism we find in First World War poetry involves no such slippage or sleight of hand, for there is no contradiction between the real experience from which it derives and which it expresses, and the movement in certain poems towards linguistic and formal fragmentation and doubleness. As we argue elsewhere:

> Such attempts to find a language and form to express the existential contradictoriness of living up close to death are in a continuum with the fragmentariness and dislocation we find in Pound and Eliot. But while theirs is a willed response to modernity, the war poets are responding directly to

---

[10] Michael H. Levenson, *A Genealogy of Modernism: A Study of English Literary Doctrine 1908–1922* (Cambridge: Cambridge University Press, 1984), 132.
[11] Eliot's working title, 'He Do the Police in Different Voices', underlines this (Eliot, *The Waste Land: A Facsimile*, see page heads and 125).

> a constitutively incoherent set of experiences. Eliot's commitment to the impersonal voice and to the use of allusiveness and symbolism in its service, lead to its being expressive of the fracture and dissolution associated with the event of the war, but without directly referring to it ... The war poets, on the other hand, are always engaged with experience at the level of the human. Their use of fragmented form, intercutting of voices (sometimes to the point of cacophony), their pushing of language sometimes to its limits, are all in the service of showing both the humanity of man to man, and at the same time therefore what is lost of the human when both mind and body are stretched to their limits.[12]

In highlighting this continuity with modernism, then, we want to preserve the very qualities of these poems which have led to their being seen characteristically in contradistinction to poetic modernism, that is their referential and historicist dimensions.

We'll make a methodological analogy here with the feminist recuperation of women poets of this period. Jane Dowson suggests that we talk of 'modernisms' rather than a singular 'modernism':

> One central strategy is to unsettle the binary concepts which falsely sever 'experiment' from 'tradition' and which support a hierarchical model of modernist poetics. The omission of women from histories of literary modernism is particularly invidious because of its elevated status and metonymical 'intellectuality'. It assigns women to modernism's antithetical ground of the 'popular' or 'sentimental'.[13]

First World War poets are similarly omitted, being assigned in their case to the non-intellectual, non-avant-garde ground of the realist and the documentary. This challenge to a monolithic modernism is now found increasingly within modernist studies itself. Peter Nicholls's 1995 revisionist account signals multiplicity in his very title: *Modernisms: A Literary Guide*.[14] Chris Baldick, attempting to rescue the 1920s from the narrative march of modernism, challenges the imposed model for this period in which 'a radical new tendency to Experiment does battle with the doomed rearguard of Tradition'; his later detailed discussions show the way in which 'that heroic myth' glosses over 'the real complexities of literary diversity and debate in the 1920s'.[15] Alysson Booth, addressing specifically the relationship between

---

[12] Palmer and Minogue, 'Modernism and First World War Poetry', 245.
[13] Jane Dowson, *Women, Modernism and British Poetry, 1910–1939: Resisting Femininity* (Aldershot: Ashgate, 2002), 1. See also Angela K. Smith, *The Second Battlefield: Women, Modernism and the First World War* (Manchester: Manchester University Press, 2000), 3–6.
[14] Peter Nicholls, *Modernisms: A Literary Guide* (Basingstoke: Macmillan, 1995).
[15] Chris Baldick, *Literature of the 1920s: Writers among the Ruins* (Edinburgh: Edinburgh University Press, 2012), 24.

modernism and the First World War, argues for 'an expansive concept of modernism ... that displays itself as deeply engaged in a broader Great War culture'.[16] She adds: 'I don't set out in this book to construct rigid categories of modernist versus antimodernist texts ... for even individual writers fluctuate back and forth along the spectrums that roughly delineate the differences ... between modernism and the forms that might seem to constitute its opposite'.[17] We too want to draw back from any narrow, polarised concept of modernism – away thus from high modernism – to look at the ways in which poets who drew on and represented their experience of the First World War can be seen as contributing to modernism.[18] In order to show that this dimension of First World War poetry is not a matter of odd or rogue examples, in this chapter we draw primarily on hard cases, poems that have not been seen standardly as modernist, by Arthur Graeme West, Wilfrid Gibson, Edmund Blunden, Robert Nichols and Siegfried Sassoon. We end with poems by Ivor Gurney and Mary Borden.[19]

The narrative of Arthur Graeme West's 'The Night Patrol' is driven by dead bodies; they are the one constant. As we said in our Introduction, they become the landmarks by which the night patrol can find their way back to their own lines. At first, the descriptions of the dead don't distinguish them as particular corpses or groups of corpses, focusing rather on their effect on the senses:

> Only the dead were always present – present
> As a vile sickly smell of rottenness;
> The rustling stubble and the early grass,
> The slimy pools – the dead men stank through all,
> Pungent and sharp; as bodies loomed before,
> And as they passed, they stank: then dulled away
> To that vague foetor, all encompassing,
> Infecting earth and air.[20]

The next lines – 'They lay, all clothed, / Each in some new and piteous attitude' – lead us to expect a conventionally human response, but then

---

[16] Booth, *Postcards from the Trenches*, 4.
[17] Ibid., 7.
[18] For this reason we do not use HD's work as an exemplar. The high modernist mode of her Imagist collection *Sea Garden* (1916) deliberately distances itself from its historical context, and thus from any direct engagement with remembering the dead – an example of what Margot Norris calls 'Modernism's suppression of the war dead' (Norris, *Writing War in the Twentieth Century* (Charlottesville: University Press of Virginia, 2000), 35).
[19] Chapter 3 focuses on David Jones and Isaac Rosenberg and the way their poetry challenges and remakes modernist myth-making.
[20] 'The Night Patrol' in West, *The Diary of a Dead Officer*, 81–3.

comes the disaffect as we realise that the individual poses are being carefully marked only so that they can be remembered as guide posts on the way back.

This retreat into disengagement, marked in a number of the poems we discuss, is both a defining response to the horror of being surrounded by death, and a characterising element in these poets' modernism. For West this was caught up peculiarly with the business of representation, as we see from his *Diary of a Dead Officer*, published posthumously in 1919 (where he expresses doubts about the rightness of the war similar to Sassoon's more widely known ones). In one passage he recalls seeing a fellow soldier's charcoal drawing entitled '"We want more men!" showing Death, with the English staff cap on and a ragged tunic, standing with a jagged sickle among a pile of bleeding, writhing bodies and smoking corpses'. His response is 'impotent horror' and he notes that the 'huge gaunt figure' of Death 'haunted me horribly'.[21] At another point in his diary he attempts an analysis of his own fear, noting rationally that 'I mind being killed because I am fond of the other life, but I know I should not miss it in annihilation'. Frustrated, he 'cannot bind the fear down to anything definite', concluding:

> I think it resolves itself simply into the realisation of the fact that being hit by a shell will produce a new set of circumstances so strange that one does not know how one will find oneself in them. It is the knowledge that something may happen with which one will not be able to cope … Something unknown there is. How will one act when it happens?[22]

'Something unknown there is': this is at the heart of the modernist impulse, as it recognises the unknown but at the same time tries to give it form in words. What is touching in West's account is his imagined, yet unimaginable, shaping up to it.

Small wonder that West felt isolated in the conventions of the army; but he felt the same with regard to his fellow poets. In 'God! How I Hate You, You Young Cheerful Men!', his ire is directed at those who had 'seen the trenches, glimpsed the huddled dead' but still produced 'pious poetry' and 'sentimental elegies'.[23] He gives a traditional poetic description of a dead man, to counter the hated sentimentality:

> a sentry shot at night,
> Hunched as he fell, his feet on the firing-step,

---

[21] Ibid., 23.
[22] Ibid., 68.
[23] Ibid., 79.

> His neck against the back slope of the trench,
> And the rest doubled up between, his head
> Smashed like an eggshell, and the warm grey brain
> Spattered all bloody on the parados[24]

Nothing modernist here. But if we put this sensuous description, reflecting the poet's deliberate gaze, together with that 'Something unknown there is', we see the split between the all too graspable physical and the formless unknown which it also generates.

Between the satirical response of the caricatured drawing which so horrified him, and the sentimentality of the standard poetic elegy, West's well-observed poetic sketches of dead bodies won't suffice. In 'The Night Patrol', he depicts instead the refusal to represent the dead in any standard way, capturing the internal dissociation which seems the only (perhaps was the only actual) response. Leed argues that this 'transgression of categories' is endemic in the experience of the First World War: 'In providing bridges across the boundaries between the visible and the invisible, the known and the unknown, the human and the inhuman, war offered numerous occasions for the shattering of distinctions that were central to orderly thought, communicable experience, and normal human relations.'[25] In such a universe, where the usual orders and significances placed on life are rendered meaningless, a tragic stance is aggrandising and falsifying, because it accords moral meaning when that has been removed. Another mode has to be found; and for many writers, that mode was bathos.

Bathos is an under-recognised element of modernist technique, perhaps because it teeters on the edge of the comic in one direction and of the valueless in the other. Wherever it is used (and we may more readily think of the eighteenth-century mock-heroic as its natural home), it works by drawing together two terms inherently different in value and rendering them as apparently of the same value by placing them on a par with each other, grammatically, structurally and ostensibly morally. In the mock-heroic, it is used to comic effect, the reader understanding that the apparent parity speaks of a real disparity; the comedy is derived from the double understanding. In its modernist use, however, the laconic placing of the apparently important and the unimportant side by side is used to produce the deflation of meaning. The suggested parity is real (say between a dead body and a signpost) but at the same time it depends on a disparity which

---

[24] Ibid., 80.
[25] Leed, *No Man's Land*, 21.

is serious – the dead body isn't, in any normal terms, merely a signpost, and to regard it as such is to denigrate its significance. But in this otherworld, that distinction has collapsed. Pushed to its extreme, this leads to a feeling that there is no meaning, or that the world is meaningless. Pushed further, it leads to a sense of the absurdity of existence. In the physical and psychological world of the First World War, that absurdity was actual. Santanu Das, in his brilliant evocation of the relationship between the material, the psychological and the conceptual at the Front, puts it thus: 'When contingency becomes the ruling principle, as in the world of the trenches, and cancels human motive or meaning, life becomes absurd'.[26] In poetry, bathos answered to that absurdity.

Wilfrid Gibson's 'Between the Lines' is written in the omniscient third person but narrated as from the point of view of a first person consciousness, that of Tom Dodd, who has been shot in action and wakes to find himself between the opposing lines, but not knowing which is which. He crawls into the relative safety of a shell-hole, and from here conducts the free indirect inner monologue which is the body of the poem. The narrative is initially conventional, reflecting alternately on his civilian life as an assistant in a haberdasher's and his current soldier's life. Though the poet never drops his conventional *abab* rhyme structure, the in-and-out pattern of consciousness cuts across this, and soon the two sets of experience and time frames run into each other:

> Politely talking weather, fit to drop,
> With swollen ankles, tired …
>   But he was tired
> Now. Every bone was aching,[27]

This device of a repeated word, here 'tired', to move from past to present is used to different effect as his mind wanders over the past 'fourteen days and nights in that wet trench'. And so he comes to the nub of the poem: the death of his friend Dick.

>   He'd slept and fed
> And sung and smoked in it, while shrapnel screamed
> And shells went whining harmless overhead –
> Harmless, at least as far as he …
>   But Dick –
> Dick hadn't found them harmless yesterday,

---

[26] Das, *Touch and Intimacy*, 48.
[27] Wilfrid Gibson, 'Between the Lines' in Kendall, *Poetry of the First World War*, 67. The ellipses in all the lines we quote from this poem are Gibson's.

Dodd goes on to recall Dick going to get 'butter in a lordly dish' because he couldn't 'stick / Eating dry bread':

> Butter enough for all, and held it high,
> Yellow and fresh and clean as you could wish –
> When plump upon the plate from out the sky
> A shell fell bursting ... Where the butter went,
> God only knew! ...
>   And Dick ... he dared not think
> Of what had come to Dick ... or what it meant –[28]

Here Gibson catches that suddenness of death plummeting from the sky on to the attempted domesticity which was a feature of the Front. We see the butter, 'yellow and fresh and clean'; we see the importance of the butter, carrying with it civilised values ('butter in a lordly dish'). And we see, not Dick blown to kingdom come, but rather the butter: 'Where the butter went, / God only knew! ...'.

Edmund Blunden describes, in his memoir *Undertones of War* (1928), a similar occasion when the suddenness of death flings itself on an essayed normality, here involving a cup of tea:

> Not far away from that shafthead, a young and cheerful lance-corporal of ours was making some tea as I passed one warm afternoon. Wishing him a good tea, I went along three firebays; one shell dropped without warning behind me; I saw its smoke faint out, and I thought all was as lucky as it should be. Soon a cry from that place recalled me; the shell had burst all wrong. Its butting impression was black and stinking in the parados where three minutes ago the lance-corporal's mess-tin was bubbling over a little flame. For him, how could the gobbets of blackening flesh, the earth-wall sotted with blood, with flesh, the eye under the duckboard, the pulpy bone be the only answer? At this moment, while we looked with dreadful fixity at such a horror, the lance-corporal's brother came round the traverse.[29]

Just as Gibson shows Tom Dodd thinking determinedly of the butter, Blunden's incredulity at what has happened, for all its open-eyed emphasis on the horror of the exploded body, fixes on the mess-tin which 'three minutes ago ... was bubbling over a little flame'. In Gibson's poem, the very ceremony of the butter in a dish is set against the brutality of the circumstances, so that the randomness of a shell falling at such a time becomes something more, a hit against normality, civilisation and any impulse to the ordinary. And the shell is, of course, huge against the

---

[28] Ibid., 67–8.
[29] Blunden, *Undertones*, 67.

smallness of the butter. 'When plump upon the plate from out the sky / A shell fell bursting …': here the butter takes the place of Dick's body; and there is something horrible about the word 'plump' which has its meaning of 'straight down upon', but also reminds us of the softness of flesh. Dick is gone; but we know it only through the butter. The small acts of domesticity, associated in Blunden with the mess-tin and in Gibson with the butter, ranged as they are in a stupid hopefulness against the deadly shells, speak of the human in some way more than the body itself. They are displacements of the body, but extensions of them, and expressions of the human tendency to nurture normality, to combat inhumanity with the everyday. The gobbets of flesh, the eyeball under the duckboard, are almost too grotesque to comprehend, and in Gibson's poem are not even put into words. The blowing apart of the body has to find an equivalent in something else, something at once more manageable yet in its very lack of equivalence, absurd. Displacement becomes the aesthetic of this world.

Das has given us a new understanding of the role of the senses in both the experience and the literary expression of the First World War. In his chapter 'Geographies of Sense', he explores the importance of 'the phenomenological geography of the trenches – a landscape not understood in terms of maps, places and names, but geography as processes of cognition, as subjective and sensuous states of experience'.[30] His general term for this is the haptic, a way of understanding the self in relation to the surrounding world through the senses, which became particularly powerful in the trenches, where the normal modes of understanding the world fell away, as the normal world itself fell away. The haptic involves an empathy between the sensual self and the surrounding sensual world, and Das argues that it was instrumental in the new modes of literary expression required by this 'phenomenological geography'.[31] We want to suggest that, in this world where the senses could be assaulted so powerfully, perhaps one defence of those experiencing it was not an embrace of but a denial or reversal of the haptic. Das's evocation of the dissolution of boundaries in the chapter 'Slimescapes' recognises that the 'threat, both physical and psychic, of *dissolution into formless matter* … brought the soldiers to the precipice of non-meaning in a world that was already ceasing to make sense'.[32] One defence against this dissolution into non-meaning was, at the level of actual experience, a refusal of sensual

---

[30] Das, *Touch and Intimacy*, 73.
[31] Ibid., 73–5.
[32] Ibid., 37. The italics are Das's.

and psychological empathy and the withdrawal of engagement. That withdrawal is certainly present at the level of representation. If one is not to succumb to the horror of disintegration either into the slime of the corpse itself or into the corpse-ridden mud-sucking landscape, the best defence may be alienation. Blunden's closing of his account of the death of the 'cheerful lance-corporal' reflects a sense of cosmic incongruity. As he puts it, laconically: 'The bay had to be put right, and red-faced Sergeant Simmons, having helped himself and me to a share of rum, biting hard on his pipe, shovelled into the sandbag I held, not without self-protecting profanity, and an air of "it's a lie; we're a lie".'[33] The comment 'it's a lie; we're a lie' cuts through the deliberate distancing, but still we are held away from the brutal actualities of what is being shovelled. We are told only 'Sergeant Simmons … shovelled into the sandbag I held'; there is a blank where the object of the verb 'shovelled' should be. Emotion is limited to the sergeant biting hard on his pipe, and the two men dosing themselves with rum. As readers we take part in the averting of eyes which both constitutes the lie but recognises its necessity.

These displacements raise questions for the reader; do the techniques of bathos or displacement deny our own emotional response? If the poem passes over or withdraws from what we should rightly feel, is it denying us the possibility of that feeling? It is clear in Blunden's description of the shovelling that deep feelings lie below. But in some of the ostensibly colder accounts, as in West's account of using the corpses as geographical markers, what is properly recognised is that that is what the corpses are good for. They have ceased to remind the living soldiers of a shared humanity and become merely useful to their survival. Sometimes the levelling of disparate terms reflects this real reduction of moral responses to the lowest level. Sometimes the knowledge and painfulness of the disparity are inherently acknowledged.

These questions are addressed tangentially in Gibson's poem, through the self-questioning of Dodd himself, as he becomes aware that he has not felt as he should about his friend's death:

> And he'd liked Dick … and yet when Dick was hit,
> He hadn't turned a hair. The meanest skunk
> He should have thought would feel it when his mate
> Was blown to smithereens – Dick, proud as punch,
> Grinning like sin, and holding up the plate –
> But he had gone on munching his dry hunch,
> Unwinking, till he swallowed the last crumb.[34]

[33] Blunden, *Undertones*, 67.
[34] Gibson, 'Between the Lines' in Kendall, *Poetry of the First World War*, 68.

The unfailing rhyming quatrains are betrayed by the run of the narrative consciousness; and significant here is the conversational voice, playing to itself but also to the reader. No officer's voice, thinking about duty and his men, but an ordinary man thinking about the death of another ordinary man. Not only does he have to deal with his friend's instantaneous death but he also has to come to terms with his own apparent lack of proper emotion. These discontinuities find expression in similar disruptions in the text, marked particularly by the many ellipses, reflecting perhaps the wandering consciousness of a wounded man, but also signalling different levels of time and place. These ellipses also signal vacancies in language:

> And Dick … He dared not think
> Of what had come to Dick …

Or indeed what Dick had come to. 'Smithereens' is what Dick has come to. Again, the horror of the event, a man's body reduced to small fragments widely scattered, is both undercut and intensified by the demotic language and conversational tone. 'Smithereens' has the light quality of the colloquial yet at the same time it is graphic without being specific. In this it speaks of the void left when trying to articulate such events (and indeed of the emptiness for the bereaved when there was no body left to mourn). The central or standard feeling of grief may be hidden in the ellipses of the poem, or displaced bathetically on to the dish of butter, as it has been displaced for Dodd himself since otherwise it would be intolerable, but it remains a presence in the poem by virtue of that glaring displacement. The reader has to engage with these challenges to expectation, but in so doing understands the emotion more fully. She understands that displacement is necessary, but understands too that it may mask a deep distress.

We can see this clearly in Edmund Blunden's 'Pillbox', which uses bathos as a deliberate technique to make the reader more rather than less aware of the inherent tragedy of a death which is described in the most quotidian of ways.

> Just see what's happening, Worley! – Worley rose
> And round the angled doorway thrust his nose
> And Serjeant Hoad went too to snuff the air.
> Then war brought down his fist, and missed the pair![35]

The rhyming couplets announce a traditional form; but as with Gibson's poem, this is continually cut through, initially by the dramatic headlong run of the narrative, and then by the use of direct speech, articulated on

---

[35] 'Pillbox' in Blunden, *Poems*, 157.

the page in italics, which renders it both more urgent and more ordinary. Or maybe it is just that the typographical representation lends us, as directly and unfussily as possible, the real voices. The tragedy at the heart of the poem is that Hoad, 'scratched by a splinter', has suffered a wound not just eminently survivable but a guarantee of being sent home; yet he doesn't survive. It's as though the blood released by the minor flesh wound also allows out all that he has been suppressing: 'the blood came, / And out burst terrors that he'd striven to tame'. Hoad dies from his terrors, and the horrible irony of the poem is that he could have lived. All of this is voiced in the quietest and most colloquial terms for the major part of the poem, yet as readers we see dramatised fully the scene of the raving man convinced he's *'blown to bits'*. Back in the safety of the pillbox, he is surrounded by his mates urging him on – urging him to life. There is something classical or religious about the scene, though the language is resolutely ordinary for the first fifteen lines of eighteen. There is a slight difference in register between the voice of the poet/narrator (the officer) and the italicised speech of the men, but all are felt to be leaning over and around the man, tending to him and giving succour on equal terms. This comes to a climax in the most bathetic of languages, yet with the strongest appeal one of the men can think of: *'Think of Eastbourne and your dad.'* Eastbourne; your dad: a whole life of loss is conjured up there, not against the run of the ordinary language, but because of it. Nothing else is needed to convey the tragedy of Hoad, dying when he doesn't need to.

Blunden's poem is without sentimentality just because of the bathos and the understated colloquial language; yet, and perhaps thus, the gods might weep. Blunden adds one line which dares to call up this possibility, but makes it continuous with the language of Hoad's friends:

> He yielded. Worley with a tot of rum
> And shouting in his face could not restore him.
> The ship of Charon over channel bore him.
> All marvelled even on that most deathly day
> To see this life so spirited away.

Here is the poem's one 'officer' touch, but it works triumphantly to align the pointless death of an ordinary soldier with classical tragedy, since in the flow of the poem there is no distinction between 'The ship of Charon' and *'Eastbourne and your dad'*. Bathos makes the reader's full apprehension of the particular nature of the tragedy possible here, without allowing him the ease of the sentimental.

It's no accident that in two of our three examples so far, the mise-en-scène is No Man's Land, a place of isolation, exposure and disorientation, of greatly increased risk of death or injury – and 'everywhere the dead'.[36] The recreated act of crossing this geographical space allows a matching reflective inward journey and these are brought together in the imaginative space of the poem. We enter the speaker's consciousness, which may move beyond the strictures of actual place to enter a separate level of psychological reality. The move to modernism springs naturally from the inherent displacement and dislocation here, intensified by the constant awareness of death, but always anchored in the actual.

Robert Nichols's 'Comrades: An Episode', uses the same scenario to dramatise the business of one man's dying. This time an officer is featured, stranded on the wire, his mind wandering back and forth across time and space as if to defeat the immobility of his body. On the surface, this is the most traditional of our examples, as the officer voice tries to make sense of his surroundings and his place within them, countering rather than succumbing to the unsettling nature of his position. The bathos that exists is that of mishandled poetic tone rather than alienated displacement. But perhaps for that very reason the eruptions of difference and dis-ease strike powerfully. The poem begins in an apparently omniscient third person voice, with a structured sequence of events suggesting a sort of normality: 'He fell. / Night waned. He was alone. A heavy shell / Whispered itself passing high, high overhead.'[37] But this omniscient consciousness is dictated, as it were, by Gates, the officer at the centre of the poem.

> His wound was wet to his hand: for still it bled
> On to the glimmering ground.
> Then with a slow, vain smile his wound he bound,
> Knowing, of course, he'd not see home again –
> Home whose thought he put away.[38]

At this point, the poem erupts interestingly with the speech of Gates's men: ' "Where's Mister Gates?" "Out on the wire." / "I'll get him," said one …'. The interplay between Gates's self-narrated perception of what's happening to him in a poetic language proper to an officer, and the men's more direct colloquial voices (' "Corporal didn't see 'un fall out on

---

[36] 'The Night Patrol' in West, *Diary of a Dead Officer*, 82.
[37] Robert Nichols, 'Comrades: An Episode' in Brian Gardner (ed.), *Up the Line to Death: The War Poets 1914–1918*, revised edition (London: Methuen, 1976), 38. First published in Robert Nichols, *Ardours and Endurances* (London: Chatto & Windus, 1917).
[38] Ibid., 39.

patrol, / Or he'd 'a got 'un"') immediately gives us two different perceptions and consciousnesses of the event. Gates is too far away to actually hear the men; only we as readers hear them, as geographical distance is closed up and languages jostle each other. They are, certainly, set somewhat crudely and stereotypically against each other. But beside both is also set the voice of war: 'Meanwhile the Maxims toc-toc-tocked; their swish / Of bullets told death lurked against the wish'.

Clever to rhyme 'swish' with 'wish'; the inanimate is far more powerful than the animate, the voice of the shell and the machine gun is more intimate, more particular than the human voice. When the men 'whispered' it was to keep hidden; the whisper of the shell on the other hand announces its approach. The 'swish' of the bullets echoes this sinister quietness. Men are shown as powerless, hearing the shell or bullet but not knowing where it will strike. Gates himself is particularly vulnerable, and we remember his 'slow, vain smile' as he bound – pointlessly – his wound, 'Knowing of course he'd not see home again'. The poem continues quite lazily in this three-part interplay of voices and tones, Gates seeing 'the morn / Break in a rosy peace through the lone thorn / By which he lay', emphasising the slowness of his dying, punctuated by the oft-repeated 'alone'. Then there is another sudden switch as Gates hears his men's voices in his consciousness, drawn from memory, echoing the earlier talk which only we as readers have been privy to:

> Suddenly he heard Corporal Timmins' voice: 'Now then,
> 'Urry up with that tea.'
> 'Hi Ginger!' 'Bill!' His men![39]

From this point on, the poem moves into a more straightforwardly self-sacrificial sentimentality which is fatal to two of Gates's men (who go over the top to bring him in), including the idealised, eroticised Corporal Timmins, 'straight and blond and wise, / With his quiet-scanning, level, hazel eyes', and the poem ends with Gates's too-innocent dying utterance, '"O my men, my men"'.[40]

It is easy to mock or parody this. But Nichols attempts a moving interpolation of voices, of men, of officer, of weaponry. He fails, yes; but nonetheless the poem is not a straight representation of an officer's death in the arms of his beloved men; the very interplay of voices allows the reader

[39] Ibid., 40.
[40] Ibid., 41.

to see what lies between, and we are left in no doubt of the dominant voice, that of the Maxim gun, the swishing bullet, the whispering shell.[41] The uneasy dialogue in this poem between aureate dream and trenchspeak prevents the ending from providing an easy romantic close.

None of these poems fit easily into the First World War canon. West, little known as a poet, tries various modes to catch that thing he can't quite catch. Blunden's bathos, heart-rending if we see it right, has scarcely been noticed by critics, and he remains stuck in the category of pastoral poet.[42] Gibson and Nichols do something which many canonical poems do not: they explore at length, slowly and sometimes in an old-fashioned way an individual consciousness, struggling with possible or imminent death, in a poetic mode which is trying to find itself. Striking in all these poems is the use of italics, ellipses, dashes which stand for ordinary speech, for what cannot be said, for what has passed in the time when consciousness has been absent, or for a break in the normal order of things, for example when two realities are brought together across time. These breaks in the fluidity of the text remind us of Leed's aperçu that 'Death, customarily the "slash" between life/not life, became for many in the war a "dash"' – signifying something unfinished, as yet unknown yet hanging there, a space where a word should be but which no word can articulate. At the same time, these poems use the language of men, in the Wordsworthian sense but brought to the level of the properly colloquial. The 'big words' are refused, because the monolithic values they represent have been leached of meaning; in their place come more ordinary utterances making us aware of the tragic within the everyday.[43] Heteroglossia might be the theoretical term here, but as readers we experience it as a genuinely mixed speech which is sufficiently flexible as a form to reflect both the mixedness of ranks and officers in the trenches, and the integral and original shifts of time, geography and consciousness. These poems can falter in tone; but,

---

[41] See our discussion in Chapter 7 of the way the machinery of war is shown to mimic the human voice in Owen's 'The Last Laugh'. This is also a motif in Ford Madox Ford's *Parade's End* (1924–8; New York: Alfred A. Knopf, 1992), especially 588–9.

[42] He was suffering from this as early as 1930; in the Preface to his *Poems 1914–30* (which includes 'Pillbox' and other fine war poems), he says ruefully: 'The titles and contents of my books "The Waggoner" and "The Shepherd" have, I apprehend, done me a slight injustice; that is, they have labelled me among poets of the time as a useful rustic, or perhaps not so useful –' (Blunden, *Poems*, vi).

[43] Randall Stevenson gives an extensive account of the way the war emptied the 'big words' of meaning in *Literature and the Great War*, 47–53; the chapter as a whole, 'Unspeakable War', deals with the larger question of a loss of faith in the reliability of language during the war.

caught in the half-ground of poetry as the men they figure are caught in No Man's Land, or in the halfway house of the pillbox, they can give us a better insight into what was happening to poetry at this time than more fully achieved poems. They show the process of struggle by individual poets to reflect their understanding of what seemed a new, a cataclysmic experience.

Baldick, as part of his argument that there is a continuum rather than an opposition between tradition and experiment in post-First World War literature, highlights 'anachronism and related disorderings of the reader's time sense' as the most innovative features of the literature at this time, spanning both modernist and non-modernist writing.[44] In the work of West, Gibson, Blunden and Nichols, stemming from the war itself, these dislocations of time, and cognate disruptions of geography and consciousness, have perhaps gone unnoticed because they have been seen as arising naturally out of the stresses of battle, rather than being related to the modernist preoccupations of their contemporaries. Booth makes a similar point about war prose: 'I suggest that war books tend to be understood as written in a realist style not so much because they differ from modernist works as because civilians are willing to see war – but not peace – as a fundamentally disordered and unpredictable experience'.[45] These poems may be realist, then, in the sense of responding to 'a fundamentally disordered and unpredictable experience', but thereby they are also more rather than less likely to be modernist. They may vary in the extent of their modernist technique, but in all of them we come up against one of the abiding concerns of modernism: the frailty of life's apparent substance, the void lying below it. In the final part of this chapter we will look at some poems of the First World War which catch this sense of the underlying void, through their explorations of dying, death and the consciousness of death in the living.

Siegfried Sassoon resented the predominance of modernism in postwar poetry, and attacked it where he could.[46] Yet some of his most interesting poems, which run counter to (though temporally alongside) his characteristic satirical mode, are those which try to capture the half-world between life and death, the dying subject on the way to extinction, but just sufficiently alive to be aware of what awaits. Here we'll look first at

---

[44] Baldick, *Literature of the 1920s*, 26.
[45] Booth, *Postcards from the Trenches*, 12.
[46] See Max Egremont, *Siegfried Sassoon: A Biography* (London: Picador, 2005), 400, 406, 495; John Stuart Roberts, *Siegfried Sassoon* (London: Richard Cohen Books, 1999), 294–5.

'Died of Wounds' and 'The Death-Bed', which in their preoccupation with the expression of this half-state are, in our redefining sense, modernist. Sassoon's editorial specificity of time and place are belied by the wandering consciousness they depict.[47] In both, the subject – unlike that of Gibson, Nichols and Blunden – is safe in a hospital bed; however, the safety is illusory, as the titles disclose.

'Died of Wounds' is observed by, as it feels, the poet in the next bed. The subject's consciousness is reflected only in his babblings, which are resolutely fixed in the immediate past, but rendered in his present tense because the past is still his present consciousness. Dickie is still beside him, the assault is still to be made; he is in that moment where his death is yet to be decided. ' "They snipe like hell! O Dickie, don't go out" ...' is the more distressing because the gap in time means that Dickie *has* gone out, to whatever fate; the speaker of the poem *has* been fatally wounded.[48] But the shift in consciousness takes us back to a time when this might still have been prevented.

The temporal dislocation is here dramatised in a conventional way, with the direct speech of the dying man set against the narrative of the observer. In 'The Death-Bed', Sassoon uses free indirect narrative to allow the reader access to the dying man's consciousness, uncontrolled by speech marks. This is the same technique as is used by Nichols and Gibson, but here the first four stanzas focus exclusively on that singular consciousness, which seems to float free from its bearings. The effect is to lead us unimpeded into the man's mind as it wanders between consoling sensual memories (set off by the particularities of experience in the ward) and the struggle with death itself. The sense of struggle and distress in 'Died of Wounds' is here replaced by an atmosphere of calm, 'silence and safety', as the sip of water the man is given transmutes at once into memories of 'Water – calm, sliding green above the weir. / ... He dipped contented oars, and sighed, and slept'.[49] We might feel shades of Brooke's contented pastoral universe of death here, but Sassoon shows us this as the delirium of the dying man. It lies in the present consciousness (which will soon cease) rather than the world of after-death.

There is a turn in the poem at the fifth stanza where the poetic voice becomes objective again, placed outside the man's consciousness: 'He

---

[47] Siegfried Sassoon, *The War Poems* (London: Faber & Faber, 1983). Sassoon's contextualising addenda are printed below each poem as though to locate the poem securely; see 41 and 53 respectively.
[48] 'Died of Wounds' in ibid., 41 (and Sassoon, *Collected Poems*, 28).
[49] 'The Death-Bed' in ibid., 52 (and *Collected Poems*, 34).

stirred, shifting his body'.[50] As he shifts, so does the poem, appearing now to dramatise a struggle between the man and the death which awaits him:

> But someone was beside him; soon he lay
> Shuddering because that evil thing had passed
> And death, who'd stepped towards him, paused and stared.

The apparent possibility of choice continues in the sixth stanza where the poetic voice now addresses us (readers and common humanity) directly, urging us to lend our weight to his struggle:

> Light many lamps and gather round his bed.
> Lend him your eyes, warm blood, and will to live.

The sense of a shared humanity, of bodies gathered round to urge the dying man to life, is reminiscent of Blunden's 'A Pillbox', and both poems conjure up the tragic moment of a life in the balance. But there is no bathos here. Sassoon holds the poem in dramatic stasis between the living, highly imaginative delirium of the dying man and the theatricalised figure of death (which recalls the grim reaper figure in the caricature by which Arthur Graeme West was haunted). The poem's title has, however, already prefigured this man's fate: 'But death replied: "I choose him." So he went'. The man's choice has been illusory all along, and his visions of peace are made a mockery. The words 'silence and safety' which in stanza one express his inward state, 'soaring and quivering on the wings of sleep', are now repeated in the penultimate line of the poem, but they are the 'silence and safety' after death – which he cannot know. The objective third person of the last stanza sends the reader back into the 'normal', non-poetic world, but to the sound of 'the thudding of the guns'. This the subject of the poem can no longer hear.

The pattern of narration in the poem – from free indirect third person, to externalised third person, to a direct address as it were to the reader by the narrative voice and finally to objective third person commenting on the disappearance of the consciousness we have earlier inhabited – follows the process of dying. It is no less dramatic in the hospital bed than in No Man's Land, since it remains the drama of the slow putting out of a life which we are allowed to share. The laconic 'So he went' uses a verb people do use about the moment of death. But the doubleness of the verb ('went' in answer to death's call, implying an act in life, and 'went' in the final sense of 'never to return') demonstrates the power of ordinary language to answer

[50] Ibid., 53 (and *Collected Poems*, 35).

to a great event even when it seems to underplay it, as with Blunden's *'Think of Eastbourne and your dad'*. The poem dramatises disturbingly the uncanny experience of being at a death-bed, of experiencing the moment when a consciousness is suddenly no more – the slash rather than the dash between life/not-life.

By February 1917 Sassoon's experiences at the Front had led him to write that 'the soldier is no longer a noble figure; he is merely a writhing insect among this ghastly folly of destruction ... God is a buffoon, who skulks somewhere at Base with tipsy priests to serve him'.[51] In 'The Effect' we see the poetic expression of this sense of the absurd. The poem is again contextualised by documentary reference, and though it was written when Sassoon was recuperating at home in the summer of 1917, we're told in his footnote that it originates from earlier 'Hindenburg Line material', which exists in a prose version.[52] Sassoon takes a line from the war correspondent's report which forms the epigraph, 'He'd never seen so many dead before', and spins the poem on this line:

> '*He'd never seen so many dead before.*'
> The lilting words danced up and down his brain,
> While corpses jumped and capered in the rain.
> No, no he wouldn't count them any more ...

Here inner and outer reality and the very language in which they might be described all collapse into a grotesque *danse macabre* in which words and dead bodies occupy the same crazy space. The most fearful thing for the writer is that the bodies seem to come to life again though they are clearly dead, a horrid animation which robs them of their humanity: 'When Dick was killed last week he looked like that, / Flapping along the firestep like a fish'. Here is the same lack of affect that we saw Tom Dodd struggling with after the death of his own friend 'Dick' in Gibson's 'Between the Lines'. Dick or Dickie is a common name running through these poems, and could strike the twenty-first century reader as comic or open to parody, but only because it is both innocent and of its time. Here the familiarity of the name adds to the bizarre contrast of the image – 'flapping along the firestep like a fish'. Though there is an insistent rhyme in the poem to give it form, there is also a sense of the writer's being barely in control of his own horror, and the poem ends on a note of music hall surrealism: '"*Who'll buy my nice fresh corpses, two a penny?*"'. This poem relates to a real place and set of

---

[51] Entry for 22 February 1916; Sassoon, *Diaries 1915–1918*, 133–4.
[52] 'The Effect' in Sassoon, *War Poems*, 87.

events, but its imaginative force lies in the way consciousness is dislocated to keep pace with the dislocation of normal relationships and associations. If the dying body of a friend is reduced to 'flapping like a fish', while dead bodies seem to jump into life under the pelting rain, where can the mind go except to retreat into reductive farce?[53]

Sassoon's 'Repression of War Experience' was written in the same 1917 summer as 'The Effect', at a key moment for Sassoon – after he had written his proclamation of dissent from the war, but before it was read out in Parliament, and just before he was sent to Craiglockhart War Hospital. The title is that given to a public lecture by his psychiatrist at Craiglockhart, W. H. R. Rivers, though the poem in fact pre-dates Rivers's lecture. Possibly the title was borrowed retrospectively. It is, in any case, ironic, since the poem is about the impossibility of repressing war experience. If 'The Effect' recognises the grotesquerie of death robbed of any dignity or heroism ('flapping like a fish'), 'Repression of War Experience' brings the psychological horror of that knowledge of death into the safety of the book-lined room and the English garden, where 'thoughts you've gagged all day come back to scare you':

> The garden waits for something that delays
> There must be crowds of ghosts among the trees, –
> Not people killed in battle – they're in France –
> But horrible shapes in shrouds[54]

The mad logic of reminding himself that the ghosts can't be people killed in battle because they're in France can't, in the end, keep at bay what the poem is always trying to suppress, repress: the sound of the guns. We know that Sassoon could hear the sound of the guns at Weirleigh; whether he is referring to actual guns or imagined ones we can't know. The poem runs together seamlessly what exists in the imagination and what exists 'objectively', so that the 'horrible shapes in shrouds' are as present as the books, the candles and the pipe. This is what is so fearful. Sassoon had written a much grimmer account (in a letter to Bertrand Russell) about this eruption of past horrors into present normality, when he was in the Fourth London Hospital with a wound to the shoulder, in April 1917:

---

[53] This is one of several First World War poems in the genre of the *danse macabre*. See also Blunden's 'Concert Party Busseboom' and 'The Midnight Skaters' (Blunden, *Poems*, 104, 148); John Rodker's 'Hymn to Death, 1914 and On' (Hibberd and Onions (eds), *Winter of the World*, 273); Rosenberg's 'Louse Hunting' (Rosenberg, *Isaac Rosenberg*).

[54] 'Repression of War Experience' in Sassoon, *War Poems*, 84 (and *Collected Poems*, 89).

> And when the lights are out, and the ward is half shadow and half glowing firelight ... then the horrors come creeping ... : the floor is littered with parcels of dead flesh and bones, faces glaring at the ceiling, faces turned to the floor, hands clutching neck or belly; a livid grinning face with bristly moustache peers at me over the edge of my bed, the hands clutching my sheets.[55]

But in the poem it is the safety of Weirleigh, his own home, which is invaded by these palpable visions. 'Home' must have been a locus of extreme desperation when, looked for so long, it did not bring the promised peace, but instead a mockery of that peace. It is worse for the subject of the poem that he is cocooned in the book-lined room, yet still the sounds and sights, the realities of the Front, enter in and disrupt. As a result the cocoon itself, the shelves of books with their wisdom, the comforts of the pipe, the normal pleasures of the rose-filled garden are all emptied of their normality and robbed of their existential comfort. Everything is stripped away.

Sassoon's stripping away will seem very different from its high modernist version, because his and the poetry of his First World War contemporaries were placed at that time in opposition to modernism, an opposition he enthusiastically articulated. The resulting split between a realist and a modernist poetic was deeply damaging to English poetry. Margot Norris argues that the split was institutional, ideological and structural; what she calls 'Modernism's suppression of trench poetry' emerges as a result of its antipathy to the referential, a defence mechanism which allows it to escape any possible suppression or containment by the war itself: '[Modernism's] formal prolepsis or anticipation of the war in violent disjunctions, illogical parataxis, mutilated figurations ... gave war a rhetorical poetic performance. Modernism's institutional gesture took form as displacement, extrusion, and silencing of the trench poetry that clearly aspired to become poetry *as* historical referent.'[56] We argue rather that the split was not necessary but contingent, that within 'trench poetry' modernist forms were emerging as a response that was not rhetorical or performative but referential, in the ways we have argued. The dominance of high modernism almost eclipsed this: Ivor Gurney, for example, might have been a voice bridging the divide, but the modernist dimension of his post-war poetry, which now seems striking,

---

[55] Sassoon, *Diaries 1915–1918*, 161.
[56] Norris, *Writing War*, 35, 36.

was not recognised.⁵⁷ However, his poetry survived, against many odds, and now helps us to see the poetry of this whole period differently. Another unrecognised voice was that of Mary Borden, offering a rare female perspective from the point of view of someone working at the sharp end of the conflict, as a nurse in France. The poetry of Gurney and Borden is more thoroughgoingly modernist than our other examples.

Gurney's poetic voice is always idiosyncratic, fixing on something unnoticed by others, or expressing that thing in an unusual way so that we understand it differently. He often uses juxtaposition, not in an obvious way but to bring us up short as readers, making us think about the oddity we are presented with. He also recognises that sometimes a thing can't quite be said. In 'On Somme' he writes: 'men were enduring there such / And such things, in wire tangled, to shatters blown'.⁵⁸ In two lines we have what can't be conveyed, next to what must be conveyed. Gurney's post-war poem 'Swift and Slow' contrasts what might seem more fearful, the suddenness of death at the Front, with the slow act of surviving. He begins with the 'swift' of the title:

> Death swooped suddenly on men in Flanders
> There were no tweedle-dees or handy-danders
> The skull was cleft, the life went out from it ...⁵⁹

There's no compromise in this; it is almost comic in its language and its rhyming of 'handy-danders' with 'Flanders'. Here is another version of the laconic, but in the service of making clear a brute reality: 'Death swooped', 'the skull was cleft, the life went out from it'. If we compare 'the life went out from it' with Sassoon's 'So he went', we feel at once the tougher imaginative understanding in Gurney's phrase, partly because it is preceded by the graphic 'cleft'. The loss of consciousness in death is linked inexorably to the physical 'cleft', so that we can see only too clearly how and why the life is leaving the body. The verb 'went' is re-empowered with physicality.

The second half of the poem deals with the 'slow' of the title:

> But here having escaped the steely showers
> Endured through panged intolerable hours
> The expensive and much-determined doom,
> Find slow death in the loved street and the bookish room.

---

⁵⁷ For more on Gurney's struggles to publish post-war, see Sally Minogue, 'Portrait of the Artist: Ivor Gurney as Modern Maker', *The Ivor Gurney Society Journal*, 11 (2005), 34–5, and '"That Awkward Squad": Ivor Gurney and John Clare', *The Ivor Gurney Society Journal*, 13 (2007), 28.
⁵⁸ 'On Somme' in Gurney, *Collected Poems*, 206.
⁵⁹ 'Swift and Slow' in ibid., 88.

Echoes of Sassoon's 'Repression of War Experience' here; but Gurney points up more sharply the implication of his contrast. We are sent back to the beginning of the poem to see that when 'Death swooped' that was the blessing. Harder by far is the post-war 'slow death', made worse and mocked because it happens 'in the loved street and the bookish room'.

In 'Farewell', another post-war poem, Gurney expresses in his highly individual style the discontinuity between remembering a dead comrade so powerfully that he seems still alive, and the fact that he is dead:

> Don Hancocks, shall I no more see your face frore,
> Gloucester-good, in the first light? (But you are dead!)
> Shall I see no more Monger with india-rubber
> Twisted face? (But machine-gun caught him and his grimace.)[60]

Tim Kendall notes that 'Names, for Gurney, not only conjure a physical reality, they become that reality.'[61] Kendall is thinking here of place-names; but for Gurney, the given names of people were also powerful. In this poem, his use of names is especially touching, as is his attached realisation, 'But you are dead!' This is at the heart of the First World War poets' modernism. Gurney's final line ('You dead ones – I lay with you under the unbroken wires once.') can only address the dead ones as still present – '*you* dead ones'. Leed describes the difficulty that the disorder of war brought to the business of shaping past memories in writing, since the normal sequencing of events could not be brought to bear: 'The shards of experience that appear in the memoirs and journals can be recognised by their curvature as fragments of a once whole vase, as chips of a cognitive, conscious structure that contrasted sharply with what was normal before the war and after it.'[62] Gurney, with the freedom of the poet, spans rather than separates past and present consciousness, but only by placing the shards of memory against each other, and against the present, without trying to find a right order. 'I lay with you under the unbroken wires once' is all that can be evinced to explain the poet's insistence on the still-presentness of the dead.

Mary Borden's apprehension of death is of a different kind. In 'Unidentified' she employs a markedly new poetic – wandering unrhymed lines, variable in length, often so long as to escape the standard representation of lines of poetry on the page, and from the outset a direct address to the reader: 'Look!'[63] Throughout the poem she makes demands

---

[60] 'Farewell' in ibid., 266; 'frore': frozen.
[61] Kendall, *Modern English War Poetry*, 102.
[62] Leed, *No Man's Land*, 125.
[63] Mary Borden, 'Unidentified' in Kendall, *Poetry of the First World War*, 81.

of the reader, forcing us to face up to the hard, everyday struggle of the man she depicts. Clearly this is an unusual struggle:

> Look at his grizzled head jammed up into that round, close hat of iron.
> See how he hunches up his shoulders;
> How his spine is bent under his clumsy coat like the hard bending of a taut strung bow;

Yet at the same time it is the struggle of any one, any where, the struggle of existence:

> He waits for death –
> He knows –
> He watches its approach –
> He hears it coming –[64]

Borden engages us, through the unequivocal demand of her address, with the central issues of existence which the soldier represents and carries within him. As readers, we can't escape what she is showing us:

> It is his self you see – His self that does remember what he loved and what he wanted, and what he never had – His self that can regret, that can reproach his own self now – His self that gave its self, let loose its hold of all but just its self –
> Is that then nothing, just his naked self, inviolate; pinning down a shaking world like a single nail that holds;
> A single rivet driven down to hold a universe together –[65]

This is a profoundly modernist image, and yet at the same time it offers hope. The man is after all pinning down a shaking world and holding a universe together, even as he is about to be obliterated. Lawrence uses a similar image to depict the significance of the individual consciousness in the closing passage of *Sons and Lovers* (1913), where Paul Morel reflects on what he can be now that his mother is dead: 'Where was he? – one tiny upright speck of flesh, less than an ear of wheat lost in the field … On every side the immense dark silence seemed pressing him, so tiny a speck, into extinction, and yet, almost nothing, he could not be extinct.'[66] Crucial to both images is that the human body, and with it the individual consciousness, is both utterly vulnerable but also

---

[64] Ibid., 82.
[65] Ibid., 84.
[66] D. H. Lawrence, *Sons and Lovers*, ed. Helen Baron and Carl Baron (1913; Cambridge: Cambridge University Press, 1992), 464.

determinedly upright, still standing against all the forces conspiring to bring it down. Walter Benjamin, reflecting on the First World War, notes the same paradox of existence: 'A generation that had gone to school on a horse-drawn streetcar now stood under the open sky in a countryside in which nothing remained unchanged but the clouds, and beneath these clouds, in a field of force of destructive torrents and explosions, was the tiny, fragile human body.'[67]

In the end, it is that 'tiny, fragile human body' that figures in all the poetry we've considered, and from it spring those characteristically modernist concerns with the nature and the limits of the self in relation to the known, and unknown, world. Leed suggests that the ubiquity of death at the Front altered this relationship radically: 'Death began to define the range of events that removed the footsoldier further and further from the values, sensory certainties, and hierarchies of status that had once rendered his experience unambiguous and his "self" identifiable.'[68]

The prime objection to interpreting First World War poetry as having some features also characteristic of modernism is that modernism has been seen as constitutively anti-realist, not just in terms of techniques, but in terms of ideology. Georg Lukács warns against confusing the solitariness of man dramatised in traditional realist literature with the essential solitariness of man identified in modernism. In realism, 'solitariness is a specific social fate, not a universal *condition humaine*'.[69] Lukács was on the side of specificity; but in the examples discussed here we are arguing that the two are not competing but continuous. The specificity which underpins the First World War poems we discuss is not in any doubt; but neither is the way they connect with that essential solitariness which marks the human condition. The wound of the war is also the wound of being human, and the poems we have discussed struggle with the challenge of expressing both. Remarkably, that existential understanding also enters the critical writing in a powerfully imaginative way, as we see in the work of Leed and Das. Das ends the main body of *Touch and Intimacy in First World War Literature* with an image of touch through writing, and he imagines both Vera Brittain's hand and the hand of the 'mutilated body' she has nursed 'meeting ours as we turn the pages of the book – each alone'.[70] The paradox

---

[67] Walter Benjamin, 'The Storyteller', *Illuminations*, ed. Hannah Arendt, trans. Harry Zorn (London: Pimlico, 1999), 84.
[68] Leed, *No Man's Land*, 23.
[69] Georg Lukács, *The Meaning of Contemporary Realism*, trans. John and Necke Mander (1958; London: Merlin Press, 1963), 20.
[70] Das, *Touch and Intimacy*, 228.

is that while we are each alone, as these poems recognise profoundly, the poems themselves span our separation.

The struggle to maintain the identifiable self whilst recognising the forces conspiring to render it 'unidentified' is there in West's 'We turned and crawled past the remembered dead'; in Gibson's 'His lying in that little hole, sore hit, / But living, while across the starry sky / Shrapnel and shell went screeching overhead –'; in Blunden's 'The poor man lay at length and brief and mad / Flung out his cry of doom'; in Nichols's/Gates's ' "Well, I must die alone" '; in Sassoon's ' "They snipe like hell! O Dickie, don't go out" '; in Gurney's 'Death swooped suddenly' and his 'But you are dead!'; and in Borden's 'his naked self, inviolate; pinning down a shaking world'. It is there too in the less evidently referential poems of the modernist revolution, but in a more conceptual and distanced way. The poets of the First World War preserve their concern for the human speaking to and of the human, perhaps because, actually or imaginatively, they 'lay with you under the unbroken wires once'. Whether we think that the stripping away of the existential comforts of the everyday world that we find in high modernism is purer, because it is free-floating, or whether we think that the stripping away we find in the First World War poets is more powerful because it is answering to the specifics of the 'fundamentally disordered and unpredictable experience' of war, they are not competing claims. These writers are in the same business.

CHAPTER 3

'Fierce Imaginings'
The Radical Myth-Making of David Jones and Isaac Rosenberg

The First World War might seem to call for a poetry of reportage, and poems which give vivid descriptions of traumatic personal experience are often the most valued, particularly those which describe a soldier's moment of death or his body after death. These are poems which reject or evade what Sandra M. Gilbert calls the 'consolatory mythology' in which the spirit ascends from the corpse: 'even while the war poets did indeed yearn for the symbolic resurrection promised by traditional forms, they were forced in the rats' alley to which history seemed to have led them not just to demystify but to desacralize'.[1] This need to 'desacralize' soldiers' deaths is a response to 'the unprecedentedly bleak materiality of death in the Great War'.[2] It leads to '*testimonial* gestures' which, Gilbert suggests, may take the form of 'a meditation on the scene of dying, [or] a preoccupation with the literal body of the dead'.[3] And yet, while this rejection of mythic frameworks is powerful in delivering a sense of horrific reality to an often ignorant or self-deceiving civilian readership, it runs the risk of offering nothing in its place. Such poems, in urging the meaninglessness of soldiers' deaths, may offer no way of feeling about those deaths beyond despair. The clearest examples can read like reportage in the service of an (albeit compelling) political position.

Because this seems reductive, and because the job of poetry has traditionally been to say something meaningful about death, many poets clung to traditional elegiac forms, a decision which Gilbert describes as 'a willed reversion to archaic modalities'.[4] Such poems continued to seek a sense of consolation through recourse to mythologies of symbolic

---

[1] Sandra M. Gilbert, ' "Rats' Alley": The Great War, Modernism, and the (Anti) Pastoral Elegy', *New Literary History*, 30.1 (1999), 182, 183.
[2] Ibid., 181.
[3] Ibid., 188. Wilfred Owen's 'Dulce et Decorum Est' is an example of the first, Robert Graves's 'A Dead Boche' the second.
[4] Ibid., 184.

resurrection. We have seen, in Chapter 1, how many poems represent the dead as sentient, suggesting an afterlife of sorts; more specifically, poets continued to draw on Christian notions of sacrifice and resurrection. As Paul Fussell notes, 'the sacrificial theme, in which each soldier becomes a type of the crucified Christ, is at the heart of countless Great War poems'.[5] His examples include Robert Nichols's 'Battery moving up to a New Position from Rest Camp: Dawn', which speaks of soldiers 'whose feet, hands, and side / Must soon be torn, pierced, crucified', and Siegfried Sassoon's 'The Redeemer', in which the Christ-like soldier is 'not uncontent to die / That Lancaster on Lune may stand secure'.[6] Other instances include Rudyard Kipling's 'Gethsemane', which equates death by poison gas with the crucifixion, and Marjorie Pickthall's 'Marching Men':[7]

> Under the level winter sky
> I saw a thousand Christs go by.
> They sang an idle song and free
> As they went up to calvary.

In these poems, the poet gives value to soldiers' deaths by making them analogous to the most meaningful death of all. Their sacrifice redeems England, as Christ's redeemed humanity.[8] Writing of the expectations placed by these poems on bereaved women, Judith Kazantzis comments: 'Christ, then, is crucified, and the duty of the woman, bereaved and despairing, becomes clear ... She will immortalise him in her obedience to the values for which he died. To question those values is to question the sacrifice itself – impossible. For then his death must become not only horrible but also meaningless.'[9] These poems, then, represent an attempt to sustain the elegiac tradition wherein an expression of grief is tempered by consoling notions. It is an understandable impulse, but an extraordinarily unconvincing one. A non-believer, of course, will find the analogy simply meaningless, but for a believer it is also highly problematic on several counts. Firstly, while there was only one Christ, there were hundreds of thousands of dead

---

[5] Paul Fussell, *The Great War and Modern Memory* (Oxford: Oxford University Press, 1975), 119.
[6] 'Battery moving up to a New Position from Rest Camp: Dawn' in Nichols, *Ardours and Endurances*, 34; 'The Redeemer' in Sassoon, *Collected Poems*, 17.
[7] Rudyard Kipling, 'Gethsemane' in Kendall, *Poetry of the First World War*, 31; Marjorie Pickthall, 'Marching Men' in George Walter (ed.), *The Penguin Book of First World War Poetry* (London: Penguin, 2006), 43.
[8] In Pickthall's words: 'That heaven might heal the world, they gave / Their earth-born dreams to deck the grave' ('Marching Men' in Walter, *First World War Poetry*, 43).
[9] Judith Kazantzis, 'Preface', *Scars upon My Heart*, ed. Reilly, xix.

soldiers whose deaths could not *all* be supremely meaningful. Secondly, those soldiers were quite unlike Christ in that they were themselves killers (indeed, they could be executed for turning the other cheek). Thirdly, soldiers were not crucified: horrific as that ancient torture is, crucifixion is a form of public execution which gives significance to the victim. It is preceded by a judgement, the sentence is pronounced, and the death therefore demonstrates a *point* (even for the common criminal, let alone the Son of God). Death on the Western Front had none of these characteristics – it came randomly and without adjudication. Furthermore, unlike crucifixion, it often involved the destruction of the body; there was no possibility of resurrection here. There may be something moving in every failed attempt to sustain 'archaic modalities', but they *are* failures.

Even so, the desire for a mythic framework that ascribes meaning, that gives a shape to grief, remains. Is there really no space between 'archaic modalities' and an uncompromising reportage of the material horror? This chapter explores how two poets, David Jones and Isaac Rosenberg, created that space by incorporating mythic elements into their work in ways which resist the false comfort of familiar mythic analogies while offering ways of thinking and feeling beyond mere horror. In this, they revive in their writing the very 'fierce imaginings' (in Rosenberg's phrase) of the traumatised consciousness snuffed out by war.[10] This is not to say that either poet withheld the material detail of soldiers' deaths or their corpses. Both give powerful testimony of the sort Gilbert privileges. Jones describes a soldier killed by shrapnel: 'the whinnying splinter razored diagonal and mess-tin fragments drove inward', and sees the corpses 'lying disordered like discarded garments or crumpled chin to shin-bone'.[11] Rosenberg describes bodies 'Burnt black by strange decay' and recounts a moment of dying: 'We heard his weak scream, / We heard his very last sound, / And our wheels grazed his dead face'.[12] Through capturing such material detail, both poets vividly express their sensory experience as witnesses. And yet, effective as their testimonial gestures are, neither found that a record of material detail was sufficient in their attempts to represent those deaths and the experience of witnessing them. Both poets brought mythic elements into their literary responses to augment or, indeed, condition their realist representations. Furthermore, both deployed myth specifically

---

[10] 'Dead Man's Dump' in Rosenberg, *Isaac Rosenberg*, 114.
[11] David Jones, *In Parenthesis* (1937; London: Faber & Faber, 1978), 157–8, 182.
[12] 'Dead Man's Dump' in Rosenberg, *Isaac Rosenberg*, 115, 116.

to address the strangeness of the moment of death – a strangeness which their experience of war enforced.

In Parenthesis traces the process by which the disorienting and phantasmagorical environment of war affects Private John Ball's perception of the deaths happening around him. His imagination, in response, turns increasingly to the mythic to express the experience. This process intensifies and accelerates in the final section of the poem, when the platoon takes part in the Somme offensive. When a man dies in his arms, Ball's first thoughts focus on the immediate horror ('the darking flood percolates and he dies in your arms'), and the narrator, in a free indirect style which attaches the thought to Ball's consciousness, laments the lack of mourning rituals:

> Nor time for halsing [embracing]
> nor to clip green wounds
> nor weeping Maries bringing anointments
> neither any word spoken
> nor no decent nor appropriate sowing of this seed
> nor remembrance of the harvesting
> of the renascent cycle[13]

Reminiscent of Wilfred Owen's 'Anthem for Doomed Youth' – where the dead go without passing-bells, prayers and choirs – this is a rational response to the horror of deaths rendered meaningless by the lack of time for such rituals. However, the darkening warscape soon affects Ball's perception and his sensory experience leads to an increasingly disoriented *imaginative* experience. His sense of sight becomes unreliable: in the depths of Mametz Wood, the enemy is invisible and his comrades 'grope in extended line of platoon through nether glooms ... warily circumambulate malignant miraged obstacles, walk confidently into hard junk. Solid things dissolve, and vapours ape substantiality'.[14] His sense of hearing is confused by the on-going barrage: 'Barrage with counter-barrage shockt / deprive all several sounds of their identity'. As the soldiers 'grope the mazy charnel-ways' they struggle to 'distinguish men from walking trees'. Ball can no longer trust his sense of touch: 'You sensed him near you just now, but that's more like a nettle to the touch; and on your left Joe Donkin walked, where only weeds stir to the night-gusts if you feel with your hand'. At this moment, a flare goes up, allowing Ball to see the corpses around him, and the grim reality becomes enmeshed with myth and childhood fantasy:

[13] Jones, *In Parenthesis*, 174.
[14] Ibid., 179.

>   he saw many men's accoutrements medleyed and
> strewn up so down and service jackets bearing below the shoulder-numerals
> the peculiar sign of their battalions.
>   And many of these shields he had seen knights bear beforehand.
>   And the severed head of '72 Morgan,
>   its visage grins like the Cheshire cat[15]

The language combines modern military register with the diction of *Le Morte Darthur* ('medley' and 'up so down' are particular Maloryisms). He conflates battalion badges with knightly shields. The name attached to the severed head recalls King Arthur's half-sister, the sorceress Morgan le Fay; its smile recalls Lewis Carroll's Cheshire Cat – particularly because, in the cat's final appearance in *Alice in Wonderland*, only his head appears. Reality is shifting, tipping, and the imagination draws on myth and fantasy. As the night deepens, this altered perception increases: 'in the very core and navel of the wood there seemed a vacuum … as though you'd come on ancient stillness in his most interior place'.[16] The trees become 'long strangers … / Stone lords coiffed'. Now, the corpses of Welsh soldiers are 'death-halsed', a compound neologism which takes its second element, meaning 'embraced', from Malory. Trying to connect the horrific sight with something familiar, Ball reaches for two similes: the dead are 'lying disordered like discarded garments or crumpled chin to shin-bone like a Lambourne find'.[17] The first is a rational attempt to find a visual match; the second continues this work but also connects the corpses with ancient Britain: Lambourn (the usual spelling) is a Bronze Age burial site in Berkshire, England. Ball's perception is further affected by his being wounded. The blood 'percolates between his toes' – the unusual verb connects Ball with the wood, whose 'clammy drippings percolate', and the man who died in his arms, whose 'darking flood percolates'.[18] In the imagination, boundaries dissolve between forest and man, living and dead. In the 'slow gyration' of the signallers' lights, the trees' 'wounded boughs seem as malignant limbs'. Now there seems to be a corpse under each terrifying tree, further transformed:

>   under each a man sitting;
> their seemly faces carved in a sardonyx stone; as undiademed princes turn
> their gracious profiles in a hidden seal, so did these appear, under the
> changing light.[19]

---

[15] Ibid., 180.
[16] Ibid., 181–2.
[17] Ibid., 182.
[18] Ibid., 183, 174, 182.
[19] Ibid., 184.

These powerful descriptions are of a warscape which is more than just horrific; it is mind-altering. The mythic elements of the text arise from this experience.

Paul Fussell famously attacks *In Parenthesis* for its mythic elements which, he argues, romanticise the war by 're-attaching traditional meanings to the unprecedented actualities'. He adds: 'The effect of the poem, for all its horrors, is to … validate the war by implying that it somehow recovers many of the motifs and values of medieval chivalric romance.'[20] One of Fussell's examples is this moment when a rusted picket-iron (a metal post used to stake out barbed wire) sticking up from a water-filled shell-hole is likened to King Arthur's sword Excalibur:

> to his immediate front, below the shelving ramp, a circular calm water graced the deep of a Johnson hole; corkscrew-picket-iron half submerged, as dark excalibur, by perverse incantation twisted.[21]

If Jones was asserting a simple equation – picket-iron equals Excalibur – then Fussell would be right but, as Fussell says himself of this episode: 'John Ball … *perceives* a flooded shell hole in Arthurian – indeed Tennysonian – terms': the observation comes via the soldier's consciousness.[22] This is a thought that occurs to *him*; it is part of a process by which he tries to make sense of an environment of unprecedented horror – and yet he also recognises the incongruity of the comparison: he can see that the picket-iron doesn't look like Excalibur, it is 'by perverse incantation twisted'. A certain wryness enters the Arthurian diction here: there is no wizardry in the mud of the Western Front and 'perverse incantation' becomes a darkly humorous euphemism for the truly perverse forces which have created the war. Fussell misses the ambiguity of the image: the picket-iron is a *joke* Excalibur, suggesting the distance between Arthurian knights and modern soldiers and, in representing Ball's thought processes, asserts his ordinariness. There is a school-boyishness to the thought, which makes us care for him. Indeed, Ball's tenuous attempt to perceive the picket-iron in a way that makes it meaningful is a moving representation of the very unprecedented nature of the war which Fussell wants preserved. The same, then, is true of Ball's perception of the corpses in Mametz Wood. They are not uncrowned princes, but appear to be so, 'under the changing light'. In the conduct of the battle, the signallers' lights perform an

---

[20] Fussell, *Great War*, 146, 147.
[21] Jones, *In Parenthesis*, 50.
[22] Fussell, *Great War*, 148; emphasis added.

essential communicative function but their effect on the soldier's senses is transformative.[23]

It is true that John Ball's is not the sole mediating consciousness of the text, and much of the narrative is delivered by a narrator who introduces mythic material independently. But Jones's narrator is a version of himself and his own perception is similarly transformed. The difference is that Ball's mythic perception is an interior experience, something he keeps to himself, whereas the narrator brings this altered way of imagining into the poem, and into the open. By extensively connecting the material experience with a body of myth, he represents on Ball's behalf that disorienting transformation. For this reason, Fussell is wrong in assuming that these myths deny the 'unprecedented actualities' of the First World War – Jones never elides those actualities.[24]

Furthermore, Jones's strong affinity for his two key mythic sources, Thomas Malory's *Le Morte Darthur* and the sixth-century Welsh poem *Y Gododdin*, rests, in part, on his sense that they are *experiential* accounts of battle. In his essay 'The Myth of Arthur', he writes:

> Malory wrote his book just, and only just, in time: a little later and it would have been a romantic rather than a romance document. He was just in time to be part of that decaying world that knew the shadow of feudalism … he could still write authentically of knighthood. His data (his visual, felt, data I mean), were accurate, experiential and contractual.[25]

Jones approves of this aspect of Malory because, in his view, 'The imagination must work through what is known and known by a kind of touch'.[26] He contrasts Edmund Spenser's *The Faerie Queene* unfavourably, where the descriptions of chivalrous knights have 'lost liaison with the concrete'.[27] As Paul Robichaud notes, Jones's attitude to Malory 'shows a

---

[23] For effective responses to Fussell's reading, see Kathleen Henderson Staudt, *At the Turn of a Civilization: David Jones and Modern Poetics* (Ann Arbor: University of Michigan Press, 1994), 18–19; Thomas Dilworth, *The Shape of Meaning in the Poetry of David Jones* (Toronto: University of Toronto Press, 1988), 106–7.

[24] It is true that *during* the war Jones saw a romantic equivalence between medieval battles and modern warfare – see, for example, his sketch 'Pro Patria' which shows a medieval knight standing on a twentieth-century battlefield with the words 'pro patria' blazoned on his shield – but this naivety did not survive into the writing of *In Parenthesis*. Thomas Dilworth points out, 'He later confessed that during the war he was immature and, unlike Wilfred Owen, believed "the old lie"' (Dilworth, *David Jones: Engraver, Soldier, Painter, Poet* (London: Jonathan Cape, 2017), 44). 'Pro Patria' appeared in *The Graphic* on 15 December 1915; it is reproduced in ibid., 36.

[25] David Jones, *Epoch and Artist* (London: Faber & Faber, 1959), 244.

[26] Ibid.

[27] Ibid., 245. Dilworth adds that 'Jones could not bear *The Faerie Queene* and its "bogus" Red Cross Knight' (Dilworth, *David Jones*, 181n).

greater awareness of historical context than the Pre-Raphaelites, for whom Malory reveals a timeless chivalric world'.[28] Similarly, for Jones, *Y Gododdin* is 'an authentic account of the warriors who fell at Catraeth, composed by a "man who was on the field" '.[29] The phrase Robichaud quotes is from the final lines of *In Parenthesis* where, in fragmented prose, Jones refers to 'the man who was on the field ... and who wrote the book'.[30] Jones is quoting the medieval heroic poem *The Song of Roland*: the kind of text Fussell finds inappropriate, but which nevertheless contains within it a clear understanding of the importance of witness testimony. So, for Jones, these mythic sources contain within them a focus on soldierly experience that is at odds with 'Tennysonian' idealism – a focus he shares with the soldier-poets Fussell admires. This is myth in cooperation with the testimonial gesture, rather than in opposition to it.

Jones's use of myth can look very much like the 'mythical method' proclaimed by Eliot in 1922 as 'a step toward making the modern world possible for art', but we want to point out fundamental differences.[31] Eliot argued for a kind of literature which 'manipulat[es] a continuous parallel between contemporaneity and antiquity' to provide 'a way of controlling, of ordering, of giving a shape and a significance to the immense panorama of futility and anarchy which is contemporary history'.[32] Thus, in *The Waste Land,* Eliot seeks to redeem a barren present by suggesting a parallel with the necessary barrenness of regeneration myths. This enables him to express a cautious hope for the future at the end of *The Waste Land* with 'a flash of lightning. Then a damp gust / Bringing rain'.[33] Eliot's despairing description of the present elevates the mythic past as possessing meaning and order. As Denis Donoghue puts it: '[Eliot] believed that the futility and anarchy of contemporary history could be redeemed for a work of literature only by showing contemporary events in the critical light of a myth, a coordinate story already significantly shaped. Such a myth would redeem the penury of mere events'.[34] Conversely, the 'mythical method' as it appears in James Joyce's *Ulysses* (the book which occasioned Eliot's remarks) tends to challenge the values of the myth. By setting Leopold

---

[28] Paul Robichaud, *Making the Past Present: David Jones, the Middle Ages, & Modernism* (Washington, DC: Catholic University of America Press, 2007), 20.
[29] Ibid., 61.
[30] Jones, *In Parenthesis*, 187.
[31] '*Ulysses*, Order, and Myth' in *Selected Prose of T. S. Eliot*, ed. Frank Kermode (London: Faber & Faber, 1975), 178. Originally published in *The Dial* 75.5 (1923), 483.
[32] Ibid., 177.
[33] T. S. Eliot, *The Complete Poems and Plays of T. S. Eliot* (London: Faber & Faber, 1969), 74.
[34] Denis Donoghue, 'Yeats, Eliot, and the Mythical Method', *The Sewanee Review* 105.2 (1997), 208.

Bloom alongside Odysseus, Joyce questions ancient notions of heroism, elevating Bloom's humble humanism and quiet forbearance to suggest that this may be a truer kind of heroism.[35]

In Parenthesis sometimes seems to offer mythic parallels which follow this 'method', although the parallels are complicated by the fact that they can simultaneously invoke both the myth, as in Eliot, and the modern everyman, as in Joyce. We have seen this duality in the example above where Private Ball likens a picket-iron to Excalibur – the rusty stake is a very debased version of the magic sword, but we feel for the soldier who imagines the analogy as we feel for Bloom. If Jones's use of the 'mythical method' pulls both ways, more fundamentally his use of these ancient and medieval myths is motivated by an entirely different impulse, and one which is more mythopoeic than methodical.

Mythopoeia, or myth-making, is the way we struggle with the ineffable, face what is difficult to face. As Michael Bell argues:

> there is a crucial difference between *using* myth and being *mythopoeic*. ... A mythopoeic imagination does not *use* myth as a *method* – it *is* it ... [Eliot's] mythic allusions in *The Waste Land* made the 'modern world possible for art' by providing a satiric and plangent contrast with, rather than a mythopoeic transformation of, the modern.[36]

Mythopoeia, in contrast, is (as Bell argues elsewhere) 'a way of approaching vital problems that constantly present themselves reductively'.[37] Bell shows how, for Nietzsche and Heidegger, 'the archaic mode of thought and feeling characterised by myth was not something belonging just to the remote past, but was the unacknowledged condition of our present being. The privileging of myth, therefore, was not a regression *to* the past, but a true understanding of the present by reflection *on* the past'.[38] Bell argues that this understanding influenced modernist mythopoeia in the early twentieth century and, while he uses the term in a broad sense, his formulation is useful for framing the ways Jones and (as we shall see) Rosenberg draw on mythic fragments to forge a response to the intense, traumatic experience of seeing others killed in war.

---

[35] As Declan Kiberd notes: 'Soldiers were dying in defence of the outmoded epic codes which permeate *The Odyssey*. ... the very ordinariness of the modern Ulysses, Mr Leopold Bloom, becomes a standing reproach to the myth of ancient military heroism' (Kiberd, 'Introduction', *Ulysses*, by James Joyce, annotated students' edition (London: Penguin, 1992), x).
[36] Michael Bell, 'Myths and Texts', *A History of Modernist Poetry*, ed. Alex Davis and Lee M. Jenkins (Cambridge: Cambridge University Press, 2015), 53, 55.
[37] Michael Bell, *Literature, Modernism and Myth* (Cambridge: Cambridge University Press, 1997), 2.
[38] Bell, 'Myths and Texts', 49.

So, while Eliot and Joyce took opposite views about which side of the mythic parallel should be privileged, they are engaged in the same method. Eliot reaches for resurrection myths because he hopes for resurrection; Joyce draws on the heroic journey of Odysseus because he sees greater heroism in the mundane journey of Leopold Bloom. It is the applicability of the myth that matters. In contrast, Jones's myths are chosen not for their potential to provide a parallel or a contrast that will support a thesis, but rather because they are the 'Matter of Britain', intrinsic to the identities of the men whose lives are endangered and, often, ended here. As he writes in the Preface to his later work, *The Anathemata*: 'one is trying to make a shape out of the very things of which one is oneself made'.[39] The Matter of Britain has shaped Jones and this, therefore, shapes the work. He adds: 'I believe that there is, in the principle that informs the poetic art, a something which cannot be disengaged from the mythus, deposits, *matière*, ethos, whole *res* of which the poet is himself a product'.[40] The result is not a programmatic parallel designed to express a position vis-à-vis contemporary history, but an on-going series of connections and *failed* connections between the war as soldiers experienced it and the myths which underlie their cultural identities, their sense of being. We are given not an analogy but a process, a series of attempts, in which the meaning comes from an intimate cultural connection with the mythic material, rather than the light it may shed on the present.

Thus, the mythical material in *In Parenthesis* draws on a wide range of sources, but principally (as Jones describes it in his Preface), 'the Celtic cycle that lies, a subterranean influence as a deep water troubling, under every tump in this Island'.[41] In this body of myth, central texts for Jones are, as mentioned, *Y Gododdin* and *Le Morte Darthur*. Jones alludes repeatedly to these texts because he sees them as key elements in the Matter of Britain which are *also* strongly Welsh. They bring Wales, usually marginal to an English sense of Britain, to the centre, and so unite the English and Welsh halves of Jones's own heritage.[42] Jones's endnote on *Y Gododdin* (which concerns a terrible defeat at Catraeth) reads:

> The whole poem has special interest for all of us of this Island because it is a monument of that time of obscurity when north Britain was still largely

---

[39] David Jones, *The Anathemata* (London: Faber & Faber, 1952), 10.
[40] Ibid., 20.
[41] Jones, *In Parenthesis*, xi.
[42] In 'The Myth of Arthur', Jones says: 'What makes the Arthurian thing important to the Welsh is that there is no other tradition at all equally the common property of all the inhabitants of Britain' (Jones, *Epoch and Artist*, 216).

in Celtic possession and the memory of Rome yet potent; when the fate of the Island was as yet undecided... So that the choice of fragments of this poem as 'texts' is not altogether without point in that it connects us with a very ancient unity and mingling of races; with the Island as a corporate inheritance.[43]

This mythic inheritance is central to Jones's representation of the deaths of three key characters, killed during the Battle of Mametz Wood in Part 7 of the text. The first of these, Lance Corporal Aneirin Lewis, is the character most prone to making his own connections with ancient myth (his forename is the name of the *Y Gododdin* poet). He sees the war landscape in terms of Welsh legend. The watery lowlands of Flanders recall for him the legendary realm Cantref Gwaelod (i.e. 'the lowland hundred'), flooded due to the neglect of the drunken dyke-warden Seithenin.[44] The soldiers who do not return from reconnaissance patrols remind him of 'ein llyw olaf', meaning (as Jones's note explains) ' "Our last ruler", the last Llywelyn. Killed on December 10th–11th, 1282 near Cefn-y-Bedd in the woods of Buelt; decapitated, his head crowned with ivy'.[45] Lewis is himself killed as the platoon waits to attack:

> No one to care there for Aneirin Lewis spilled there
> who worshipped his ancestors like a Chink
> who sleeps in Arthur's lap
> who saw Olwen-trefoils some moonlighted night
> on precarious slats at Festubert[46]

The second line quoted imitates the retrospective comment of a Cockney soldier (the battalion is a mixture of Cockneys and Welshmen), then the register changes and so draws us into Lewis's own perspective. Even so, the narrator is at pains to underline the difference between 'sleep[ing] in Arthur's lap' and being killed on the Somme:

> more shaved he is to the bare bone than
> Yspaddadan Penkawr.
>   Properly organised chemists can let make more riving
> power than ever Twrch Trwyth;
> more blistered he is than painted Troy Towers
> and unwholer, limb from limb, than any of them fallen at Catraeth
> or on the seaboard-down, by Salisbury[47]

---

[43] Jones, *In Parenthesis*, 191–2.
[44] Ibid., 89. Lewis's oblique reference to this legend is explained in Jones's note on 211.
[45] Ibid., 89 and note on 211.
[46] Ibid., 155.
[47] Ibid., 155. See Jones's notes for details of the source myths (220).

The true manner of Lewis's death is beyond his mythic imagination; his body is '*unwholer*, limb from limb' than those at the battles in *Y Gododdin* or *Le Morte Darthur*.[48] This is no romanticisation, the difference is clear in Jones's mind, and yet there is also a distant fellowship asserted in the distinction. The narrator pays a kind of respect to Lewis's mindscape, speaking of his death in terms he would understand, while also asserting the 'unprecedented actualities' of this war. This is a tribute to Lewis's rootedness in the Matter of Britain, rather than a sacralisation of his death (*pace* Gilbert/Fussell) or a plangent parallel (*pace* Eliot).

Ten pages later, the death of Lieutenant Jenkins is described very differently, with a focus on the precise material details of the moment of dying. Leading his men forward in the attack, he has just given 'the conventional sign … [to] take it at the double', when:

> He sinks on one knee
> and now on the other,
> his upper body tilts in rigid inclination
> this way and back[49]

His movements are recorded, the narrator speaking as if a watching soldier. Jenkins's revolver swings out on its lanyard 'like a pendulum' and, as he falls, his helmet slips over his face: 'jerked iron saucer over tilted brow'. Here, Jones appears to follow Gilbert's prescription: this is a 'testimonial gesture' and a 'meditation on the scene of dying'. However, the account of Jenkins's death also alludes to the death of Oliver, Roland's comrade in *The Song of Roland*.[50] As Jenkins's helmet slips over his face, the narrator adds: 'nor no ventaille to this darkening'. That is to say, the image of the officer's slipped helmet calls to mind the *ventaille*, or chin-guard, worn by medieval knights. Jones borrows the word from *The Song of Roland* and Thomas Dilworth suggests that 'The deaths of Jenkins and Oliver exist here in a brilliant and original allusive double exposure triggered by Jones's use of the Old French word'.[51]

---

[48] The 'seaboard-down, by Salisbury' is the site of King Arthur's last battle in *Le Morte Darthur* (Book XXI, Ch. 3). Jones's note explains that this is Camlann, though Malory does not name it as such (Jones, *In Parenthesis*, 220).

[49] Jones, *In Parenthesis*, 166.

[50] This mythic source, while not directly part of the Celtic cycle, is connected, as Dilworth explains: 'In a sense, [Roland] is one of Arthur's knights, because his lord, Charlemagne, was the chief historical model for Arthur in the French romances that were Malory's sources. Roland dies at Roncesvalles, but, as Jones might have put it, he belongs to the dead at Camlan [sic]', (Dilworth, *Shape of Meaning*, 98).

[51] Dilworth, *Shape of Meaning*, 82.

Dilworth strains to see this as an example of Eliot's method, noting a series of parallels between the deaths of Oliver and Jenkins: 'Dying, Oliver [like Jenkins] goes blind and falls first into a kneeling posture and then flat on the ground... And as Oliver dies beside Roland, Jenkins dies beside Ball'.[52] But it is clearly the differences that matter here. Where Oliver's blindness is due to the blood in his eyes, Jenkins's is due to the slipped helmet; where Oliver dismounts from his horse to lie on the earth, Jenkins merely 'sinks on one knee / and now on the other'. Furthermore, Oliver heroically splits the skull of the Saracen who has dealt him his mortal blow, but the anonymous bullet which kills Jenkins cannot be so avenged – he merely struggles to free his face from the slipped helmet ('enfeebled fingering at a paltry strap'). The differences continue in the moment of death and its aftermath: Oliver speaks nobly with Roland but Jenkins speaks to no one; Oliver prays before dying, Jenkins just dies; Roland speaks movingly over his friend's corpse, Sergeant Quilter merely 'takes over'. In short, we find the two deaths far from each other in almost every respect, but Dilworth is right about the trigger effect of the word *ventaille* – in the context of an experiential account, it jars, discordantly connecting us with the medieval legend. For the narrator, Jenkins's slipped helmet momentarily recalls the *ventaille*, but only for the distant similarity to be rejected: 'nor no ventaille'. Again, we see the soldier's mythic imagination in tension with the grim reality and, while the mythopoeic mind reaches for *Roland,* Jones clearly makes no assertion of a parallel.

Another ten pages on, the character Dai Greatcoat receives a 'gun-shot wound in the lower bowel'.[53] Dai seems, himself, to be a mythic emanation in the text, or else a madman who believes himself to be one. He is named for a character in *Le Morte Darthur* and delivers the extraordinary 'boast' at the centre of the text.[54] And yet, his wounded body is then utterly destroyed by a shell: he becomes 'clots and a twisted clout / on the bowed back of the F.O.O. [Forward Observation Officer]'.[55] If the mythic is thus put in its place by brute fact, the soldiers respond by transforming the earth, the place where Dai's remains will rot, into a protective deity. When

---

[52] Ibid.
[53] Jones, *In Parenthesis*, 176.
[54] For more on this section, see Vincent Sherry, 'A New Boast for *In Parenthesis*: The Dramatic Monologue of David Jones', *Notre Dame English Journal*, 14.2 (1982); Dilworth, *Shape of Meaning*, 107–16.
[55] Jones, *In Parenthesis*, 177.

Dai is fatally wounded, the stretcher-bearers set him on the ground and urge him:

> curroodle mother earth
> she's kind:
> Pray her hide you in her deeps
> she's only refuge against
> this ferocious pursuer
> terribly questing.[56]

They then address mother earth directly:

> Maiden of the digged places
>   let our cry come unto thee.
> *Mam*, moder, mother of me
> Mother of Christ under the tree[57]

In thus transforming the cold earth, soldiers' imaginations work mythopoeically. By this act, Dai's 'scene of dying' (in Gilbert's phrase) is connected to the most powerful myth-making in the text: 'mother earth' is one manifestation of a series of mythic female presences who variously offer protection and intimacy, but also draw soldiers into death. The key figures are 'sweet sister death' and the Queen of the Woods, who both appear in the final pages. We are prepared for them by the soldiers' transfiguring perception of the environment in which they find themselves: in a warscape where there are no women, they imagine a female presence in the earth, the night and the moon.[58] This element of the text is intensely mythopoeic, and operates entirely around the soldiers' experience of death. As we noted in the last chapter, a repeated trope in First World War writing is the experience of seeing a man's body destroyed suddenly and brutally in the midst of an essayed normality. Such experience forcefully impressed the strangeness of death in a new way which, for Jones, called for new myths.[59]

Like the earth, the moon too has figured as a protective female presence in the poem's earlier stages: 'her veiled influence illumined the texture of that place'.[60] After rainfall, her light transforms everything: 'A silver

---

[56] Ibid., 176.

[57] Ibid., 176–7. Earlier in the narrative, John Ball, waiting to go into battle, 'pressed his body to the earth and the white chalk womb to mother him' (ibid., 154).

[58] Dilworth points out that when Jones, after being shot through the leg in July 1916, was taken to a casualty clearing station, the nurse's voice that woke him was 'the first female English voice he had heard in seven months' (Dilworth, *David Jones*, 42).

[59] For further discussion of moon, earth and mythic females, see Staudt, *At the Turn of a Civilization*, 93–9.

[60] Jones, *In Parenthesis*, 27.

hurrying to silver this waste / silver for bolt-shoulders / silver for butt-heel-irons'.[61] The moon's appearance is noted at various points, always in terms of the extent of her power to illuminate, to transfigure with light – sometimes she is obscured by cloud or diminished in size, sometimes she silvers everything. Like the earth, she is beseeched to protect: 'shine on us'.[62] In a note, Jones reminds us of 'the association of the moon with the Mother of God' and so we have an image of soldiers, deprived of all female care, imagining a kind of supernatural mothering.[63] The night becomes a more ambiguous figure, a lover with a dangerous edge. John Ball anticipates her as his battalion prepares for a night-march to the front line: 'He would hasten to his coal-black love: he would breathe more freely for her grimly embrace'.[64] The soldiers' mythopoeic impulse is to find, in their environment, elements which can be refigured in this way. Jones's own mythic creations in the final part of the text grow out of this need, and develop the earlier personifications. The night becomes 'sweet sister death' and mother earth evolves into the Queen of the Woods.

Sweet sister death is characterised as a lascivious girl who takes innocent boys against their will:

> But sweet sister death has gone debauched today and stalks on this high ground with strumpet confidence, makes no coy veiling of her appetite but leers from you to me with all her parts discovered.
> By one and one the line gaps, where her fancy will – howsoever they may howl for their virginity
> she holds them[65]

She holds them rapaciously, but there is a darkly comic edge here, with death in battle likened to a loss of sexual innocence, and the men placed in the role of the coy mistress. A related figure is the tree sprite who seizes two men crushed by a falling oak: 'the Acorn-Sprite – / She's got long Tom / and Major Lillywhite'.[66] In a note, Jones explains: 'I mean that the oak spirit, the *Dryad*, in fact, took these men to herself in the falling tree'.[67] Finally, the Queen of the Woods welcomes soldiers of both armies into death with gifts of nature:

> The Queen of the Woods has cut bright boughs of various flowering…
> Some she gives white berries

---

[61] Ibid., 34.
[62] Ibid., 35.
[63] Ibid., 196.
[64] Ibid., 28.
[65] Ibid., 162.
[66] Ibid., 178.
[67] Ibid., 223.

>   some she gives brown
> Emil has a curious crown it's
>   made of golden saxifrage.
> Fatty wears sweet-briar,
> he will reign with her for a thousand years ...
>   She plaits torques of equal splendour for Mr Jenkins and Billy Crower.[68]

The Queen of the Woods is the apotheosis of the series of female presences, created in place of the absent mothers, sisters, wives and lovers. Implicitly, this array of female figures offers a series of versions of a single mythic force.

It is true that Jones's mythic females are stereotypes which present difficulties for post-feminist readers, but there remains something moving about the way these soldiers – Jones's characters and Jones himself – seek symbolic or imaginative representations of women in a narrative that is otherwise inescapably masculine.[69] It is also true that the stereotypes, and their neat oppositions, are destabilised in the text. As is characteristic of his heterogeneous method, Jones sidesteps essentialism by having the mythic female appear in a variety of guises.[70] There is something even-handed about Jones's attributing to the female both the power of death and the ritualistic comfort of flowers. The image of 'sweet sister death' is anyway a deeply ironic one. Many of the young men who died in battle were killed before they had had any sexual experience: they were truly innocent. Jones reverses the conventional balance of sexual power to enforce the bitterness of that innocence, that cutting-off of a man's life before it has begun. This is not an attack on women in the manner of, say, Sassoon's 'Glory of Women'. It shows one aspect of the mythologising to which women-deprived soldiers are drawn and is placed alongside the countervailing Queen of the Woods.

The Queen of the Woods, although benign, is the more familiar stereotype – the caring, nursing, mothering female principle – and so, perhaps, a more problematic one for the post-feminist reader. But here Jones unsettles this more standard image of women by also unsettling our understanding of men. For it is not only the Queen of the Woods who acts as the assuaging figure dispensing tenderness. In *In Parenthesis*, men care

---

[68] Ibid., 185. See Dilworth, *Shape of Meaning*, 140–1, for explanation of allusions in each of the Queen's gifts.

[69] Two actual females appear very briefly: Veronica Best runs the refreshment hut in the training camp (Jones, *In Parenthesis*, 4), and Alice runs an estaminet behind the lines (ibid., 104–6, 112–13).

[70] Jones even gives a female personality to the rifle: 'Marry it man! Marry it! / Cherish her, she's your very own ... Fondle it like a granny –' (ibid., 183–4).

for other men, and they do it when men fall apart as they are not meant to do. Here, John Ball's friends care for him in a moment of terror:

> his friends came on him in the secluded fire-bay who miserably wept for the pity of it all and for the things shortly to come to pass and no hills to cover us… and '45 Williams was awfully decent, and wipe every tear, and solidified eau-de-cologne was just the thing so that you couldn't really tell[71]

They do it also when the body falls apart under the barrage:

> burdened bearers walk with careful feet
> to jolt him as little as possible …
> you mustn't spill the precious fragments, for perhaps these raw bones live.[72]

When Dai Greatcoat is dying, the forces of both male and female tenderness come to the fore: 'Lift gently Dai, gentleness befits his gunshot wound in the lower bowel – go easy – easee at the slope'.[73] Tenderness is, then, shared both between the actual men and the mythical Queen of the Woods; and the casual carnage of the Front is likewise shared between mythical 'sister death' and her victims – who are, in actuality, the victims of well-directed bullets or random shells fired by other men. That combination of randomness and organisation is what Jones, and his soldier-characters, attempt to give comprehensible form to through the invoking of myth. And, as always in this poem, the myth-making springs directly from experience.

But myth never outweighs or smooths over the brutality of events in the final section of *In Parenthesis*. The great strength of Jones's vision is that the minutiae, the actualities of the experience, draw myth to themselves, but remain themselves. The carrying of Dai Greatcoat brings together the often-represented cry of the dying soldier to his mother with the larger mythical references to a maternal deity: '*Mam*, moder, mother of me / Mother of Christ under the tree'.[74] That the line leads with the simple child's term (and Welsh term) '*Mam*' reminds us again that the experiential underpins the mythical. In this context it is only natural to invoke mother earth, to enjoin the dying man to get as close to the earth as possible, 'down on hand on hands down and flattened belly and face pressed' – the instinct of all soldiers at the Front, whether dying or trying to stay alive.[75]

---

[71] Ibid., 153.
[72] Ibid., 175.
[73] Ibid., 176.
[74] Ibid., 176–7.
[75] Ibid., 176.

One of the sadnesses *In Parenthesis* brings before us is that whether it is Dai Greatcoat, or Mr Jenkins, or Lance Corporal Lewis, or one of the lesser characters like Talacryn or Wastebottom who is annihilated – they are annihilated. The fate of Private Ball is left open: he may survive or he may not, and we fear for him as the text closes. What does indubitably survive is the poem itself. *In Parenthesis* is a prime example of what, for Jones, all art is: 'a recalling, a re-presenting again, anaphora, anamnesis'.[76] As Jones draws on ancient sources (which for him were current in the experience of war: 'I suppose at no time did one so much live with a consciousness of the past'[77]) to re-present his more recent past, so the poem now performs for us a further act of rescue and reclamation of a historical moment now a hundred years distant from us. As the soldiers' myth-making brings them some comfort, so the text's myth-making can bring *us* a sort of comfort. This is much needed in Part 7, which is coruscatingly accurate about the ways men die in battle: they receive no 'halsing' or 'anointments' other than what the Queen of the Woods can bring.[78] Equally, the text's mythopoeic structures can unsettle us as they accentuate the darkness of this moment in history. They can show the existence of a continuity of tradition which derives from the soldiers' own pasts, but one whose meaning is repeatedly questioned by the form of the poem.

While the female image in *In Parenthesis* draws on material in J. G. Frazer's *The Golden Bough* about the goddess Diana, it also expresses a very modernist heap of fragments – the motherly earth is set against the mischievous acorn sprite, the rapacious strumpet sister death against the sweetly welcoming Queen of the Woods. These fragments Jones shores against his comrades' ruin, creating a troubling confusion of consolation and anguish. Jones shows us how soldiers make myths to handle the traumatic experience of comrades' deaths and, in presenting all soldiers as myth-makers, explains and justifies his own extreme case. Rather than importing myth to sacralise, or to draw a parallel, Jones uses myth in a way that is more complex, creative, ambivalent and consequently more *moving* than Gilbert allows for, or Eliot achieved.

---

[76] 'Art and Sacrament' in Jones, *Epoch and Artist*, 167. Adrian Poole argues that even Jones's archaisms should be seen as an act of rescue: 'There is also a commemorative intent, a purposive anamnesis, in recalling the words in which these precedents have been memorialised' (Poole, 'David Jones', *The Cambridge Companion to the First World War*, ed. Santanu Das (Cambridge: Cambridge University Press, 2013), 150).
[77] Jones, *In Parenthesis*, xi.
[78] Ibid., 174.

David Jones's mythical female figures have a notable precedent in the poetry of Isaac Rosenberg, in particular in his late poems, 'Dead Man's Dump' and 'Daughters of War'. In the first of these, Rosenberg, like Jones, personifies the earth as a woman:

> Earth has waited for them
> All the time of their growth
> Fretting for their decay:
> Now she has them at last![79]

There is a strange ambiguity here: 'Earth' is both an anxious mother who waits and frets, and a seductress who 'has them at last!' Where Jones ascribes motherly and lascivious qualities to separate female figures, Rosenberg combines these qualities in one. He does not call her 'mother earth' but simply 'Earth' and there is less distance here than in Jones between the mythic figure and the mud from which she is conjured. Rosenberg's mythopoeic impulse, driven by the same pressing need to express the inexpressible, has a different, darker quality to it. The relationship between Earth and the dead soldiers is made ambiguous by missing pronouns:

> In the strength of their strength
> Suspended – stopped and held.

Is it Earth that is 'suspended' in the ebbing strength of the dead (as solid particles are suspended in a liquid – soil in blood, perhaps), or is it the soldiers' strength which is 'suspended', in the sense of being halted ('stopped and held')? This is myth-making *in process*; the coordinates have not been fixed. And where Jones's mother earth is a deity to be invoked ('let our cry come unto thee'), Rosenberg's Earth is challenged as an interlocutor to provide answers to the mystery of the moment of death, the moment where a mind, with all its 'fierce imaginings', disappears in an instant:

> What fierce imaginings their dark souls lit
> Earth! Have they gone into you?
> Somewhere they must have gone,
> And flung on your hard back
> Is their soul's sack,
> Emptied of God-ancestralled essences.[80]

---

[79] 'Dead Man's Dump' in Rosenberg, *Isaac Rosenberg*, 114. Jones and Rosenberg were not alone in this. See also Richard Aldington's 'An earth goddess: after the advance 1917' in Aldington, *Images of War* (London: Beaumont Press, 1919), 36.
[80] 'Dead Man's Dump' in Rosenberg, *Isaac Rosenberg*, 114–15.

During the writing of this poem, Rosenberg struggled to express the ineffable substance of which the 'soul's sack' is emptied.[81] In one draft of the poem, the soul's sack is:

> Emptied of all that made it more than the world
> In its small fleshy compass

In another draft, these lines read:

> Emptied of all that made the young lean Time
> Eye with thief's eyes, shouldering his masters [sic] load
> Of proud Godhead ancestralled essences.[82]

The second is evidently an attempt to improve on the first. Here, as Jean Liddiard says, Rosenberg is 'wrestling with the notion of the sudden wrenching of the "dark souls" from the corpses, how the living human being with its capacity to encompass and challenge the universe becomes in a violent instant detritus'.[83] The final version is the strongest, as well as the most concise, but its power rests in the fact that the poet addresses the question not to the reader, nor to himself, but to Earth. Addressed to the reader, these questions would become simply rhetorical, a way of grabbing the reader's collar and demanding that she share the poet's trauma; addressed to the self, they would become an expression of that trauma with the reader as onlooker. Addressed to Earth, they draw us into the soldier's mythopoeic way of thinking: we may resist the absurdity of talking to the mud, but we also want the answers to these urgent questions and hope (in vain) that Earth will reply.

The figure of Earth interrupts, and so disrupts, two allusions to the story of Christ's crucifixion which are, in themselves ambiguous. The poem begins:

> The plunging limbers over the shattered track
> Racketed with their rusty freight,
> Stuck out like many crowns of thorns[84]

Jean Moorcroft Wilson reads this use of Christian imagery as straightforward sacralisation, as though it is of a piece with the Christ analogies in

---

[81] 'Soul's sack' is borrowed from John Donne's 'Elegy IX: The Autumnal'.
[82] Both versions were enclosed in a letter to Gordon Bottomley, June 1917; the first is in a typescript of the entire poem, the second is handwritten on a separate scrap of paper (reproduced in Figure 1.1, on p. 20). See Isaac Rosenberg, *Poetry out of My Head and Heart: Unpublished Letters and Poem Versions*, ed. Jean Liddiard (London: Enitharmon, 2007), 101, 103. All drafts referred to here are available to view in their original form at the *First World War Poetry Digital Archive*, www.oucs.ox.ac.uk/ww1lit/collections.
[83] In Rosenberg, *Poetry out of My Head and Heart*, 49.
[84] 'Dead Man's Dump' in Rosenberg, *Isaac Rosenberg*, 113.

the poems discussed at the start of this chapter. She suggests that the 'crowns of thorns' in the poem's third line 'point[s], metaphorically, to a crucifixion of latter day Christs, the soldiers, which lends a dignity and nobility to their apparently meaningless deaths'.[85] This reading is problematic: the simile refers not to the soldiers but to the barbed wire piled on limber carts, one of which the poem's speaker is pushing. True, soldiers will be caught in this barbed wire which may then add a kind of jagged crown to their outlines, but there is dark irony in the image of soldiers delivering cartloads of thorny crowns to the battlefield. Rosenberg thus draws our attention to one of the problems with a Christian parallel: there are just too many deaths for each one to be meaningful in the way that Christ's death was meaningful.[86] Later in the poem, Rosenberg describes stretcher-bearers adding the body of a just-dead soldier to a pile of corpses:

> They left this dead with the older dead,
> stretched at the cross roads.[87]

The body is, literally, stretched out on the ground, but the image also evokes the *Calvaires*, crucifixes on which a sculptured Christ is stretched, which stood (and continue to stand) at country crossroads across northern France.[88] Again, there is irony in the analogy between a pile of rotting corpses and the single figure of the meaningfully killed Christ. The body on the cross is elevated; it is also whole. The soldiers' bodies are piled on the road and 'Burnt black by strange decay'.[89] Christ ascends to sit 'at the right hand of God'; the soldiers are 'Joined to the great sunk silences'.[90] These allusions to Christian myth are not simply satirical – they offer an unresolved combination of solace and irony – and between them comes Earth, Rosenberg's central mythic representation of the moment of death. Unlike Jones's mother earth, she is no 'Mother of Christ under the tree', and her presence destabilises the poem's Christian allusions. As Santanu Das notes, 'Dead Man's Dump' 'yokes together sense and symbol', offering

---

[85] Jean Moorcroft Wilson, *Isaac Rosenberg: The Making of a Great War Poet* (London: Phoenix, 2009), 350.
[86] The image is further modified by the next three lines: 'And the rusty stakes like sceptres old / To stay the flood of brutish men / Upon our brothers dear'. The simile connects the metal posts which will hold the barbed wire to the legend of King Canute and the waves. As Moorcroft Wilson notes, this suggests 'how ineffectual the barbed wire is likely to be in keeping back the enemy' (ibid., 350), but the main effect arises from the incongruity of the conjoined images: the 'dignity and nobility' attached to the Christian image is undercut by the folklorish anecdote.
[87] 'Dead Man's Dump' in Rosenberg, *Isaac Rosenberg*, 115.
[88] See Nicholas J. Saunders, 'Crucifix, Calvary, and Cross: Materiality and Spirituality in Great War Landscapes', *World Archaeology*, 35.1 (2003), 7–21.
[89] 'Dead Man's Dump' in Rosenberg, *Isaac Rosenberg*, 115.
[90] Mark 16:19; Rosenberg, *Isaac Rosenberg*, 116.

the 'flames, corpses, explosions' of the testimonial gesture, but also 'a profound questioning of the relation between the living and the dead', conducted through the figure of Earth.[91]

In 'Dead Man's Dump', the poet's unprecedented proximity to, and experience of, countless deaths makes his questioning of Earth urgent and insistent: 'have they gone into you? / ... Who hurled them out? Who hurled?'[92] But Earth does not reply. In 'Daughters of War', Rosenberg develops his myth-making to offer a kind of answer, while carefully resisting the false comforts of a 'consolatory mythology'. Rosenberg's approach is recognisably indebted to the work of one of his talismanic figures, William Blake. Blake developed his own unique mythological universe as a way of exploring pressing questions of his day. His mythopoeia challenges the authority of established myths (the kind on which Eliot's 'method' relies) by forcefully suggesting that there is a lack therein; that aspects of human experience have not been adequately accounted for there; that there is therefore a need to invent. Rosenberg, like Blake, was driven to myth-making by a disillusionment with the patriarchal, Judeo-Christian God (in which several of his earlier poems trusted: see 'A Ballad of Whitechapel', and 'God looked clear at me through her eyes'). In the poem 'God', he begins by expressing a revulsion for God's indifference and cruelty:

> In his malodorous brain what slugs and mire
> Lanthorned in his oblique eyes, guttering burned!
> His body lodged a rat where men nursed souls...
> On shy and maimed, on women wrung awry,
> He lay, a bullying hulk, to crush them more.[93]

And yet, the image is of a decaying force: 'Ah! This miasma of a rotting God!'[94]

Michael Bell, tracing the development of thought which led to 'modernist mythopoeia', notes that Blake 'sought to create a mythology out of traditional elements including Christianity'.[95] The same can be said of Rosenberg, but in place of Christianity, he turns to Jewish folklore. As Ian Parsons has said: '[Rosenberg] was profoundly influenced by Hebrew mythology and legend ... but it was his own myths that he wove round the archetypal characters that he drew from those sources'.[96] Beth Ellen

---

[91] Das, 'War Poetry and the Realm of the Senses', 98, 97.
[92] 'Dead Man's Dump' in Rosenberg, *Isaac Rosenberg*, 114–15.
[93] 'God' in ibid., 97–8.
[94] Ibid., 98.
[95] Bell, *Literature, Modernism and Myth*, 13.
[96] Parsons, 'Introduction' in *Rosenberg, Collected Works*, xxi–xxii.

Roberts has shown how he drew on Eastern European Yiddish legends, arguing that the outbreak of war 'unleashed' Rosenberg's creative use of these myths which, like Jones's Arthurian material, are fitted to the horrifying phantasmagoria of modern warfare.[97]

Roberts notes that 'One startling and persistent image which appears in his work from the onset of war until his death is the concept of a female supernatural force'.[98] She locates the source for this figure in the medieval kabbalistic legend of Lilith, first wife of Adam, the first man. Lilith proves to be sexually ungovernable, so God replaces her with the more subservient Eve. She escapes to become a seductive demon.

> Lilith, who appears as the catalyst for action in Rosenberg's verse plays 'The Amulet' and 'The Unicorn,' holds a position in Jewish legend as a usurper of the power of the masculine God, as a seducer of men, and as a killer of children. This same mythical demon lurks unnamed in much of Rosenberg's poetry of the war period.[99]

From this source, Rosenberg develops the figure of a terrible goddess who usurps the Old Testament God and more accurately represents the horror of the age. She appears forcefully in 'The Female God', a poem written shortly after Britain's entry into the war. The speaker of the poem addresses this new deity:

> You have dethroned the ancient God.
> You have usurped his sabbaths, his common days.
> Yea! every moment is delivered to you.[100]

As these lines suggest, the speaker's attitude to the female God is ambiguous. It is uncertain how he feels about her usurpation. She is both lover and tyrant. She is, in part, an incarnation of the desired women of Rosenberg's earlier love poetry (in both cases, he focuses repeatedly on the eyes and hair), but she is a giantess on which tiny human figures struggle: 'In the fierce forest of your hair / Our desires beat blindly for their treasure'. Human spirits are overwhelmed: 'Like a candle lost in an electric glare / Our spirits tread your eyes' infinities', yet their devotion is total: 'Our Temple! our Eternal! our one God!' Written in the autumn of 1914, this poem represents the early stages of Rosenberg's mythopoeic response to the war. As Roberts comments: 'the advent of war precipitated the change in the manner in

---

[97] Beth Ellen Roberts, 'The Female God of Isaac Rosenberg: A Muse for Wartime', *English Literature in Transition 1880–1920*, 39.3 (1996), 320.
[98] Ibid., 320.
[99] Ibid., 321.
[100] 'The Female God' in Rosenberg, *Isaac Rosenberg*, 72.

which females appear in his poetry ... the descent of the world into war must have appeared to Rosenberg as the waxing of Lilith's power'.[101]

In 'Daughters of War', Rosenberg develops this myth-making to focus powerfully on the moment of death.[102] Rosenberg describes a host of supernatural females who live beneath the battlefield and take soldiers as their lovers, an act which brings those soldiers into death. There is an allusion here to the Valkyries of Norse mythology, Odin's handmaidens who lead warriors killed in battle to Valhalla, but they are also 'these strong everliving Amazons' and so become a combination of the maidens who honour the slain and the female warriors who rape and murder helpless males. In alluding to Valkyries and Amazons to convey this duality, Rosenberg reaches for mythic references more widely known, but these Daughters are clearly a development of the Lilith-inspired 'female god', the terrible, gargantuan seducer who is both feared and loved.[103] So, the consoling image of the dead dancing with these Daughters is set against the disturbing image of a 'soul aghast'. The Daughters are terrible but they are not vindictive. They send an 'Amazonian wind' which breaks open soldiers' faces 'So the soul can leap out / Into their huge embraces', but they have no other way of getting their lovers, 'No softer lure than the savage ways of death'. The emotion which motivates them is both 'love' and 'love-heat'. They embrace the dead *and* seize them. They are both loving and fatal; consoling yet terrifying. This ambiguity in Rosenberg's mythic women remains unresolved and captures movingly the shifting emotions of the experiencing poet.

Like the feminised Earth in 'Dead Man's Dump', the Daughters are both loving and lascivious. However, they also *supplant* Earth as a female force: their act of seduction/murder takes place 'shut from earth's profoundest eyes' and, in the moment of consummation/death, 'the earth-men's earth fell away'. The Daughter who speaks describes how her sisters ' "force their males / From the doomed earth" '. This is another kind of usurpation, by which the female force has been separated from the material reality of the battlefield – the mud – and exists beyond it, or beneath it. This separation allows a re-emphasis on the physical realities of death: Rosenberg describes 'corroding faces / That must be broken – broken for evermore / So that the soul can leap out'. For these lines, an earlier draft had: 'perishing faces / That must be utterly perished / For

---

[101] Roberts, 'Female God', 325, 327.
[102] Rosenberg, *Isaac Rosenberg*, 116–19. Blake's influence is evident in the poem's title, which recalls *Visions of the Daughters of Albion*.
[103] Interestingly, 'everliving Amazons' was a late amendment; in earlier pencil drafts, Rosenberg wrote 'immortal girls', then 'everliving girls'. This suggests that Rosenberg felt a need in the final version to clearly underline the Daughters' darker side with reference to a more familiar myth.

the soul to rush out'.[104] To emphasise the materiality of death, Rosenberg replaces 'perishing' and 'perished' with the more concrete 'corroding' and 'broken'. In the earlier draft, the souls 'rush out', which implies that the soul is a kind of wind; in the later version, the souls 'leap out' which is, again, more concrete, connecting the exit of souls from bodies to the movement of rats. The soul *leaps*, just as, in 'Break of Day in the Trenches', 'a live thing leaps my hand, / A queer sardonic rat'.[105] Thus, Rosenberg rejects the conception of the soul as an airy spirit and instead conceives of the soul as part of the horrific warscape. This radically transforms the pile of decayed corpses in 'Dead Man's Dump': those dead were out of reach of the imagination, 'Joined to the great sunk silences'. Here, the physicality of corroding faces, broken skulls, leaping souls, connects the appalling reality to the mythic vision: it is by that leap that the souls of the dead are brought into the 'huge embraces' of the Daughters of War.

Another effect made possible by the separation of earth and goddess is that, unlike the mute earth, these Daughters have a voice. Indeed, of all the mythic female figures who appear in the work of Jones and Rosenberg, the Daughter who occupies the final third of the poem is the only one who speaks.[106] Earth had no answer to the poet's urgent questions about the moment of death but here, in the final part of the poem, one gargantuan Daughter speaks.

> 'My sisters force their males
> From the doomed earth, from the doomed glee
> And hankering of hearts.
> Frail hands gleam up through the human quagmire, and lips of ash
> Seem to wail, as in sad faded paintings
> Far sunken and strange.
> My sisters have their males
> Clean of the dust of old days
> That clings about those white hands,
> And yearns in those voices sad.
> But these shall not see them,
> Or think of them in any days or years,
> They are my sisters' lovers in other days and years.'[107]

---

[104] See Rosenberg, *Poetry out of My Head and Heart*, 68.
[105] 'Break of Day in the Trenches' in Rosenberg, *Isaac Rosenberg*, 106. The idea of the soul as a wind is also expressed/negated in 'Dead Man's Dump': 'None saw their spirits' shadow shake the grass'. See pp. 40–1 in this volume.
[106] Jones tells us that the Queen of the Woods 'speaks to them according to precedence' and 'calls both high and low' for Dai Greatcoat (Jones, *In Parenthesis*, 185–6), but does not tells is what she says: her voice goes unrepresented.
[107] 'Daughters of War' in Rosenberg, *Isaac Rosenberg*, 118–19.

What this Daughter emphasises is that, in her sisters' embrace, the dead are separated from all community with the living.[108] However, the lines' ambiguousness has led to different readings. Deborah Maccoby assumes that the 'frail hands' belong to 'mortal women mak[ing] a last vain effort to hold on to the dying young men'.[109] This is suggested by the way the men are forced 'from the ... hankering of hearts' and allows the word 'their', in the line 'My sisters have their males', to refer to the mortal women whose men have been taken. However, in attempting to make the entire speech fit her reading, Maccoby stumbles: 'the mortal women are ... immersed in dust and in the "human quagmire", bogged down in clinging squalor'.[110] It seems more likely that, in describing how 'Frail hands gleam up through the human quagmire, and lips of ash / Seem to wail', the Daughter is referring to the dying men on the field of battle. The human quagmire is no metaphor: it is a pile of mulching corpses and, among them, near-corpses. Her sisters 'have *their* males' just as they 'force *their* males': the pronoun indicates the Daughters' ownership. The men, in their embrace, are 'Clean of the dust of old days / That clings about those white hands'. While Maccoby's reading invokes a moving image here of men separated from their vainly waiting women, whose white hands are dusted with flour perhaps, it is at least as likely that the distinction is between the newly dead and their dying comrades. This 'dust' is the dust of the shell burst which covers the poet's ear-lodged poppy in 'Break of Day in the Trenches'. That poppy was 'safe – / Just a little white with the dust'[111] and these men are similarly 'safe'.

The ambiguity is fitting. By confusing or conflating mortal women and dying comrades, Rosenberg makes us think of both and draws our attention to the different kinds of severance each death entailed. For each death, he suggests both the soldiers' trauma in seeing it, and the non-combatants' trauma in *not* seeing it. This ambiguity is redoubled in the final three lines: the pronouns are confusing – 'these shall not see them' – and can be read in a number of ways, suggesting again the severance of all kinds of human relationship. Perhaps the dominant reading is that

[108] Rosenberg, in a letter to Gordon Bottomley, describes the end of the poem as 'an attempt to imagine the severance of all human relationship and the fading away of human love' (19 August 1917; ibid., 344).
[109] Deborah Maccoby, *God Made Blind: Isaac Rosenberg, His Life and Poetry* (London: Symposium, 1998), 189.
[110] Ibid.
[111] That the dust is caused by a shell burst is not explicit in the poem, but see the earlier version, 'In the Trenches': 'Down – a shell – O! Christ. / I am choked ... safe ... dust blind' (Rosenberg, *Isaac Rosenberg*, 105).

'these' are the dead, while 'them' refers to their still-dying comrades. For Rosenberg, there is no community of the dead; not for him the image of the ghostly legions: they are each alone in their embrace with one of the Daughters of War. They are out of time, or in another *kind* of time (another dimension?) and so cannot be communicated with:

> '... these shall not see them,
> Or think of them in any days or years,
> They are my sisters' lovers in other days and years.'[112]

This is an altogether darker mythic vision than Jones's. Where the Queen of the Woods welcomes the dead, as it were, into a woodland community, Rosenberg's dead are utterly isolated not just from the living but also from each other. This darkness is compounded by the way the poet shifts between two distinct positions or personae in the poem. In lines 6–14, he is a visionary poet, in the Blakean manner, who tells us: 'I saw in prophetic gleams / These mighty daughters in their dances' and 'I heard the mighty daughters' giant sighs'. The emphasis is on the poet's visionary perception ('I saw', 'I heard'). But a few lines later, the speaker uses the first person plural to place himself in the ordinary ranks ('We were satisfied ... / To take our wage of sleep and bread and warmth') and then firmly locates himself among the corpses when he speaks of 'our corroding faces'.

These two personae are united in the rendering of the Daughter's voice. She speaks at the precise moment of death, 'as the earth-men's earth fell away', and hers is a voice that only the dead can hear: their 'new hearing drunk the sound'. It is the visionary poet, quietly returning, who translates for us: it is he who allows her music/thought (lines 46–7) to be 'Essenced to language'.[113] The awkwardness of what follows, with its obscurities of expression and grammar, is not a failure of technique but a representation of the titanic difficulty of that act of translation. But it is a voice that the living cannot hear, which, finally, places the visionary among the dead. Rosenberg is both chronicler and victim, both outside the myth and in it, in a way that David Jones's narrator is not.

Rosenberg wrote to Laurence Binyon, in autumn 1916: 'I will not leave a corner of my consciousness covered up, but saturate myself with the strange and extraordinary new conditions of this life and it will all refine

---

[112] 'Daughters of War' in ibid., 119.
[113] Rosenberg worked hard to render this voice. In the same letter quoted above, he told Bottomley: 'I have tried to suggest the wonderful sound of her voice, spiritual and voluptuous at the same time' (ibid., 344).

itself into poetry later on'.[114] There was no 'later on' for Rosenberg, but here, in 'Daughters of War', he created the beginnings of a mythopoeic response to the horrors around him.

Both Jones and Rosenberg use myth to address the problem of representing the war in general, and its deaths in particular. In this strange other-world, the truth of the experience rests not only in the material detail, but in the 'fierce imaginings' of those who experienced it. Both poets offer a mythopoeic vision which goes beyond the limits of mere testimony into the traumatised imagination. Neither poet heroises the soldiers in their myth-making. *In Parenthesis* sets the warriors of myth against, alongside and within the ordinary bloke, with his moments of courage, fear, duty, humiliation and trauma. Similarly, for Rosenberg, the dead are both the heroic 'sons of valour' and simple 'earth-men', happy merely to take their share of 'sleep and bread and warmth'. Neither relies on the accreted authority of canonical myth, but rather on their sense of the poet as a visionary, shaping their cultural inheritance in new ways.

That said, their approaches are distinct. Where Jones's use of myth rests on an extraordinary breadth of learning, Rosenberg's derives from a knowledge of Jewish mythologies accumulated through his upbringing. Where Jones lays great importance on his textual sources (identifying them directly in his notes), Rosenberg detaches his myth-making from its sources. Rosenberg produces a profoundly disturbing mythic vision of the moment of dying, unleavened by the camaraderie so central to *In Parenthesis* – and there may be a reason for this beyond Rosenberg's prickly character. Jones writes in his Preface that the events of *In Parenthesis* don't extend beyond July 1916 because, after that date, the character of the war altered:

> From then onward things hardened into a more relentless, mechanical affair, took on a more sinister aspect. The wholesale slaughter of the later years, the conscripted levies filling the gaps in every file of four, knocked the bottom out of the intimate, continuing domestic life of small contingents of men... How impersonal did each new draft seem.[115]

As casualties mounted, the necessary drafts of new recruits broke the sense of fellowship between men. Rosenberg was himself one of those late arrivals. 'Daughters of War' was begun around October 1916 and completed after June 1917: it is a poem of the second, darker, more appalling half of the

---

[114] Ibid., 320.
[115] Jones, *In Parenthesis*, ix.

war.[116] Thus, where the Queen of the Woods offers the dead her flowers, the Daughters of War break open their faces to capture the soul.

Jones's mythical methods work movingly in several directions at once – and this fragmentary experience feels very much part of the high modernism of the 1920s. Rosenberg's mythopoeia is more single-minded – 'Daughters of War' creates a powerfully realised myth – and yet, within this myth there is a complexity of unresolved feeling which also brings Rosenberg's work into the orbit of modernism. For both poets, the mythical element in their work is not an intellectual move, it is not a 'method', but rather an imaginative response to the horror arising from their experience. The result, in each case, is a powerful meditation on the moment of dying.

---

[116] Rosenberg, *Isaac Rosenberg*, 390.

CHAPTER 4

Memorial Poems and the Poetics of Memorialising

In our Introduction, we set the hastily scrawled 'tablet' commemorating a fallen comrade in Walt Whitman's 'As Toilsome I Wander'd Virginia's Woods' against civic war memorials such as the one at Sorigny that Roland Barthes found so hideous. We also suggested that, while the commemorative writing of the individual may seem a less compromised kind of memorial than the stone monuments created by public bodies, even the most independent poet must negotiate the forces of broader cultural memory. Even so, the poem as memorial seems to have a powerful capacity to remember while expressing a critical distance from the civically developed set of approved values to which public monuments (mostly) adhere.

Public war memorials are attempts to symbolise, through a combination of form, symbol and inscription, an agreed national or communal response to the deaths of those killed. They are inevitably the products of protracted and complex debates.[1] Poems which reflect on the war dead are each the product of a single consciousness; while the writer is no less enmeshed in cultural memory than committee members, the poem is the result of an internal debate only. These distinctions are most graphically delineated where the two forms engage with each other: when poems are inscribed on monuments and when monuments are the subject of poems.

Poetic inscriptions on monuments, like monuments themselves, tend to the conservative, reinforcing the values the monument embodies. We take as an example the war memorial local to us, located in the Buttermarket, in the centre of Canterbury, only a few paces away from the Cathedral gates (see Figure 4.1). The poetry inscribed on one face of the memorial is as follows:

---

[1] See Prost, 'Monuments to the Dead', quoted in our Introduction (p. 11). For an account of the politics of war memorials, see Kristin Ann Hass, *Carried to the Wall: American Memory and the Vietnam Veterans Memorial* (Berkeley: University of California Press, 1998), 9.

> True love by life
> True love by death is tried
> Live thou for England
> We for England died

The Imperial War Museum's records show that this quotation is used relatively frequently on First World War memorials, but its source is not conclusively documented.[2] On the Buttermarket memorial, it appears below a commemorative prose inscription to 'the officers, non-commissioned officers and men of Canterbury who gave their lives for God, King and country'. The tone is thus set for a celebration of sacrifice, but the first two lines of the quatrain could come from any context, and the clever repetition, syntactical symmetry and inversion lend the lines an axiomatic quality. The remaining two lines are a classic case of prosopopoeia, the dead men whose names are inscribed on the memorial seeming to speak directly to us, as it were from within the memorial itself. They offer first an injunction, 'Live thou for England', then the ultimate moral claim to support that injunction: 'We for England died'. Hard for the reader to dissent from words which, oracle-like, seem to come from the dead themselves.

Martial self-sacrifice, religion and nationalism come together strikingly in a more familiar poetic inscription, this within the Cathedral itself, on a First World War memorial tablet to the 16th Queen's Lancers (see Figure 4.2):

> If I should die think only this of me
> That there's some corner of a foreign field
> That is for ever England

Rupert Brooke's famous lines, like those on the Buttermarket memorial, are unashamed in their singular appeal to England, in spite of the fact that men from all parts of the United Kingdom, including the whole of Ireland, made the same sacrifice, as did huge numbers from the Empire.[3] The bold lettering and the very placing of the lines within the Cathedral again make it difficult for the reader to take issue, except through outright rejection; there's no room for nuance.

---

[2] It has been suggested provisionally that the author is Arthur Campbell Ainger, an Eton master and a recognised hymn-writer. See the discussion thread on the *Great War Forum*, September 2008: http://1914-1918.invisionzone.com/forums/index.php?/topic/105748-true-love-by-life-true-love-by-death-is-tried-live-thou-for-england-w/.

[3] The *Great War Forum* discussion, mentioned above, includes an image of a grave marker for a Scottish soldier, where the Buttermarket lines are adapted, replacing 'England' with 'Britain'; this example only points up the reductive nature of the original lines.

Figure 4.1 The Buttermarket War Memorial, Canterbury.
Photograph © Nina Carrington.

By contrast, when monuments are the subject of poems, the effect is more often to question the values and the meanings which the monument appears to embody. In this chapter, we explore this intersection of commemorative practices, starting with the First World War but then moving beyond it to later decades and later wars. We begin with early poetic responses to the monuments of the First World War, then look at four later poems – one reaching back a century to the American Civil War, another considering a Northern Irish First World War memorial sixty years after the deaths it commemorates, and finally two poems of the late-twentieth century which offer contrasting responses to the Vietnam Veterans Memorial in Washington.

Memorial Poems and the Poetics of Memorialising 113

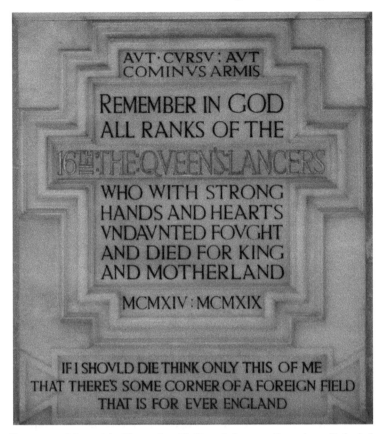

Figure 4.2 Memorial tablet to the 16th Queen's Lancers, Canterbury Cathedral. Photograph © Nina Carrington.

This chapter stands as a pivotal point in our work. Later decades of the twentieth century are also the focus of the latter part of this book, which looks at the influence of the poetry which emanated from the First World War on later poets and on British cultural and artistic expressions of, and responses to, memorialisation. This midway chapter, then, acts both as a retrospective and as a jumping off point, looking at the moment when memorials to the dead of the war were being freshly minted, and then at more recent poetic responses to such memorials and the reflections they provide on the act of remembering.

Cultural histories about public war memorials tend to be aligned to one of two poles. The first position is most fully expressed by Jay Winter, who characterises the building of memorials as an act of compassion towards grieving families, a valuable expression of sympathy and formal recognition of their loss. Winter emphasises the way First World War memorials developed bonds between fellow mourners and provided communal recognition of the mourners' suffering. They became 'foci of the rituals, rhetoric and ceremonies of bereavement'.[4] Winter acknowledges that memorials are also 'carriers of political ideas', but sees this as secondary to the humane function of offering consolation to the bereaved.[5] Whatever the political symbolism in evidence, these memorials 'provided first and foremost a framework for and legitimation of ... grief'.[6]

This interpretation endorses the account of the New Menin Gate given by Field Marshal Herbert Plumer at its unveiling in 1927. This memorial, designed by Sir Reginald Blomfield, commemorates the soldiers killed around Ypres whose bodies were never found. It combines the forms of a triumphal arch and a mausoleum and, at its unveiling, had 54,889 names inscribed on its panels. Speaking to an audience of several thousand bereaved relatives, Plumer said:

> One of the most tragic features of the Great War was the number of casualties reported as 'Missing, believed killed.' ... when peace came and the last ray of hope had been extinguished the void seemed deeper and the outlook more forlorn for those who had no grave to visit, no place where they could lay tokens of loving remembrance. The hearts of the people throughout the Empire went out to them, and it was resolved that here at Ypres, where so many of the 'Missing' are known to have fallen, there should be erected a memorial worthy of them which should give expression to the nation's gratitude for their sacrifice and its sympathy with those who mourned them. A memorial has been erected which, in its simple grandeur, fulfils this object, and now it can be said of each one in whose honour we are assembled here to-day: 'He is not missing; he is here.'[7]

In contrast, a more critical position sees public war memorials as attempts by the state to defend its waging of war by hijacking the human impulse of grief at the loss of young life. In this account, the government plays on the need of grief-stricken relatives to believe that their loved one's death was not in vain. The dead are 'sanctified' and 'glorified' in the name

---

[4] Winter, *Sites of Memory*, 78.
[5] Ibid.
[6] Ibid., 93.
[7] Quoted in Charles Harington, *Plumer of Messines* (London: John Murray, 1935), 303.

of grand abstracts such as Liberty, Honour and Peace. Their deaths are presented as necessary sacrifices for the greater good and received with humble gratitude. Samuel Hynes calls these monuments 'official acts of closure': 'They embody, in permanent form, ideas about war – heroic, romantic, histrionic, occasionally tragic … They belong to the discourse of Big Words, and by existing they affirm the meaning and value of those words, in spite of all the dying.'[8] War memorials, in this account, constitute propagandistic attempts to enforce unity, encouraging the people to forget the state's errors, complicity and false rhetoric, all of which would muddy the narrative. As the character Irwin, in Alan Bennett's play *The History Boys*, puts it: 'It's not so much lest we forget as lest we remember … so far as the Cenotaph and the Last Post and all that stuff is concerned, there's no better way of forgetting something than by commemorating it'.[9] The rhetoric of war memorials may even reinforce forgetting, in that it elicits a brief, sentimental response, but doesn't allow a questioning of the values the monument represents. There is a sleight of hand when we look at memorials which, unless we force ourselves to think hard about what each of those names means, leads to a generalised response of sadness which doesn't connect to the reality of each life, and each life lost, represented there.

Many poems written after the First World War movingly express this range of responses to public memorials, from both sides of the argument. Rudyard Kipling's 'London Stone', written for Armistice Day 1923, portrays the Cenotaph as a gathering place for the bereaved where they may comfort each other in their shared pain – though Kipling, grieving for the death of his son John at the Battle of Loos, is careful not to underestimate the power of grief, nor to suggest it can be erased by monuments and rituals. Thus, the purpose of the two-minute silence on Armistice Day is not to soften the pain, but to sharpen it:

> For those minutes, let it wake
> (Grieving – grieving!)
> All the empty-heart and ache
> That is not cured by grieving.[10]

---

[8] Samuel Hynes, *A War Imagined: The First World War and English Culture* (London: Pimlico, 1992), 270.
[9] Alan Bennett, *The History Boys* (London: Faber & Faber, 2004), 25.
[10] Rudyard Kipling, *The Collected Poems of Rudyard Kipling* (Ware: Wordsworth, 2001), 827.

Kipling urges mourners not to seek a false sense of consolation: 'For those minutes, tell no lie', and rebukes the complacency of St Paul's famous rhetorical questioning of death – 'O death, where is thy sting? O grave, where is thy victory?'[11] – with the simple assertion: 'Grave, this is thy victory; / And the sting of death is grieving'. Daniel Karlin calls this Kipling's 'impulse to honesty'.[12] Thus, when the poet asks whether there is any comfort to be had 'from earth or heaven', he answers himself: 'Heaven's too far and Earth too near'. However, at this point, the poem turns on a *but*: 'But our neighbour's standing here, / Grieving as we're grieving'. It is the Cenotaph that has brought these neighbours together and made them aware of each other's grief.

> What is the tie betwixt us two
> (Grieving – grieving!)
> That must last our whole lives through?
> 'As I suffer, so do you.'
> That may ease the grieving.

This offers a tentative response to Kipling's earlier poem, 'My Boy Jack', written after his son was reported 'missing, believed killed' in 1915. There, the speaker asks: '"Oh, dear, what comfort can I find?"', and a voice replies: '*None this tide, / Nor any tide, / Except he did not shame his kind*'.[13] Eight years later, Kipling is able to suggest that the Cenotaph creates a space for encounters that 'may ease the grieving' – not by effacing it but by allowing the bereaved to experience it anew in the company of fellow mourners.

Karlin notes that Kipling was a key figure in the devising of consoling rituals after the war.[14] He was deeply involved in the Imperial War Graves Commission, wrote the speech delivered by King George V on a war graves pilgrimage in 1922 and was instrumental in the creation of the Tomb of the Unknown Warrior at Westminster Abbey. Also, 'He devised the ceremony of sounding the Last Post at the Menin Gate in Ypres, the monument so hated by Siegfried Sassoon'.[15]

Sassoon's vituperative sonnet, 'On Passing the New Menin Gate' represents the other pole in the debate about public memorials. He calls the memorial 'this sepulchre of crime', suggesting a devious attempt by the

---

[11] 1 Corinthians 15:55.
[12] Daniel Karlin, 'Kipling and the Limits of Healing', *Essays in Criticism*, 48.4 (1998), 334.
[13] Kipling, *Collected Poems*, 228.
[14] Karlin, 'Kipling and the Limits of Healing', 334–5.
[15] Ibid., 335.

state to avert criticism of its prosecution of the war.[16] He sees in the Gate's design not the 'simple grandeur' which Field Marshal Plumer claimed for it at the unveiling, but merely 'pomp'. He finds repulsive the gap between the memorial's grandiosity and the ignominious, muddy deaths of simple conscripts. The poem begins: 'Who will remember, passing through this Gate / The unheroic Dead who fed the guns?' The rhetorical question suggests that the memorial will fail to call to mind those whose names are inscribed upon it because it is too grand a sight to recall enlisted men whose ordinariness was their defining characteristic. They are the 'doomed, conscripted, unvictorious ones'. In the second quatrain, Sassoon spits this out with increased ire, in a sarcastic cannonade of plosives:

> Crudely renewed, the Salient holds its own.
> Paid are its dim defenders by this pomp;
> Paid, with a pile of peace-complacent stone,
> The armies who endured that sullen swamp.

The architect Reginald Blomfield had based his design on 'a long and vaulted tunnel-like gateway' that he had seen in seventeenth-century fortifications at Nancy, aiming thereby to mark the entry point by which so many British troops approached the Ypres salient.[17] The massive and monolithic nature of the Menin Gate, 104 feet wide, 133 feet deep and with 69-foot high walls, was in part determined by the need to find space for the names of the missing, which were its *raison d'être*, to be inscribed on the inner side of the central arch. Sassoon pays no attention to the specifics of the design, asserting disdainfully in his very title that he is passing by rather than passing through the Gate.[18] In the poem he does not approach it, let alone inspect it, and the only specific detail he gives is inaccurate: 'here with pride / "Their name liveth for ever," the Gateway claims'. This inscription does not appear on the Menin Gate.[19] Sassoon ignores the several inscriptions that do appear on the memorial, preferring this one because of its focus on the *names* of the dead. He is horrified by the 'intolerably nameless names' that cover the memorial's panels. There

---

[16] Sassoon, *Collected Poems*, 188.
[17] David Crane, *Empires of the Dead: How One Man's Vision Led to the Creation of WWI's War Graves* (William Collins: London, 2013), 207.
[18] This is probably a fiction. Sassoon's own note in *War Poems* tells us that the poem was begun in Brussels on 25 July 1927, the day after the memorial's unveiling ceremony, which suggests that he had crossed the Channel on purpose to be present (Sassoon, *War Poems*, 143).
[19] It does appear (with 'ever' rendered as 'evermore') on the 'Stone of Remembrance', the white stone altar designed by Edwin Lutyens that features in British military cemeteries across the Western Front. The line, taken from Ecclesiasticus, was chosen by Kipling, at Lutyens's request.

are simply too many of them, he suggests, for each individual name to mean anything. For the soldier who has fought intimately alongside other soldiers, individual names acquire a greater meaning, and as Kristin Ann Hass suggests, 'This use of names ... both asserted an individual memory and lost that memory in the mass of names'.[20]

Vera Brittain, visiting the Thiepval Memorial (dedicated to the missing of the Somme) in 1933, also focuses on the names:

> Upon the arch, inside and all around it, are inscribed the 73,367 names of those who fell on the Somme and whose bodies were never found or never identified. It made me realise what a comparatively few of the dead must have been found and buried beneath dignified tombstones inscribed with their names, for there appeared to be numbers of these memorials to the missing ... I don't think this fact has ever been made public.[21]

Brittain's apparently cool, perceptive analysis belies the hot feelings aroused not just by the memorials but by the carefully tended cemeteries 'full of roses, pansies and lavender'. Like Sassoon, she is incensed by the way these memorials gloss over the complicated truth of war and its losses: 'I thought what a cheating and a camouflage it all is, this combined effort of man and nature to give once more the impression that war is noble and glorious, just because its aftermath can be given an appearance of dignity and beauty.'[22] It is no surprise that Kipling, the grieving father, takes such a different view from Sassoon, the betrayed soldier; but Brittain's response is interesting because she is bereaved and thus she might have an interest in preserving the glory of the men she has lost.[23] Yet here she responds very much like Sassoon, with the fury of a sense of injustice – perhaps because her experience as a grieving civilian was countered by her experience as a nurse who witnessed the reality at close quarters. While all are grounded in the same historical moment, each responds through specific personal experience. Kipling needs to believe in the possibility of a measure of consolation, not least because he has been the source of many of the mantras of consolation offered in memorial inscriptions. Sassoon has

---

[20] Hass, *Carried to the Wall*, 55–6.
[21] Vera Brittain, *Chronicle of Friendship: Vera Brittain's Diary of the Thirties 1932–1939*, ed. Alan Bishop (London: Gollancz, 1986), 134.
[22] Ibid., 135.
[23] Her visit to Thiepval was made during a journey to the grave of her fiancé Roland Leighton who had died of wounds on 23 December 2015. Brittain's biographers note that, during the war itself, she sustained a position generally supportive of the war, and even of the gloriousness of sacrifice, her pacifism developing only subsequently (Berry and Bostridge, *Vera Brittain*, 85, 109 and *passim*).

seen and suffered the grim reality of war and cannot brook attempts to lessen or overlay its horror. Brittain has been changed by her several losses (lover, brother, friends), and by her experience nursing both British and German patients, into a political being, seeing behind the public show to the structures beneath. What none of these three writers allows for is the possibility of internal conflict in the response to public memorials – the response of, say, a wounded soldier wheeled forward to lay a wreath, or a mother who *wants* to agree with Field Marshal Plumer but cannot quiet her anger at the patriarchal rhetoric which led to war, or a soldier from an ethnic minority or colonial background with a complex relationship to national identity.

Charlotte Mew's intriguingly confused poem of 1919, 'The Cenotaph', offers such a response. As Tim Kendall acknowledges, while the poem 'is tempted to find some divine recompense for the dead ... its mazy obscurities betray the strain on such hope'.[24] Mew begins with a sympathetic account of the monument, suggesting its power to heal. The first six lines develop an opposition between two locations: 'there', where the battle-torn fields are still soaked with 'the wild sweet blood of wonderful youth', and 'here' where bereaved women 'from the thrust of an inward sword have more slowly bled'.[25] *There*, each grave holds 'too long, too deep a stain', but *here* the Cenotaph provides a symbolic grave at which the nation's women can express and share their grief by laying flowers around its foot.

In these lines, Mew bolsters the sense of consolation by reviving the rhetoric of Rupert Brooke's *1914* sonnets – 'the wild sweet blood of wonderful youth' recalls Brooke's third sonnet, where 'The Dead' have 'poured out the red / Sweet wine of youth'.[26] Similarly, when Mew describes the flowers spread at the foot of the Cenotaph –

> Violets, roses, and laurel, with the small, sweet, tinkling country things
> Speaking so wistfully of other Springs,
> From the little gardens of little places where son or sweetheart was born and bred.

---

[24] Kendall, *Modern English War Poetry*, 76. Mew engages with the concept of a cenotaph, but the features she describes don't match those of the actual Cenotaph in London. The poem was written before the temporary wood-and-plaster cenotaph created for Peace Day in 1919 was replaced by a permanent stone version, so Mew may have envisaged something different. For an account of the Cenotaph's design and early popularity see Alex Moffett, '"We Will Remember Them": The Poetic Rewritings of Lutyens' Cenotaph', *War, Literature & the Arts*, 19.1–2 (2007), 230–4; Winter, *Sites of Memory*, 102–6.
[25] Charlotte Mew, 'The Cenotaph' in Reilly, *Scars upon My Heart*, 71.
[26] 'The Dead' in Brooke, *Collected Poems*, 314.

– she recalls the assumption of Brooke (and Georgian officer-poets in general) that every soldier was an English country lad, stepped from the pages of Housman (and never the slums of Whitechapel or Glasgow). This movement in the poem is brought to a rhetorical climax, with the long lines giving way to a shorter, four-beat line and then two two-beat lines, indented and exclamatory:

> In splendid sleep, with a thousand brothers
>   To lovers – to mothers
>   Here, too, lies he

Mew echoes Field Marshal Plumer's declaration at the Menin Gate that 'He is not missing; he is here!' and affirms the one clearly intended meaning in the Cenotaph's design – that it is an empty tomb representing the graves of all those buried across the sea (*cenotaph* is from the Greek *kenos* 'empty' + *taphos* 'tomb'). Up to this point, Mew would seem to express, with great compassion, Kipling's (and Winter's) position. However, this reading is troubled, first by an ambivalence evident in the form, secondly by a conspicuous omission and, most emphatically, by the poem's ambiguous coda.

The insistent rhyming (ten of the poem's twenty-five lines rhyme *shed*, *tread*, *bled* etc.) may suggest the closure that the monument hopes to represent, but this sense is undermined by the long, rambling lines, each of a different length and with no clear metre. Like the fields of Flanders described in the first line, these lines are 'measureless' – there is no comfort in them. The rhymes, when they come, may remind us distantly of the satisfactions of a well-made sonnet, but fail to supply them by being too far, and too variously, apart. In this context, their repetitiveness suggests an over-insistent desire for a sense of closure where none is truly felt or anticipated.

This note of anxiety draws attention to the fact that, for all that Mew echoes Brooke's rhetoric, she cannot bring herself to repeat the central consolations of his third sonnet – that the soldiers are enriched by death ('Blow out, you bugles, over the rich Dead!') and that their deaths enrich us also ('There's none of these so lonely and poor of old, / But, dying, has made us rarer gifts than gold'), causing 'Holiness', 'Honour' and 'Nobleness' to return to our lives.[27] Writing in 1919, and specifically from the position of the nation's grieving women ('the watchers by lonely hearths'), Mew cannot go this far. She does not imagine the dead as being capable

---

[27] Ibid.

of feeling anything at all – they are *dead* ('young, piteous, murdered') – but focuses instead on the feelings of the women who have 'more slowly bled' and whose hearts 'must break' to see the coverlet of flowers at the memorial's foot. As Kendall points out, whatever the consolations offered by the memorial, for Mew 'the dead undergo no transformation, and reap no reward for their sacrifice'.[28]

The ambivalent form, coupled with this retreat from Brooke's fantasy of the happy dead, suggests an inner turmoil that belies the speaker's assertion of the consolation offered by the monument. That sense is redoubled in the poem's closing lines:

> God is not mocked and neither are the dead
> For this will stand in our Market-place –
>   Who'll sell, who'll buy
>   (Will you or I
> Lie each to each with the better grace)?
> While looking into every busy whore's and huckster's face
> As they drive their bargains, is the Face
> Of God: and some young, piteous, murdered face.

Initially, this passage seems to affirm that the Cenotaph will purify our future lives, conditioning our behaviour by constantly reminding us, as we go about our daily business, of the dead, and the ideals for which they died and which we have a duty to uphold. The phrase 'God is not mocked' comes from Paul's Epistle to the Galatians: 'God is not mocked: for whatsoever a man soweth, that shall he also reap', suggesting that, if we sow the correct commemorative seeds, we shall reap a transformed future.[29] Here is a form of consolation we might believe in – a softer version of Brooke's notion that our civilisation is ennobled by the soldiers' deaths, as if Mew seeks to salvage something from those naive 1914 sentiments. And yet, even *this* thought is interrupted by the anxious enquiry in parentheses. The grammatical sense of the final six lines is difficult to follow and the poem's rhetoric is supplanted by a moment of modernist interior monologue. The confusing punctuation adds to this effect. The question mark which follows the parentheses invites us to treat the last three lines as a discrete sentence, which leaves us wanting a further clause at the end to answer that 'While …'. We have to retrace our steps to try to make grammatical sense, and the experience is one of listening to disjointed thoughts.

[28] Kendall, *Modern English War Poetry*, 77.
[29] Galatians 6:7.

By shifting the question mark to the poem's end, making one long sentence of the final nine lines, we may make grammatical sense of them, but they still present contradictory sentiments. The main clause asks rhetorically who will continue in thoughtless commerce when confronted by the memorial, symbolising the sacrificed dead, and Christ. And yet, this affirmation of the Cenotaph's power to ennoble our future behaviour is undercut by the cynicism evident in the parentheses, suggesting that human nature cannot be purified and that, while we may behave with 'better grace' in the shadow of the monument, this will be a matter of decorum, rather than morality. Further, Mew describes the people apparently affected by being in the monument's shadow as busy whores and hucksters, introducing more doubt about the monument's power to purify. The poem manages to end on a strong note of closure, in the triple repetition of the end-rhyme 'face'. Yet there is no real closure. The three faces are those of the common people, God and the dead, among whom nothing can be resolved. The very image of three faces is redolent with this poem's ambiguous, anxious spirit: when there are three faces, none can fully face another without turning away from the third.

The critical view that only combatants could write truly about the experience of war has long been laid to rest. But the fact remains that it was difficult for contemporary female poets such as Mew to find a poetic place in representing a conflict that was experienced at first hand only by men. Yet, with the Armistice, her voice is surer than either Kipling's or Sassoon's in its very uncertainty, for here she can represent some of the confusions and strains involved in both being a mourner and imagining the mourned, in the experience of confronting a memorial intended to act for both. Mew is not afraid to seem poetically ungainly because the poem is a sort of dialogue with herself in the face of something that attempts to resolve what she knows can't quite be resolved. The very difficulty of interpreting her final lines also allows the reader into this irresolution.

Modernism was the tool that allowed penetration of the interstices between a unified understanding of the individual within the world and the fractures within the individual, and between the self and the world, which some see the First World War as instigating. Mew's poem takes frail steps towards that new consciousness. As the modernist voice in poetry matured, it allowed a challenge to monuments and a questioning of them, whilst recognising their iconic power to speak to both private and public grief. Our defining examples here show mature reflections on the complexities of the memorial within a poetic tradition imbued with modernism: Robert Lowell's 'For the Union Dead' and Seamus Heaney's 'In Memoriam Francis Ledwidge'.

Lowell's poem is triggered by the Boston monument, dedicated in 1897, to Colonel Robert Shaw, a white officer who led the first black Northern regiment in the Civil War and was killed in action, with many of his troops, in 1863. It conjures the Shaw monument whilst also reminding us that Shaw's father 'wanted no monument / except the ditch, / where his son's body was thrown'.[30] But perhaps Shaw's father would have accepted the more flexible memorial of Lowell's poem, just because it *can* reflect upon the fact that he wanted no monument; and at the same time it can remind us of the deadly ditch that lies behind every war memorial. The paradox of words is that they can sometimes affect us more than the actuality they refer to and represent. Lowell's poem can take us in and out of the monument, letting us see it within its place in history as well as taking us beyond that immediate history.

The poem looks at the Shaw monument but also through and beyond it to what the American Republic has become: 'a savage servility / slides by on grease'. This larger context of greedy and grubbing capitalism, which makes the very Statehouse shake, sets Shaw's sacrifice and that of his black regiment in a questioning frame. Lowell layers the poem with historical strata: his younger and older self are set in the same pose against the glass of the 'old South Boston Aquarium', but the once-clear glass through which he gazed at 'the cowed, compliant fish' is now 'broken' and 'boarded' (an oblique reference to the once-clear glass of the Republic). Though there is a considerably insistent 'I' throughout, the voice veers between distance and involvement, allowing the reader in and out alongside.

Yet the monument remains at the centre of this poem. However Lowell frames, circumscribes, historicises Shaw and his men, the impulse at the heart of the poem is to memorialise – but not to memorialise in the same way as the memorial. That is of its moment, and that moment is carefully recreated in the midst of the poem: the monument is to Shaw, the white officer, not to his black regiment, and the poem gives him due imaginative weight, which is not given to the black men. Similarly, the monuments to the Union soldier, replicated on 'a thousand small town New England greens', are both materially and representatively white. In these ways Lowell's poem reflects faithfully cultural history as it is reflected in stone. But even stone, as he notes, can be shaped by and through time: 'The stone statues of the abstract Union Soldier / grow slimmer and younger

---

[30] 'For the Union Dead' in Robert Lowell, *For the Union Dead* (London: Faber & Faber, 1965), 70–2.

each year –'. Lowell catches the poignancy of the statues growing slimmer and younger through weathering, even while the bodies they represent have long decayed. It is as though we see the dead men going backward to youth, the mutability of the flesh more searing somehow when reflected in the mutability of the stone which is meant to be an enduring memorial. Again here we see both the death that has been and the death that will be, in the one moment. As Lowell says, 'The ditch is nearer'.

Lowell addresses a politics and a cultural and civic history, connecting the personal and the public through the address to the memorial, in a way that the memorial itself, fixed always in its aesthetic and historical moment, cannot. His poetic representation and commentary allow us as readers to figure the monument itself in our mind's eye; to see the now-dead persons both in and beyond that history; to have some understanding both of the existential moment of the soldier ('He rejoices in man's lovely, / peculiar power to choose life and die –') and of the moment of bitterness of the bereaved in the face of the meaningless monument; and to place all of this in the larger and generally more dispiriting history of the American Republic. But irreducibly in the centre of the poem the monument 'sticks like a fishbone / in the city's throat'. And, for the reader, Lowell's poem does the same job – it brings the ditch nearer.

Where Lowell takes on the history of the American Republic, Heaney addresses a more local Republicanism. But whilst the historical frame of his 1979 poem 'In Memoriam Francis Ledwidge' is specific, and its political elements still active, the consciousness of the poem's voice is personal, human. The poem centres on the First World War memorial at Portstewart in Northern Ireland.[31] Heaney deliberately brings himself into the poem, allowing 'the worried pet // I was in nineteen forty-six or seven' to inform, and perhaps undercut, the voice of the mature poet's overview.[32] He allows himself to be more vulnerable than Lowell (whose recovered childhood self is fixed firmly in the cooler gaze of his adult eye). Heaney deliberately conflates the extant memorial figure with the Francis Ledwidge he imagines, linking them through, and with, his Aunt Mary. Again, time periods are shuffled like cards. The pre-war 'literary, sweet-talking, countrified' Ledwidge is juxtaposed with the 'haunted Catholic

---

[31] The Portstewart memorial shows a soldier in the 'on guard' position, whereas Heaney describes a soldier in action, with a 'cape / That crumples stiffly in imagined wind' as he makes a 'hunkering run'. Critics have assumed that Heaney is describing the Portstewart memorial, and the references in the poem clearly support this, but Heaney, like Sassoon and Mew before him, makes somewhat free with the material details.
[32] 'In Memoriam Francis Ledwidge' in Seamus Heaney, *Field Work* (London: Faber & Faber, 1979), 59.

face' in the trenches, but both are underlain by 'a Boyne passage-grave'. That Neolithic grave is drawn from Ledwidge's landscape, reminding us of a history deeper than the last few hundred years, and matched in its end-line place in the stanza with the 'bloom of hawthorn', thus borrowing comfort from nature. But deeper history is finally less consolation than irony. The 'Boyne passage-grave' foreshadows Ledwidge's own grave, with its echoes of the tunnels and trenches of the front line.

What draws the reader into the poem are the persons of Ledwidge and of Aunt Mary, placed together by their being contemporaries in the same culture, religion and landscape, but divided by their gender. Aunt Mary lives, while Ledwidge dies; there are no monuments to Aunt Mary, but then they are not called for in the same way since she had a long life and he a short, sacrificial one. Personal tragedies and losses remain just that, whatever the larger history from which they spring, or the larger way in which they are commemorated; the wider historical ironies are at the outreaches of the poem. Here the representational nature of the bronze memorial, its human scale, the fact that we (through the poet's eyes) can walk all round it and equate its three-dimensionality with our own make the ironies of its bronze fixedness all the more poignant.

Heaney has been criticised for this – for an essentially bourgeois stance, his gaze levelled at the detail, at the individual; and where he embraces the political, he has been criticised for reinforcing sectarian positions, exemplified here by his representing nature as inherently Catholic ('the May altar of wild flowers, / Easter water sprinkled in outhouses').[33] This is to ignore the way that, in this poem, he carefully builds in the complexities of North and South, Catholic and Protestant, ensuring that they interweave and criss-cross through the fabric of the poem:

> In you, our dead enigma, all the strains
> Criss-cross in useless equilibrium
> And as the wind tunes through this vigilant bronze
> I hear again the sure confusing drum
> You followed from Boyne water to the Balkans

The allied strains of the dead bronze and the dead man pick up the historical tensions that both embody. Heaney chooses this memorial, partly for biographical reasons, to bring in 'the worried pet' he once was, and to allow

---

[33] See Jim Haughey, *The First World War in Irish Poetry* (London: Associated University Presses, 2002), 252–6; Edna Longley, *Poetry in the Wars* (Newcastle-upon-Tyne: Bloodaxe, 1986), 185–210 *passim*; James Simmons, 'The Trouble with Seamus', *Seamus Heaney: A Collection of Critical Essays*, ed. Elmer Andrews (London: Macmillan, 1992), 63.

an oppositional parallel between Ledwidge and his own Aunt Mary. More importantly, however, the linking of this Portstewart memorial with the Boyne poet Ledwidge re-unites North with South as in the pre-partition days of the First World War, and reminds us that Catholic Nationalist and Unionist Protestant fought alongside each other – and alongside the British whose sovereignty divided them so deeply. That Ledwidge could be a key member of the nationalist Irish Volunteers pre-war, and a friend and admirer of the Easter Rising luminary Thomas McDonagh, yet also be a volunteer for the British Army when the First World War broke out, is one enigma Heaney's poem investigates. His almost shocking use of the insignia of loyalism, the drum and the flute, to capture Ledwidge's own brand of loyalty, and his doubling of the same flute to stand for Ledwidge's poetic voice, insist against Jim Haughey's reading of the poem, and even reclaim them as tropes of a potential unity.[34]

But a deeper enigma underlies the political and historical one, which is the confrontation between living and dead that both the memorial and the poem seek to grasp. The Ledwidge of the poem and the hunkering figure of the bronze soldier are fixed in time, frozen in both action and inaction, recalling to us both their once-aliveness and now-deadness. Facing the Portstewart bronze in his own reimagining, the older Heaney looks back ruefully at his unknowing childhood self, ignorant as yet of the death that has been and the death to come, unconscious of the import of the memorial. Ledwidge – another Catholic poet – is brought live into the poem through the words from his letters, yet he is irreducibly 'rent / By shrapnel', consorting 'underground' with 'true-blue ones', fixed firmly in that history and in a death beyond history. The Boyne passage-grave and the Flanders grave come to the same thing – the ditch that was the only monument Shaw's father wanted for him. This then is the deeper enigma Heaney faces in the poem, that of his own inevitable death. Aunt Mary has known the fullness of life that Ledwidge couldn't, but she will go too, as will the poet himself. What the memorial brings us up against is what the poem finally brings us up against too – 'all of you consort now underground'.

The poems we have considered so far are responses to memorials that in themselves did not attempt to embody the complexities that the poems reflect. We end with poetic responses to a monument, the Vietnam

---

[34] 'Judging by the way Heaney's poem associates Irishness with landscape and Catholicity, we see further evidence of his love affair with romantic nationalism', (Haughey, *First World War in Irish Poetry*, 254).

Veterans Memorial, that was conceived and executed in a much more self-conscious way than any of those earlier ones, and that deliberately tries to embody and account for the contradictory impulses felt by those who come to see it. The complexity of the Memorial is well reflected in Yusef Komunyakaa's 1987 poem, 'Facing It', but before turning to that, it is important to recognise a more simply antagonistic poetic response.

The soldier-poet W. D. Ehrhart, in his 1984 poem 'The Invasion of Grenada', dismisses the very idea of a memorial to those killed in Vietnam:

> I didn't want a monument,
> not even one as sober as that
> vast black wall of broken lives.[35]

Enjambment tricks the reader into pausing at the end of the second line – 'not even one as sober as that' – suggesting a speaker who concedes that the memorial is, at least, appropriately solemn. But, with the third line, we realise we must retrace and read 'not even one as sober as that vast black wall of broken lives'. Here is another voicing of the anger Sassoon feels when confronted by so many engraved names.[36] Like Sassoon, Ehrhart refuses to consider the form of the memorial. He opposes its existence and will not engage with it, whatever it looks like. Thus it is presented as merely the first item in a list of attempts at commemoration, all of which he rejects: postage stamps, memorial highways. None of these gestures can compensate for what's missing:

> What I wanted was a simple recognition
> of the limits of our power as a nation
> to inflict our will on others ...
> What I wanted
> was an end to monuments.

Ehrhart shares Sassoon's feeling (and that of Colonel Robert Shaw's father a hundred years earlier) that any memorial is a traducement of the reality of war, a covering up of the dirty deaths of soldiers, reasserting the deceitful rhetoric and national narratives that their experience has taught them to be false. Their poems speak directly of the anger of surviving combatants confronted with monoliths that they feel cannot possibly contain their experience, because they remain monoliths. Their bitterness stems from

---

[35] W. D. Ehrhart, 'The Invasion of Grenada' in Reese Williams (ed.), *Unwinding the Vietnam War: From War into Peace* (Seattle: Real Comet, 1987), 282.
[36] The Vietnam Veterans Memorial had 57,939 names inscribed on its surfaces when first dedicated in 1982.

a belief in the value of individual life; the memorial for them seems to obliterate that value.

The link between Ehrhart's poem and its title is implicit. The United States invaded Grenada in October 1983, eleven months after the Vietnam Veterans Memorial was dedicated. What bothers Ehrhart is that the memorial has made no difference to America's self-justifying view of itself as the world's policeman. As Neil P. Baird puts it, 'For Ehrhart ... one of the consequences of the way public memory is being shaped by these memorials is the cultural reinscription of the values of American power and dominance, resulting in the invasion of Grenada, another possible Vietnam in Ehrhart's eyes'.[37] The Memorial portrays the named dead as victims, effacing their role as killers. In so sanctifying the dead, it may sustain the rhetoric necessary for further invasions.[38]

Yusef Komunyakaa's 1987 poem, 'Facing It', is a very different response. If Sassoon's anger anticipates Ehrhart's, Mew's complexity and ambivalence anticipate Komunyakaa's. His African-American identity functions in ways similar to Mew's gender in generating a nuanced, ambivalent response to the public memorial. Komunyakaa engages intensely with the Vietnam Veterans Memorial's radical design, seeking a way of engaging with it that might 'ease the grieving'. It is worth pausing to describe those aspects of the design to which his attention is drawn, and which themselves attempt to undercut or question the inherently monolithic nature of a memorial.[39]

Firstly, the walls of the Memorial are not white, but black. In a passionate attack on the design, one veteran, Tom Carhart, argued that 'Black is the universal color of shame, sorrow and degradation in all races, all societies worldwide', but this is a mistaken assumption – Donald Ringnalda points out that 'in Vietnam *white* is the color of sorrow' and the monument's

---

[37] Neil P. Baird, 'Virtual Vietnam Veterans Memorials as Image Events: Exorcising the Specter of Vietnam', *Enculturation*, 6.2 (2009), n.p., http://enculturation.net/6.2/baird.

[38] Ehrhart, in his essay 'This Is All We Wanted', goes further than Sassoon in the valuing of individual lives, including in the reckoning the lives of Vietnamese soldiers and civilians. He calls the Memorial 'a sober reflection upon our 58,000 dead that avoids any acknowledgement of some three million dead Asians' (Ehrhart, *The Madness of It All: Essays on War, Literature and American Life* (Jefferson, NC: MacFarland, 2002), 87).

[39] For more detailed descriptions of the Memorial, see Hass, *Carried to the Wall*, 14; Elizabeth Hess, 'Vietnam: Memorials of Misfortune', *Unwinding the Vietnam War: From War into Peace*, ed. Reese Williams (Seattle: Real Comet, 1987), 264; Donald Ringnalda, *Fighting and Writing the Vietnam War* (Jackson: University Press of Mississippi, 1994), 236–40. For a philosophical enquiry into the radical nature of the Memorial see Charles L. Griswold, 'The Vietnam Veterans Memorial and the Washington Mall: Philosophical Thoughts on Political Iconography', *Critical Inquiry*, 12.4 (1986). For accounts of the controversy surrounding it, see Hess, 'Vietnam', 262–70; Ringnalda, *Fighting and Writing*, 232–4.

designer, Maya Lin, argued that she found black 'a lot more peaceful and gentle than white'.[40] Moreover, Carhart seems unaware of the effect his statement may have on veterans whose skin is black.

Lin had further reasons for choosing black granite: 'I wanted something that would … turn into a mirror if you polished it'.[41] The choice of material, then, is related to another unique feature of the Memorial: its surface is highly reflective. Visitors see their own mirrored faces gazing out from behind the chiselled letters, which are matt grey against the shiny black surface. As Arthur C. Danto observes: 'Through an uncanny reversal, the names of the dead appear more real, more substantial than we do'.[42] Ringnalda describes the effect well: 'Its polished black granite reflects its surroundings – visitors, grass, trees, water, clouds, airplanes taking off overhead … it integrates the visitor in a complex mobile collage in which the viewer watches himself look as others watch him look at names of the dead'.[43]

Finally, the walls of the Memorial are engraved with the names of the American servicemen and women who were killed or went missing in action in Vietnam – and, unusually, they are listed in order of death or disappearance. The big First World War monuments characteristically list names first by regiment, then by rank, and then alphabetically, thus inscribing each name in a network of military classification and record-keeping. The Vietnam Veterans Memorial chooses to place its names in a narrative, rather than administrative, frame. This means that 'soldiers who died together are listed together', so that visitors seeking the name of a loved one will also read the names of soldiers unknown to them who were killed on the same day, possibly in the same place.[44] A further effect of this arrangement is that specific names are harder to locate – they must be searched for with the help of guides and a printed directory. Unlike the Menin Gate and the Thiepval Memorial, most of the names are in easy reach, and sets of steps are available for those wishing to touch the names beyond reach. Grant F. Scott contrasts the Vietnam Veterans Memorial with the grander, neighbouring memorials on the Mall: 'Unlike its neighboring cousins, the Veterans memorial does not just encourage

---

[40] Carhart quoted in Hess, 'Vietnam', 265; Ringnalda, *Fighting and Writing*, 232; Lin quoted in Hess, 'Vietnam', 272.
[41] Hess, 'Vietnam', 272.
[42] Quoted in Grant F. Scott, 'Meditations in Black: The Vietnam Veterans Memorial', *Journal of American Culture*, 13.3 (1990), 37.
[43] Ringnalda, *Fighting and Writing*, 237.
[44] Hass, *Carried to the Wall*, 15.

us to touch its surface, but absolutely mandates it' and Hass suggests that each engraved name 'asks to be touched'.⁴⁵

In his polemical study of Vietnam War poetry, Ringnalda accuses weaker poems of resorting to 'preachy didacticism' and merely 'rail[ing] against the Establishment'. He argues that 'Instead of watching themselves look at Vietnam, most of the poets just look'.⁴⁶ In contrast, Ringnalda likens the strongest poems to the reflective Vietnam Veterans Memorial itself: 'Like Maya Lin's Vietnam Veterans Memorial, they show us that we can gain healing power from facing more than 58,000 "unpleasant facts". By eliciting thoughtful reflection rather than ... the reification of warrior nostalgia, they show us how to remember the war without conferring dignity on it.'⁴⁷ It is interesting that Ringnalda uses the Memorial as a point of analogy for the strongest poems: 'Facing It' is one of his exemplars and it takes the form of a meditation on the Memorial itself.⁴⁸ Komunyakaa – the only one of the later twentieth-century poets we discuss here who served in the war whose memorial he considers – waited fourteen years before writing any poems about his experience of Vietnam.⁴⁹ This was one of the first. That is to say, he was able to find a way of speaking by engaging with the Memorial's reflective qualities, which enabled him to 'watch himself look', rather than simply look.

Conditioning that unflinching self-observation is Komunyakaa's acute awareness of the ambivalent position of black GIs who fought for their country while, at home, that country remained segregated and African-Americans continued to suffer racist oppression.⁵⁰ In several poems in the collection *Dien Cai Dau* (1988), which 'Facing It' concludes, Komunyakaa shifts between racial and national identities, writing as both an American and an African-American, exploring tensions and contradictions without seeking to efface them.⁵¹ In 'Facing It' he does this intensely. Intrinsic

---

⁴⁵ Scott, 'Meditations in Black', 39; Hass, *Carried to the Wall*, 14.
⁴⁶ Ringnalda, *Fighting and Writing*, 138.
⁴⁷ Ibid., xii–xiii.
⁴⁸ It is both a distinguishing and a constitutive feature of Komunyakaa's poem that he engages accurately with the material detail of the monument, unlike the other poets we discuss.
⁴⁹ Komunyakaa 'served in Vietnam as a correspondent and editor of *The Southern Cross*' (Yusef Komunyakaa, *Dien Cai Dau* (Middletown, CT: Wesleyan University Press, 1988), 64).
⁵⁰ William M. Ramsey points out that Komunyakaa, who was brought up in Louisiana, would be familiar with the many public monuments commemorating the Confederate dead in Southern towns and so 'he would innately resist grand narratives that sustain themselves by suppressing the truth of micro-narratives pertaining to the oppressed' (Ramsey, 'Knowing Their Place: Three Black Writers and the Postmodern South', *The Southern Literary Journal*, 37.2 (2005), 125).
⁵¹ The collection's title is a Vietnamese phrase meaning 'Crazy Head'.

to this expression is his use of what might be called jazz forms. 'Facing It' has the feel of a jazz improvisation – firstly in its form and secondly in the way it presents its images. The form of this thirty-one-line poem seems to be free, with line-breaks and moments of rhyme and rhythm randomly scattered. However, like improvised jazz, there is a structure underpinning the apparent free play. This structure, comprising two parts of equal length separated by a shorter central section, mimics the verse-bridge-verse structure of many jazz songs. It is within this framework that the poem presents its series of images, which are ambiguous, disconnected and contradictory, and yet comprise a coherent whole. Where Ehrhart makes an assertive statement but offers no concrete images, Komunyakaa does the precise opposite. In the poem's first movement (lines 1–13), the speaker contemplates not the Memorial but his reflection in it – which seems to vanish, reappear and alter its nature. From the first sighting, its connotations are unsettlingly ambiguous: 'My black face fades, / hiding inside the black granite'.[52] Is it that the black granite of the Memorial erases his own blackness, making him one with all the names on the wall regardless of race? Perhaps, and yet the image also suggests a camouflaged soldier fading into the background, waiting to ambush the poet – a reading encouraged by the likening of his reflection to a 'bird of prey, the profile of night', which eyes him.[53] To approach the Memorial with an appropriate sense of unity, he must set aside his identity as an African-American, but this can only be a temporary move. At any moment, the ambush will be sprung, the bird of prey will dive.

This double-edgedness slices into the self-admonition: 'I said I wouldn't, dammit: No tears'. Are his tears for fallen soldiers, or for the divided self? The divided nature of the self is evident in the next line: 'I'm stone. I'm flesh'. The first of these two-word sentences can be read as a command to the self not to cry – in which case, the second sentence reads as an admission that he has failed. He is not stone, he is only flesh, and so he has shed tears. Yet, in a real sense, his reflection *is* stone; stone is the element in which it moves, while the onlooking poet is flesh and breathes air.

The poet's two selves, one stone, the other flesh, can never unite. In this reading, the ghostly self in the granite comes to stand for the ghost Komunyakaa might well have become. Stared at by this ghost, when he searches through the engraved names, he does so 'half-expecting to

---

[52] 'Facing It' in Komunyakaa, *Dien Cai Dau*, 63.
[53] *Dien Cai Dau* begins with 'Camouflaging the Chimera', which describes this process of melting into a landscape and waiting, 'ready to spring the L-shaped / ambush' (Komunyakaa, *Dien Cai Dau*, 4).

find / my own'. Yet his reflection is not a separate being. In his final attempt to pin down the image, he writes:

> I turn
> this way – the stone lets me go.
> I turn that way – I'm inside
> the Vietnam Veterans Memorial
> again, depending on the light
> to make a difference.

It is he, not some doppelgänger, who is 'inside' the Memorial. And, what is more, he is in there by his own volition – he turns to catch the light, allowing himself to be reflected, and so gives himself up to the Memorial, hoping that this surrender of the self will 'make a difference'.

In this extraordinary image, the two parts of the poet's divided self are separated, literally, by the engraved names of the dead. He is now ready to shift his focus (again, literally) from his other self, watching himself looking, to those names. This middle section of the poem, though, brings no relief. The Memorial fails to deliver on its promise of consolation. The light makes no difference – he reaches out to touch the name of a dead comrade and the tentative, shifting optical effects created by the morning light on the wall are rudely wiped out by a stronger, more insistent light: 'I touch the name Andrew Johnson; / I see the booby trap's white flash'. It is as if the act of touching the wall sets off the lethal device, ignites the painful memory.

The poem's final movement presents a series of ambivalent and suggestive images. In the first, 'Names shimmer on a woman's blouse'. This is the first female presence in the poem, suggesting a turn to life, possibly to desire, and the names shimmer as if they are insubstantial, not engraved – and yet, 'when she walks away / the names stay on the wall'. The note of hope fades, the image reinforces the sense of the Memorial's failure to console.

Briefly, the poet's attention is drawn upwards to reflections of a 'red bird', 'The sky' and 'A plane in the sky'. For the veteran, these are disturbing images – the wings of the bird 'flash', the verb linking this movement to the 'booby trap's white flash'. The bird's colour suggests a jungle creature, perhaps, 'wings cutting across my stare' – the image interrupts his thoughts, his attempts to heal. What is more disturbing is the way that the veteran is so traumatised that mundane sights in the sky over Washington carry terrible suggestiveness. Komunyakaa only has to itemise 'The sky. A plane in the sky', and the reader shares the veteran's traumatised vision. The sky is full of dangers, the plane no longer a passenger jet out of Washington

National Airport, but a terrifying presence. The wall has failed; the veteran is irrecoverably damaged.

And yet, here, the poem moves to a powerfully complex and ambiguous image:

> A white vet's image floats
> closer to me, then his pale eyes
> look through mine. I'm a window.

The poet does not turn to the human being beside him, but remains focused on the reflection – the ghost 'floats / closer', suggesting both a gesture of friendship and the insistent presence of death. And then, the white vet's eyes 'look through' the poet's eyes. Is this a moment of unity, where colour no longer matters and the white vet sees through the black vet's eyes, or is it a restatement of the distance and discord between them where the white vet 'looks through' in the sense of not seeing? The bald statement 'I'm a window' can work in either reading, drawing on contradictory connotations of the image in each case.

The poet tells us that the white vet has 'lost his right arm / inside the stone', but he is unable to turn and verify whether this is an optical effect or a brutal fact. He is not ready for the stone to let him go. The series of shifting images has cumulatively created the sense (darkly recalling Lewis Carroll's looking glass) that the world inside the black mirror is a place where fantastic metamorphoses are possible, and the poet is loath to leave, still hoping for the light to make a difference. The poem's final image, tentatively and provisionally, answers this need:

> In the black mirror
> a woman's trying to erase names:
> No, she's brushing a boy's hair.

Initially, he thinks he sees the woman touching the wall, as all mourners do, and as he has just done – but he interprets the movement of her hand as an attempt to erase the names, an act as futile as his own touching of the name Andrew Johnson. The dead will stay dead. But then he understands that, just as his traumatised imagination converted a harmless bird into a fearful sign, he has misinterpreted a motherly gesture of care. The shifting world of the black mirror has tricked him, and so shows him the nature of his damaged perception. He is able to watch himself looking – and, as he refocuses, he is able to correct himself. Kevin Stein points out that the woman's gesture brings the poet's focus 'on the future that young boy embodies, a future outside of the glass-like surface of the Memorial' and that this family's colour is not mentioned because it is no longer important.⁵⁴ The light has made a difference after all. On this note of hope and expression of common humanity, the image presages the poet's own exit from the Memorial. He is ready for the stone to let him go.

Kristin Ann Hass, in her study of the thousands of written notes and other objects left by visitors at the Vietnam Veterans Memorial, suggests that the design of the Memorial has allowed it to become a locus for a continuing debate:

> the Vietnam Veterans Memorial and the things that people leave there are part of a continuing conversation about the relationship of individuals and bodies to nations and to patriotism and nationalism… the objects … articulate a struggle on the part of ordinary Americans to be part of a conversation about how the war should be remembered and, therefore, part of a conversation about the shape of the nation.⁵⁵

'Facing it' is a profound contribution to that conversation.

T. J. Clark reminds us that rationality goes missing 'when the living and the dead confront one another. Corpses are (still) persons. They are people we cannot help treating, at one level, as entities with wishes, fears, awareness, powers over us, subservience to us. We still desire their presence – their regard'.⁵⁶ Those poets we have considered who manage to escape the monolithic even as they confront it – Mew, Lowell, Heaney, Komunyakaa – seem to catch something of this desire, and the confusion and contradiction it can generate. Mew inhabits the difficult place of the non-combatant female facing the Cenotaph embodying male sacrifice, but does not allow an oversimplified reading, rather inviting us to share some of her own confusion. Lowell's mature American modernist voice brings all the tensions of race and Republic into his historical sweep; but at the centre of the poem the confrontation remains between the living, mortal poet and the memorialising representation of a dead man and the men he led. In that sense, it remains personal. Heaney starts and ends with the personal, conflating the bronze representation of a soldier with the actual man Francis Ledwidge in 'our dead enigma'. But far from giving us an ahistorical benison in depicting the universality of death, Heaney catches that deeply human impulse to desire a reciprocity from the dead

---

[54] Kevin Stein, 'Vietnam and the "Voice Within": Public and Private History in Yusef Komunyakaa's *Dien Cai Dau*', *Massachusetts Review*, 36.4 (1995–6), 558.
[55] Hass, *Carried to the Wall*, 4–5.
[56] T. J. Clark, 'Living Death', *London Review of Books*, 7 January 2010, 10. Clark is referring to an argument in Pascal Boyer, *Religion Explained: The Human Instincts That Fashion Gods, Spirits and Ancestors* (London: Heinemann, 2001).

that cannot be given – as well as the knowledge that eventually we too will become the unreciprocating. Komunyakaa, the only poet of the four facing a memorial on which his own name might have figured, brings a particular edge and pain to his poem. He plays on the reflectiveness of the granite that was part of the conception of the Vietnam Veterans Memorial, thereby introducing his own blackness into the poem, along with the idea of confronting the self through looking at one's reflection. This poem thus announces its facing up to death, perhaps because the poet has already had to do so in actual conflict, perhaps because of the multiple ironies the poetic voice has been able to accumulate at this late point in the tradition, and that underlie the poem's punning title.

Yet Komunyakaa's voice also takes us right back to the desperate understandings of death and of the difficulties of commemoration sometimes achieved by combatant poets of the First World War. In the thick of trench warfare, the dead had to be speedily buried with but a rushed marking of the grave, as Ivor Gurney reminds us in the crisply named 'Butchers and Tombs':

> ... the time's hurry, the commonness of the tale
> Made it a thing not fitting ceremonial[57]

Instead of the desired 'Cotswold stone' each dead man is given just 'one wooden cross'. Underlying all, however, is the certainty of the deadness of the dead man; Cotswold stone nor wooden cross will hide what Gurney, in 'To His Love', calls 'That red wet / Thing I must somehow forget'.[58]

'That red wet / Thing' lies beneath all memorial monuments; it is what we are trying both to remember and to forget. The best memorial poems inscribe both impulses, whilst also allowing us to imagine what can't in the event be imagined – the experience of our own deaths. Such poems bring us face to face with the loneliness of our own extinction, not by annihilating our relationship to the world, but by enabling us to confront and experience in a living way the sudden extinction of our fellows.

---

[57] 'Butchers and Tombs' in Gurney, *Collected Poems*, 241.
[58] Ibid., 21.

CHAPTER 5

'Disquieting Matter'
The Unburied Corpse in War Poetry

> At times the living were surrounded by corpses throughout the trenches and adjacent areas. The dead were underfoot; they were used to reinforce the parapets of the trenches; they were stored in trenches awaiting burial. Some turned up in bizarre places, such as in the latrine, holding up a fragile doorway, or up a tree.[1]

Trudi Tate reminds us that, on the Western Front, corpses were everywhere. She then shows how descriptions of corpses as objects of horror and fascination abound in the prose narratives of the war, notably those by Henri Barbusse, Frederic Manning, Edmund Blunden and Robert Graves: 'Two sights are figured repeatedly in the soldiers' narratives of the Great War: corpses and bodies in pieces'.[2] To understand this horrified fascination with the corpse, Tate turns to Julia Kristeva's notion of the abject, as set out in *Powers of Horror* (1982).

> Kristeva describes the corpse, 'the most sickening of wastes', as a border, but 'a border that has encroached upon everything'. It is the most powerfully affecting example of the *abject*.... For the physical body, the abject (bodily fluids, waste, sweat, tears, etc.) simultaneously marks its boundaries and threatens to dissolve them.[3]

The conditions on the Western Front brought this sense of abjection to the soldier's consciousness with a new kind of intensity. The destruction of corpses, the fragments and globs of their rotting remains, force a traumatising confrontation with the abject as never before. As a result, soldiers' prose accounts repeatedly 'describe the fantasy relationship between the living and the dead, understood through the troubling figure of the corpse'.[4]

---

[1] Tate, *Modernism, History*, 66.
[2] Ibid., 64.
[3] Ibid., 68.
[4] Ibid., 69.

However, the same cannot be said of the poetry. It is notable that even poets who wrote such prose accounts tend to confront the corpse in their prose only. Where one does find in poetry descriptions of corpses, they tend to serve a public argument against the war rather than confronting the private horror. Robert Graves's 'A Dead Boche' is a good example:

> he scowled and stunk
> With clothes and face a sodden green,
> Big-bellied, spectacled, crop-haired,
> Dribbling black blood from nose and beard.[5]

Graves's purpose is polemical; he holds the horror up to his readers with the express aim of curing their 'lust of blood', rather than giving an account of his own experience.[6] Siegfried Sassoon describes corpses in similar terms in 'Counter-Attack':

> The place was rotten with dead; green clumsy legs
> High-booted, sprawled and grovelled along the saps
> And trunks, face downward, in the sucking mud,
> Wallowed like trodden sand-bags loosely filled;
> And naked sodden buttocks, mats of hair,
> Bulged, clotted heads slept in the plastering slime.[7]

As Lorrie Goldensohn says of this poem: 'Every verb in the stomach-turning description is picked to convey a maximum degradation of the body'.[8] Sassoon goes further than Graves, though, describing the effect of the abject on one individual:

> He crouched and flinched, dizzy with galloping fear,
> Sick for escape, – loathing the strangled horror
> And butchered, frantic gestures of the dead.

But, as in Graves's poem, the purpose here is to express a public position about the war. The poem ends with the death of the soldier who was traumatised by corpses, and its title comes to describe not just a failed military operation but also the poet's own counterblast directed at civilian

---

[5] Robert Graves, 'A Dead Boche' in Kendall, *Poetry of the First World War*, 194.
[6] This poem closely follows a prose description in Graves's memoir, *Goodbye to All That* (1929). See Kendall's note on the poem: ibid., 285.
[7] 'Counter-Attack' in Sassoon, *Collected Poems*, 68.
[8] Lorrie Goldensohn, *Dismantling Glory: Twentieth Century Soldier Poetry* (New York: Columbia University Press, 2003), 129.

readers. He demands that *they* see what the war is doing to the men they have sent to it – rather than exploring his own sense of horror.⁹

These confrontations with the battlefield corpse are public statements expressing anger rather than trauma. That said, even such descriptions as these are very rare in the poetry, and this requires some explanation. It seems that poetry as a genre is resistant to the risk of a confrontation with the abject because of its traditions of elegy and its discourses surrounding death. The grotesque fact of the corpse conflicts with a poetic commemoration of those killed. In fact, this may explain why lyric poetry was the genre to which writers were primarily attracted during the war years – its traditions provided a way of processing the experience which protected the writer from the abject, providing a bearable way to remember and a consoling way to commemorate.

Aside from the polemics above, where poetry notices the battlefield corpse, that corpse is somehow transformed. A survey of wartime anthologies bears this out, providing an overview of attempts in poetry to find a way to speak of the battlefield's corpses by those who saw them. In E. B. Osborn's 1917 anthology, *The Muse in Arms*, Dyneley Hussey's 'Ode to a Young Man Who Died of Wounds in Flanders, January 1915' makes the traditional division between body and soul – 'Thou gav'st thy body, gav'st thy soul' – but then invests the former with qualities of the latter, addressing the corpse as if it is sentient: 'Sleep on, pure youth, sleep at Earth's soothing breast /…/ Where all ungarlanded thou tak'st thy rest'.¹⁰ In Galloway Kyle's anthology, *More Songs by the Fighting Men* (also 1917), R. Howard Spring draws the corpse into a softening Arthurian myth with his title 'Hic Jacet', and with archaic diction and weaponry: 'Unrecorded and unsung, / Lay his body in the clay; / Buckler broken, sword unslung'.¹¹

These evasions are distant echoes of the tradition of Romantic elegy discussed in our first chapter, where a sense of consolation is evoked by the suggestion that the dead man will re-enter the cycles of nature. When, in 'Adonais', Shelley describes the spirit of Keats entering nature, there is a suggestion that this transfiguration is parallel to the chemical transmutation

---

⁹ In 'Repression of War Experience', where Sassoon does movingly represent that horror, the memory of the dead bodies is dismissed ('they're in France'), creating a sense of wary self-censorship (Sassoon, *Collected Poems*, 90).

¹⁰ Dyneley Hussey, 'Ode to a Young Man Who Died of Wounds in Flanders, January 1915' in E. B. Osborn (ed.), *The Muse in Arms* (London: John Murray, 1917), 132.

¹¹ R. Howard Spring, 'Hic Jacet' in Galloway Kyle (ed.), *More Songs by the Fighting Men* (London: Erskine MacDonald, 1917), 131. The inscription on King Arthur's tomb is said by Thomas Malory to be *Hic jacet Arthurus, rex quondam, rexque futurus*: 'Here lies Arthur, king once, and king to be'.

of his corporeal remains into surrounding plant life. The former idea is evident in the poem's epigraph, from Plato, which likens Keats in death to Hesperus, the evening star, giving 'New splendour to the dead'.[12] The latter is expressed in stanza 20 where Shelley imagines how 'The leprous corpse', touched by the spirit of Spring, 'Exhales itself in flowers of gentle breath'.[13] However, the flowers through which the corpse exhales 'mock the merry worm that wakes beneath', that is to say, the flowers *deprive* the worms of their food whereas, in reality, the work of worms is an essential part of nature's processes. The chemical transformation slips into a spiritual one. Similarly, the famous stanza (stanza 42) to which Owen alludes in 'A Terre' balances itself between the two conceptions. The statement 'He is made one with Nature' suggests the chemical process, but the idea is developed in a spiritual sense: Keats's voice joins the sounds of creation:

> there is heard
> His voice in all her music, from the moan
> Of thunder, to the song of night's sweet bird;
> He is a presence to be felt and known
> In darkness and in light, from herb and stone.[14]

This indeterminacy enters the poetry of the First World War as poets strive to evade the full horror of the unburied corpse. Soldiers' bodies nourish trees or flowers which then become a manifestation of their life force. In many anthologised poems of the period, we can read this trope as a moving but flawed attempt to cover over the abject corpse, to make the traumatising memory safe.

In Kyle's first anthology, *Soldier Poets: Songs of the Fighting Men* (1916), another poem by Dyneley Hussey, 'The Dead', refers more directly to soldiers' decomposing corpses but transmutes them into 'dead leaves' that 'waken in the weary earth, / Making the barren warm and rich with life, / And give to nobler flowers a glorious birth'.[15] The decomposition of corpses becomes the mulching of leaves; Hussey retreats further still from the abject in his final three lines by addressing 'the dead' as if they remain conscious:

> And your dead lives are dead alone in name,
>   For you shall live anew after the strife,
> And light in future hearts a sacred flame.

---

[12] 'Adonais' in Shelley, *Selected Poems*, 314.
[13] Ibid., 321–2.
[14] Ibid., 328.
[15] Dyneley Hussey, 'The Dead' in Galloway Kyle (ed.), *Soldier Poets: Songs of the Fighting Men* (London: Erskine MacDonald, 1916), 53.

That final line is a further evasion. True, mulching leaves *can* spontaneously combust, but it seems that, rather than extending the earlier metaphor, Hussey abandons it for a safer cliché which is even more remote from materiality, and from the abject. David Cox McEwen Osborne's poem 'Private Claye' (which appears in Kyle's *More Songs by the Fighting Men*) figures the dead soldier as a modern Adam made from English clay which, in the earth, becomes the matter from which a nation and a civilisation grow:

> From clay in strength our native oak-tree grows
> To height and girth and spread of largest span;
> The sweet and crimson riot of the rose;
> And wheat, the bread and sacrament of man.[16]

The allusion to natural processes is overwhelmed by the metaphorical; the poem conflates body and spirit in a way that, again, puts a screen around the abject. In Georges Bannerot's 'As Ye Have Sown', which appeared in Bertram Lloyd's 1919 anthology *The Paths of Glory*, the connection between corpse and nature is more actual: 'Wrought of our flesh and bone the Spring appears, / Its sap our hearts-blood's deep and glowing stream'.[17] However, any sense of a recognition of the abject corpse is countered by the poem's prosopopoeia (the dead men tell us that they have 'lain down' but, as yet, 'sleep not'), and by a romantic tone which is compounded by the notion that the corpse-fed wheat will feed the next generation: 'From the glad golden grain another life / More wondrous and more manifold shall rise'. The grain, then, has magical properties because it is fed by the remains of happy warriors.

Several soldier-poets, rather than describing or responding to the actual corpses around them, imagine the corpse that their own still-breathing body will become – a genre Tim Kendall calls 'self-elegy'.[18] Rupert Brooke, in 'The Soldier' (collected in Osborn's *The Muse in Arms*, under the title 'If I should die'), imagines his body in the earth as 'a richer dust', a faint allusion to corporeality which is supplanted in the sestet by the non-bodily 'pulse in the eternal mind' which 'Gives somewhere back the thoughts by England given'.[19] Similarly, in Kyle's *Soldier Poets*, E. F. Wilkinson,

---

[16] David Cox McEwen Osborne, 'Private Claye' in Kyle, *More Songs*, 123.
[17] Georges Bannerot, 'As Ye Have Sown' in Bertram Lloyd (ed.), *The Paths of Glory: A Collection of Poems Written during the War 1914–1919* (London: Allen & Unwin, 1919), 31. This poem is translated from the French by Stella Browne, but its appearance in a British anthology contributes to poetic possibilities in English-language war poetry.
[18] Kendall, *Modern English War Poetry*, 167.
[19] Rupert Brooke, 'If I should die' in Osborn, *Muse in Arms*, 3.

anticipating his own death, consoles his family with Shelleyan ideas in 'To "My People," before the "Great Offensive"'. His body will return to an original state – 'the clay that once was I / Has ta'en its ancient earthy form anew' – while his spirit will be everywhere in nature:

> For in the voice of birds, the scent of flowers,
> The evening silence and the falling dew,
> Through every throbbing pulse of nature's powers
>   I'll speak to you.[20]

While Wilkinson refers to the degradation of his corpse, the process is made metaphorical through the biblical 'clay' by which the soldier becomes (as in David Osborne's 'Private Claye' above) a new Adam – a purifying gesture in Kristeva's terms. In Max Plowman's poem 'When It's Over', a common soldier expresses the Shelleyan notion as he imagines himself after death:

> 'A cold body in foreign soil;
> But a happy spirit fate can't spoil,
> And an extra note in the blackbird's mirth
>   From a khaki ghost.'[21]

The speaker's dead self comprises a body and a spirit. The 'extra note' is, most obviously, a manifestation of the spirit, but might also suggest that the body has nourished the tree which nourishes the blackbird. The poem fails to make a clear distinction, and in this lack of clarity an allusion to the corpse is made safe – or safer, anyway. In the wartime anthologies, the constitutive power of elegiac conventions almost entirely precludes direct attention to the rotting corpse even for political purposes, as in the poems by Graves and Sassoon above. One very rare example is E. J. L. Garstin's 'Lines written between 1 and 2.30 a.m. in a German dug-out', which appeared in Kyle's *Soldier Poets* and contains these lines:

> And scattered over all the stricken field,
> See lie the shattered bodies of the slain
> In all the ghastly posturings of death,
> Their attitudes suggesting all their pain[22]

In fact, 'shattered' is euphemistic and 'slain' romanticises. True, 'ghastly posturings' attempts to impress an abject image on the reader's imagination,

---

[20] E. F. Wilkinson, 'To "My People," before the "Great Offensive"' in Kyle, *Soldier Poets*, 106.
[21] Max Plowman, 'When It's Over' in Osborn, *Muse in Arms*, 155.
[22] E. J. L. Garstin, 'Lines written between 1 and 2.30 a.m. in a German dug-out' in Kyle, *Soldier Poets*, 25.

but Garstin, like Graves and Sassoon, does so to support an argument against the 'frightful ingenuity' of war, and gets no closer to the horror.[23]

This exception aside, the wartime anthologies show poets drawing on the elegiac tradition to screen themselves, and their families, from the abject – while still remembering and commemorating the dead. It is certainly the case that anthologies published during or shortly after the war were likely to enforce prevailing discourses but the image of the soldier's corpse is almost equally absent from the poetry being written beyond their editors' ken. Even Owen, aiming to disabuse readers of romantic notions in 'Anthem for Doomed Youth', keeps the eye of the poem away from the bodies of 'these who die as cattle'. He does not describe or consider them when it would have been powerfully effective to do so. Tellingly, though, he focuses instead on the fact that conditions on the Western Front preclude the possibility of burial rituals: in this abattoir, there are 'no prayers nor bells; / Nor any voice of mourning'.[24] For Kristeva, it is precisely the corpse denied such rituals which presents the greatest horror: 'The purification rite appears then as that essential ridge, which, prohibiting the filthy object, extracts it from the secular order and lines it at once with a sacred facet... The human corpse is a fount of impurity and must not be touched (Numbers 19:13ft). Burial is a means of purification.'[25] Without purifying rites, the unburied corpse remains 'disquieting matter', forcing us to confront that which we 'permanently thrust aside in order to live'.[26] For Owen and others, it is as if the unburied corpse presents too great an ontological horror to be the object of sustained attention in poems which, in part, were written to process, manage and express war trauma. It threatens to destroy, with its extreme abjection, the careful containment provided by the carefully crafted elegy.

If, in 'Anthem for Doomed Youth', Owen excluded the disquieting matter of the unburied corpse, he soon began to question the over-reliance on the conventions of Romantic elegy. In 'Insensibility', he insists that 'they are troops who fade, not flowers, / For poets' tearful fooling'.[27] Then,

---

[23] Ibid., 26.
[24] 'Anthem for Doomed Youth' in Owen, *Complete Poems and Fragments*, 96.
[25] Julia Kristeva, *Powers of Horror: An Essay on Abjection*, trans. Leon S. Roudiez (New York: Columbia University Press, 1982), 65, 109. Thus, the unburied corpse is, in anthropological terms, *defilement* rather than *filth*. Kristeva clarifies the distinction: 'secular "filth," which has become sacred "defilement," is the *excluded* on the basis of which religious prohibition is made up' (ibid., 65). The biblical verses to which she refers in the quotation above are Numbers 19:16–22, which describe in detail the purifying rituals surrounding those who have touched a corpse.
[26] Ibid., 109, 3.
[27] Owen, *Complete Poems and Fragments*, 145.

in 'A Terre', as we have noted above (Chapter 1), his philosophising soldier comments ironically on Shelleyan notions.[28] The satire grows from the way the soldier shifts Shelley's pantheistic belief (' "I shall be one with nature, herb, and stone," ') towards the corporeal image of ' "Pushing up daisies" ' in the mind of even the 'dullest Tommy'. The verb 'pushing' comically draws attention to the corpse's lack of agency – it has no will or power to push. Owen upends the elegiac tradition, then, but the soldier's humour leads him to a far more disturbing thought as he imagines what will become of his own remains:

> To grain, then, go my fat, to buds my sap,
> For all the usefulness there is in soap.
> D'you think the Boche will ever stew man-soup?
> Some day, no doubt, if ...[29]

The fat on his body will become grain – this might be a literal description of chemical processes – but the sap is metaphorical, as if his mind pulls him away from contemplation of the abject. That mind then pulls him back, beyond the still-consoling idea of the corpse entering a regenerative cycle, to the gruesome rumours that the Germans were boiling corpses to make both soap and soup. The triple para-rhyme *sap/soap/soup* shows his line of thought from the consolingly metaphorical to the gruesome and the grotesque. Fearful of where his thoughts are leading, he interrupts himself ('Some day, no doubt, if ...'), returning in the following lines to a more Romantic contemplation of an afterlife in which the body enjoys itself in nature. These lines together, then, represent the soldier's stream of consciousness, wherein the abject horror of the corpse leads to self-censorship and self-protection. The conflict in his thoughts is captured in his comment about the sound of the guns: 'I'll not hear; / Or, if I wince, I shall not know I wince.' The corpse is both sentient and insentient. The soldier moves further from the abject and into a safer realm when he avers: 'Soldiers may grow a soul when turned to fronds'. Here the chemical processes of degeneration *generate* a conscious soul – although it remains a tentative notion qualified by the modal verb 'may'. Edmund Blunden also comments ironically on the evasions of the elegiac tradition in 'Vlamertinghe: Passing the Chateau, July 1917'. Here, the poet describes an abundance of flowers around 'the proud mansion' of the title but he

---

[28] Precise dates of composition cannot be recovered, but Stallworthy discovers enough to indicate that these three poems were written in this order between September 1917 and July 1918. See notes in ibid., 12, 33, 67.
[29] Ibid., 179.

rejects the idea that soldiers' blood may have contributed to this profusion. This is effected by a dramatic shift from a Romantic register to that of the dull Tommy:

> Such a gay carpet! poppies by the million;
> Such damask! such vermilion!
> But if you ask me, mate, the choice of colour
> Is scarcely right; this red should have been much duller.[30]

Blunden alludes to the consoling notion that the redness of the poppies derives from the blood of the dead only in the act of ridiculing it. Like Owen, he ventriloquises the voice of the common soldier to do so, as if the poet must reach outside of the elegiac tradition to find a jarring voice capable of undoing it.[31]

The kind of awareness shown by Owen in 'A Terre' and Blunden in 'Vlamertinghe: Passing the Chateau, July 1917' may lead to a politically motivated gruesome description of battlefield corpses as in Graves's 'A Dead Boche', but attention to the individual's trauma in this extreme experience of abjection is far more difficult to find. There are brief moments in Owen's work: in 'Asleep', the dead man's 'thin and sodden head / Confuses more and more with the low mould', and the lines we quote from 'Mental Cases' at the start of Chapter 1 indicate the damage done to men exposed to extreme abjection – in their ravished minds, they wade 'sloughs of flesh … / Treading blood from lungs', and see 'shatter of flying muscles'.[32] Richard Aldington, in 'Apathy', places the traumatic memory of a corpse at the root of his post-war inability to engage with the world around him: 'there's always something else – / The way one corpse held its stiff yellow fingers / And pointed, pointed to the huge dark hole / Gouged between ear and jaw right to the skull …'.[33] It is horror of the 'disquieting matter', which leads Ivor Gurney to remember 'that red wet / Thing' which he 'must somehow forget' in 'To His Love', but as we have noted above (Chapter 1) this oblique reference is self-erasing: he remembers that he must forget. The traumatic remembrance is limited to three monosyllables, the first two recalling the visual and tactile horror before the third reasserts the intense need to disassociate the corpse from the man it once was. Gurney, then,

---

[30] 'Vlamertinghe: Passing the Chateau, July 1917' in Blunden, *Poems*, 152.
[31] See Nils Clausson, ' "Perpetuating the Language": Romantic Tradition, the Genre Function, and the Origins of the Trench Lyric', *Journal of Modern Literature*, 30.1 (2006), for a discussion of the ways soldier-poets transformed Romantic models. On these lines, he comments: 'Blunden finds he can express new content only by transforming an antecedent genre' (ibid., 118).
[32] Owen, *Complete Poems and Fragments*, 152, 169.
[33] Aldington, *Images of War*, 46.

confronts the abject momentarily but in a way which turns immediately away: 'cover him over / ... Cover him, cover him soon!' he begs and this is, in effect, what every one of the poets so far discussed seeks to do, albeit with less self-awareness of the urgent need than Gurney shows here.[34] Their elegiac covering-over arises from a shared experience of the battlefield corpse as 'the utmost of abjection'.[35] In this they concur with Kristeva – and such poems, of course, helped to *construct* her understanding.

However, as Santanu Das points out, Kristeva's notion of the abject is rooted in psychology rather than the specific conditions of the Western Front:

> To Kristeva ... the threat to autonomy goes back to the primordial maternal lining, the suffocating presence of the mother. Bodily fluids [like the decaying corpse] are examples of what she calls the 'abject': it is that which is excluded in the process of constituting the subject and yet can never be got rid of, hovering 'at the border of my condition as a living being'.[36]

Das, focusing on 'slimescapes', emphasises that, on the Western Front, 'mud was an actual physical threat [... in which] men floundered and drowned'.[37] The same point can be made in relation to the 'corpsescapes' of the Western Front: for Kristeva, a single corpse may trigger a revulsion connected to that which we have subconsciously excluded from our subjectivity, but the soldier encounters a multitude of decaying, eviscerated and shattered corpses in an environment where he has a high chance of suddenly becoming one such corpse himself. This has its own horror beyond the psychological framework of Kristevan abjection and rooted in 'actual physical threat'.

Isaac Rosenberg's approach to this problem of representation is unique, and his poetic responses to the corpsescape offer a corrective to Kristeva. He is concerned not so much with the abject as the object: the dead body closely observed. He is, perhaps, the only writer of the First World War able to include in poetry a contemplative consideration of the unburied corpse. The 'sprawled dead' in 'Dead Man's Dump' do not re-enter nature in a regenerative cycle, but are simply destroyed by external material forces: their bones crunch under the wheels of a limber cart, their brains are 'splattered', they are piled up to turn 'black by strange decay'.[38] The consoling idea of a spirit distinct and separable from the body is negated

---

[34] 'To His Love' in Gurney, *Collected Poems*, 21.
[35] Kristeva, *Powers of Horror*, 3.
[36] Das, *Touch and Intimacy*, 37–8. Das takes the quotation from Kristeva, *Powers of Horror*, 3.
[37] Ibid., 38.
[38] 'Dead Man's Dump' in Rosenberg, *Isaac Rosenberg*, 115.

('*None saw* their spirits' shadow shake the grass') and Rosenberg replaces the tropes of elegy with philosophical questioning about the whereabouts of the 'God-ancestralled essences' of the men who have been killed. Tellingly, these questions are rhetorical and must go unanswered (they are asked of 'Earth', who cannot reply); the poem's final image of the limber wheels grazing the 'dead face' imparts not the faintest suggestion of agency, sentience or afterlife in the just-dead soldier.[39] Rosenberg creates a tone that is curious and enquiring, but no less engaged with the horror. He achieves this, in part, by close attention to his own sensory and emotional experience – he told Edward Marsh that the poem was suggested by 'carrying wire up the line on limbers and running over dead bodies lying about' – but also by placing that experience in a web of literary allusion.[40] His sources include poems by Wilfrid Gibson and Francis Thompson, Wordsworth's 'A slumber did my spirit seal', Blake's 'The Marriage of Heaven and Hell', Donne's 'Elegy IX: The Autumnal', the medieval legend of King Canute, the gospel of Matthew, Psalm 103 and the Book of Job. With these fragments and echoes he pieces together a voice that is awkward and discordant, and in so doing he slips away from the poetic conventions and public discourses in which other poets were entrapped.

Particularly interesting here is the use he makes of his earliest source, Homer's *Iliad*. We have noted, in Chapter 1, how Rosenberg evokes the Homeric idea of the spirit being exhaled in the moment of death only to remove it, and how he echoes the Homeric diction of apotheosis only to reject the idea. But Homer enters the poem earlier on, in the second stanza: 'The wheels lurched over the sprawled dead / But pained them not, though their bones crunched'.[41] This image recalls Achilles's chariot passing over the bodies of the dead at the end of book 20 of the *Iliad*.[42] Achilles, having learned of Patroclus's death, is on a grief-stricken rampage among the Trojans:

> as one who yokes broad-browed oxen that they may tread barley in a threshing-floor – and it is soon bruised small under the feet of the lowing cattle – even so did the horses of Achilles trample on the shields and bodies of the slain. The axle underneath and the railing that ran round the car were

---

[39] Ibid., 116.
[40] Letter to Edward Marsh, 8 May 1917; Rosenberg, *Isaac Rosenberg*, 331.
[41] 'Dead Man's Dump' in ibid., 113.
[42] There is also an echo here of William Blake's line in *The Marriage of Heaven and Hell*, 'Drive your cart and your plough over the bones of the dead' (Blake, *Selected Poetry*, ed. Michael Mason (Oxford: Oxford University Press, 1996), 76).

bespattered with clots of blood thrown up by the horses' hooves and from the tyres of the wheels.[43]

This is not one of those allusions to a literary past which comments ironically on a tragic present nor does it invite a straight comparison. The crushing of corpses by the limber wheels in Rosenberg's poem might seem even more egregious than the same act by Achilles's chariot wheels because it is without motive but, equally, the lack of any sense of vengeance makes the act simply unpleasant for the 'charioteer' and, fundamentally, without meaning. The corpses are not crushed by a warrior's chariot but by a cart pulled by surviving soldiers going about mundane duties. It is not even clear to which army the dead men belong. In modern warfare, the corpse can be mangled or destroyed, and it makes no difference. This allusion to Achilles's chariot in the second stanza conditions our response to the lines about the limber cart's wheels at the poem's end:

> Even as the mixed hoofs of the mules,
> The quivering-bellied mules,
> And the rushing wheels all mixed
> With his tortured upturned sight,
> So we crashed round the bend,
> We heard his weak scream,
> We heard his very last sound,
> And our wheels grazed his dead face.[44]

Vandiver, overlooking the earlier allusion, sees chiefly irony here: the mule-drawn limber loaded with barbed wire is a sorry substitute for 'the much swifter chariots of epic': its progress 'was more likely to be terrifyingly slow than to move at the speed Rosenberg describes, a speed that is more fitting for a chariot driven by a warrior', the mules 'are not war-horses but transport animals, "quivering" from fear, exhaustion, or both' and the soldiers 'are not warriors coming to save or avenge their dead comrade … but are exhausted purveyors of barbed wire'.[45] But, if we have Homer's account of Achilles's rampage in mind, we are taken beyond the familiar ironic mode: where Homer focuses on the grief and anger of the charioteer, Rosenberg shifts us into the dying consciousness of the fatally wounded soldier whose dead face will be grazed by the wheels of

---

[43] Samuel Butler, *The Iliad of Homer* (Longmans: New York, 1898), 343. We choose Butler's translation of 1898 as one which could have been read by Rosenberg but, as Elizabeth Vandiver notes, it is impossible to know how much classical literature he had read and, however much, which translations he used (Vandiver, *Stand in the Trench, Achilles*, 139–40).
[44] 'Dead Man's Dump' in Rosenberg, *Isaac Rosenberg*, 116.
[45] Vandiver, *Stand in the Trench, Achilles*, 300, 301, 302.

the approaching cart. This dead face is 'grazed' rather than 'crunched' – the light touch of the wheels leave the head intact but, if a small part of us feels grateful that the corpse is spared, we recall that in an earlier stanza, another dying soldier whose brains were 'splattered' was 'sunk too deep / For human tenderness'. Crunched, splattered or merely grazed; it makes no difference. In alluding to the *Iliad*, Rosenberg thus transforms its tropes to forge what seems (retrospectively) a modernist voice. He rejects both elegy and polemic, and combines the experiential with the literary to express an Imagist sensibility: dispassionate, precise, curious and unblinking. In doing so, he challenges the power of abjection and its hold on our imaginations.

Similarly, when Rosenberg engages with the Shelleyan elegiac trope in 'Break of Day in the Trenches' he moves beyond satire into something new. He alludes to the idea of the poppy as a manifestation of the dead but transforms it by setting it alongside the corpse-nourished rat. Poppy and rat are common images in the poetry of the war, of course, but this may be the only poem in which they appear together. They vie with each other to be the poem's central image and the familiar meanings attached to each are thus destabilised. The presence of the rat makes it impossible for the poppies to carry the traditional note of consolation. Alongside the rat, the 'Poppies whose roots are in man's veins' become unsettling, even malign.[46] They seem to adopt some of the rat's busy agency, feeling their way into the veins of the dead. As well as transforming the Shelleyan idea, Rosenberg's poppies are also a further transformation of a Homeric trope. Vandiver points out that 'this poppy's ultimate origins are in the simile of *Iliad* 8.306–8 where a dying man's head is compared to a drooping poppy'.[47] Homer's poppy droops under the weight of raindrops, but Rosenberg combines the image with the First World War's elegiac poppy trope to destabilising effect: 'his poppies drop because of the human blood at their roots' whereas the flower he has plucked is 'safe'. 'A plucked flower is in effect already dead and withers quickly, while rooted flowers normally continue to grow. But Rosenberg's poppies drop precisely because they are still rooted, in the bloodshed of the Western Front, in "man's veins".'[48] Thus, Vandiver concludes, Rosenberg's poppy 'looks back, through the re-figurings of earlier literature, to the Homeric scene where it first appears,

---

[46] 'Break of Day in the Trenches' in Rosenberg, *Isaac Rosenberg*, 106.
[47] Vandiver, *Stand in the Trench, Achilles*, 142–3.
[48] Ibid., 143.

and as it does so reverses the reader's expectations so that living and plucked flowers alike are emblems of inevitable death'.[49]

Vandiver, generally, challenges the orthodoxy that literary allusion in First World War poetry is chiefly ironic, giving many examples of Homeric allusions which are meant to be taken straight.[50] 'Sometimes heroic poetry is just heroic poetry', she says.[51] But Rosenberg's transformative allusions to Homer and to Shelley are neither ironic nor 'straight'. They are so distinctive partly because, with no public school education, he went to war, as Jon Stallworthy suggests, 'with no Homeric expectations' while the haphazard and piecemeal nature of his self-education in poetic traditions enabled a magpie approach unhampered by deference to received opinion.[52] The foregoing account of poems published in the wartime anthologies gives a sense of just how radical his achievement is in the context of prevailing literary and political discourses. Where Owen and Blunden recognise and satirise the evasions of Romantic elegy, and Gurney glances in horror at the abject, Rosenberg transforms poetic traditions to address the corpsescape of the Western Front in a way that seems to sidestep the literary and political pressures of the period and returns the abject to something we can humanly contemplate. This, in turn, makes possible a new kind of remembrance.

Rosenberg's approach to the corpse was to become a powerful example for a poet writing in the next war. At the age of sixteen, Keith Douglas chose as one of his school prizes the newly published anthology *The Progress of Poetry*, edited by I. M. Parsons, which included six of Rosenberg's poems.[53] This is almost certainly where Douglas first encountered Rosenberg's work. Indeed, these six Rosenberg poems may be the only ones Douglas ever read.[54] As Kendall notes, 'The dead body is overwhelmingly the central image in Douglas's work': Douglas is drawn repeatedly to consider the remains of the recently killed soldier, focusing disturbingly on the

---

[49] Ibid., 144.
[50] As in Patrick Shaw Stewart's plea: 'Stand in the trench, Achilles, / Flame-capped, and shout for me' ('[I saw a man this morning]' in Kendall, *Poetry of the First World War*, 117).
[51] Vandiver, *Stand in the Trench, Achilles*, 9.
[52] Jon Stallworthy, (ed.), *The New Oxford Book of War Poetry* (Oxford: Oxford University Press, 2014), xxx.
[53] Desmond Graham, *Keith Douglas 1920–1944: A Biography* (London: Oxford University Press, 1974), 41.
[54] His biographer tells us there was 'no copy of Rosenberg among KD's books, but his school prize, I. Parsons's *The Progress of Poetry* (1936), contains a good selection of the earlier poet's work' (ibid., 277). The six poems are: 'Returning, we hear the larks', 'Break of Day in the Trenches', 'Girl to Soldier on Leave', 'Daughters of War', 'Dead Man's Dump' and 'Wedded'.

sight of the unburied corpse, and on the problem of its representation.[55] In this, Rosenberg's unique voice provides him with a precedent, a fact he explicitly acknowledges in his 1943 poem 'Desert Flowers' when he writes: 'Rosenberg I only repeat what you were saying'.[56] However, in tracing the line of influence in Douglas's work we will argue that he does far more than simply repeat.[57] That self-doubting, self-deprecating judgement appears, in fact, in the midst of the period in which Douglas achieved a mature poetic voice and produced some of the century's most powerful poems about those killed in war. That period was all too brief – a matter of months before Douglas's own death in action – but it is an exhilarating example of a poet working in a tradition to produce poetry that is both part of that tradition and radically new. Here, we trace the creative journey Douglas made under the influence of Rosenberg and others, exploring how he adopted, reshaped and modified their ways of writing, specifically about soldiers killed in battle, to develop his own unique voice and vision.

It seems likely that *The Progress of Poetry* played an important part in Douglas's poetic development not just through the inclusion of Rosenberg but also through Parsons's insightful Introduction, as well as some of his other editorial choices. Parsons's Introduction makes this statement of intent:

> the history of poetry, as of any art, is of a tradition that is continually being modified even while it grows ... So that though it is true that the best poets in any age are those who are most successful in finding an idiom close enough to the world in which they live, it is also true that the poetical progress of an age can only be represented by those poets whose work is a genuine development of what has gone before. It is this development, this progression, which ... this anthology attempts to illustrate.[58]

Parsons adds that, in an age of 'radical changes', poetry will be 'affected drastically'.[59] The radical change on which he focuses is the diminishment of religious faith, and he considers the ways recent poetry has responded to this, particularly in its representations of the dead. Parsons argues that, if the waning of belief in an afterlife was a key provocation for poetic

---

[55] Kendall, *Modern English War Poetry*, 151.
[56] 'Desert Flowers' in Keith Douglas, *Collected Poems*, ed. John Waller, G. S. Fraser and J. C. Hall (London: Faber & Faber, 1966), 129.
[57] See also Kendall, *Modern English War Poetry*, 165–6.
[58] I. M. Parsons, 'Introduction', *The Progress of Poetry*, ed. I. M. Parsons (London: Chatto & Windus, 1936), xii.
[59] Ibid., xiii.

development in the years preceding 1914, the war 'gave a ghastly immediacy' to the problem of how to write about death.[60] For this reason, the work of soldier-poets lies at the heart of *The Progress of Poetry*.

In particular, Parsons praises Owen and Rosenberg. He says that Owen 'saw, as few saw clearly while the War was actually in progress, the forces really at work behind the multitude of conflicting noises – the prayers and exhortations, religious and patriotic, the explanations and justifications – indeed, the whole gamut of self-deception which inevitably accompanies war on a large scale'.[61] But his highest praise is reserved for Rosenberg. He acknowledges 'the difficulties which some readers have found' in Rosenberg's work but responds by quoting the poet's own defence:

> 'Simple *poetry* – that is when an interesting complexity of thought is kept in tone and right value to the dominating idea so that it is understandable and still ungraspable. I know it is beyond my reach just now, except, perhaps, in bits.'[62]

Parsons argues that the poems succeed as they stand: 'Difficulties and complexities there are, but they spring neither from turgidity of thought nor inadequacy of expression; they are the result of an extraordinary compression of language ... and of his own particular and highly individual vision'.[63] Finally, he avers that 'what made his poems appear difficult was neither blindness nor carelessness, but "the brain succumbing to the Herculean effort to enrich the world of ideas" '.[64]

Parsons concludes with a manifesto for what constitutes good poetry in times of radical change:

> New ways of feeling call for new modes of expression, and in every age the artists who create them are condemned by those who are unwilling to make the effort to appreciate anything to which they are unaccustomed. Yet it is these artists who are responsible not only for the developments but for the continuity in the poetry of a language.[65]

---

[60] Ibid., xxii.
[61] Ibid., xxiv.
[62] Ibid., xxvi. Parsons gives no references, but this statement appears in a letter sent by Rosenberg to Gordon Bottomley in July 1916. See Rosenberg, *Isaac Rosenberg*, 305 (where the sentence that Parsons quotes here is transcribed thus: 'Simple *Poetry* that is where ...').
[63] Parsons, 'Introduction', xxvi–xxvii.
[64] Ibid., xxvii. Here Parsons quotes a letter sent by Rosenberg to Winifreda Seaton. This letter is omitted in *Isaac Rosenberg*, but a fragment of it appears in Parsons's own *Collected Works of Isaac Rosenberg*. In that volume, Parsons dates the letter '*November–December 1917*' and transcribes it thus: 'I absolutely disagree that it [the obscurity of Rosenberg's poems] is blindness or carelessness; it is the brain succumbing to the herculean attempt to enrich the world of ideas' (Rosenberg, *Collected Works*, 266).
[65] Parsons, 'Introduction', xl.

We summarise these points from Parsons's Introduction because it seems to us that they had a profound effect on Douglas. His development shows a sharp awareness of the idea that to work in a tradition is to modify it, that drastic changes in experience necessitate drastic shifts in poetic practice, that poetry can respond to the 'gamut of self-deception' in the discourses of war with a complexity of thought which is ' "understandable and still ungraspable" ', and that 'difficulty' in poetry arises necessarily from these efforts. In what follows, we show how Douglas works with these ideas and how he responds to the various attempts collected in *The Progress of Poetry* to write about dead soldiers in a modern world traumatised by the combined effects of a loss of faith and a glut of corpses.

In his short essay of 1943, 'Poets in this War', Douglas argues that there is no significant war poetry being written because 'there is nothing new, from a soldier's point of view, about this war'. He goes on:

> hell cannot be let loose twice: it was let loose in the Great War and it is the same old hell now. The hardships, pain and boredom; the behaviour of the living and the appearance of the dead, were so accurately described by the poets of the Great War that everyday on the battlefields of the western desert … their poems are illustrated. Almost all that a modern poet on active service is inspired to write, would be tautological.[66]

In this statement, Douglas overlooks what becomes evident in his poetry: that the foreknowledge provided by the First World War *is* the drastic change which differentiates his own experience from that of Owen, Rosenberg and Sassoon. As Vernon Scannell writes: 'There were no initial fervour and excitement [in 1939] to be replaced by sick disillusionment as the appalling realities of modern warfare were experienced. The serviceman of 1939–45 could not be disillusioned because he held no illusions to start with'.[67] Much of the poetry we now see as characteristic of the First World War seeks a way of responding to the naivety of 1914. The absence of such naivety in 1939, the clear sense that war was no more than a tragic necessity, called for a new kind of poetic response.[68] In the months following the writing of 'Poets in this War', while his regiment rested in Tunisia, Douglas wrote a group of war poems, including '*Vergissmeinnicht*' and 'How to

---

[66] Keith Douglas, *The Letters*, ed. Desmond Graham (Manchester: Carcanet, 2000), 352.
[67] Vernon Scannell, *Not Without Glory: Poets of the Second World War* (London: Woburn Press, 1976), 17.
[68] As Lorrie Goldensohn says: 'in this second of the twentieth-century world wars, death in general is not less painful but at least less surprising' (Goldensohn, *Dismantling Glory*, 131).

Kill', which show him striving to achieve this response.[69] In August 1943, he was able to write, in a letter to his Oxford friend John [J. C.] Hall, with clarity about his creative processes and decisions. Responding to Hall's criticism of his recent work, he rejects both 'musical verse' and the 'lyric form' as being entirely inappropriate to his war experience.

> In my early poems I wrote lyrically, as an innocent, because I was an innocent: I have (not surprisingly) fallen from that particular grace since then. I had begun to change during my second year at Oxford ... Well, I am still changing: I don't disagree with you if you say I am awkward and not used to the new paces yet. But my object (and I don't give a damn about my duty as a poet) is to write true things, significant things in words each of which works for its place in a line. My rhythms, which you find enervated, are carefully chosen to enable the poems to be *read* as significant speech: I see no reason to be either musical or sonorous about things at present.[70]

It is possible to follow a clear line of development in Douglas's wartime poetry illustrating this assessment of his development from the spring of 1940 onward.[71] In a series of poems, Douglas adopts familiar tropes and then transforms them. This starts with the self-elegy 'Canoe', written at Oxford after he had enlisted, but some months before he took up uniform.[72] Here, Douglas anticipates his own death in action, and imagines his spirit re-entering nature. In this, he follows the self-elegies of Rupert Brooke, and closely recalls the specific elegiac gestures of E. F. Wilkinson noted above. He imagines his dead self re-entering nature as a breeze, telling his lover:

> as you lie looking up for thunder again,
> this cool touch does not betoken rain;
> it is my spirit that kisses your mouth lightly.[73]

Douglas is more romantic than Wilkinson in that this breeze is capable of thought and agency: 'Whistle and I will hear'. It has no connection with the poet's corpse; at this early stage, Douglas rejects even the tentative conflation of spirit and corpse evident in Shelley. This is a very moving poem, but it is one of anticipation rather than

---

[69] The precise date of composition for 'Poets in this War' is uncertain. Desmond Graham dates it thus: '?May 1943' (Douglas, *The Letters*, 350).
[70] Letter to J. C. Hall, 10 August 1943; Douglas, *The Letters*, 294–5.
[71] We trace Douglas's development through the poems in the order they appear in Keith Douglas, *Complete Poems*, ed. Desmond Graham, 3rd edition (London: Faber & Faber, 2000). That ordering is necessarily a little speculative, but the general direction of travel is clear.
[72] The poem was printed in the weekly student paper *The Cherwell*, of which Douglas was the new editor, on 18 May 1940 (Graham, *Keith Douglas*, 98).
[73] 'Canoe' in Douglas, *Collected Poems*, 73.

experience, written by a twenty-year-old undergraduate. Nevertheless, even here, there are signs that Douglas works uneasily in the tradition and pushes at its boundaries under the influence of both Owen and Rosenberg. Where Brooke and Wilkinson handle poetic form in ways that are conventional and conservative, Douglas introduces Owenesque techniques which counter the musicality of the lyric form and wrong-foot the reader. Envelope rhyme creates distance between rhymes in the first two stanzas, and the aural connections become fainter still in the final two stanzas where full rhyme gives way to half-rhyme. The metre alludes loosely and intermittently to iambic pentameter in a way that never settles. Strong enjambments and mid-line full stops create a jarring mismatch between grammatical units and poetic lines. These features all appear in Owen's 'Exposure' and 'Spring Offensive' (both of which are included by Parsons in *The Progress of Poetry*) and speak to a sensibility that already finds, at this early stage, the musicality and strong closure traditional to the lyric form inappropriate to the age. Indeed, Douglas goes beyond Owen by eschewing capital letters at the start of each line, taking the poem further from lyric form and closer to prose (each of the poem's four sentences starts with a capital letter, but three of these are mid-line).

The faint influence of Rosenberg is evident in the prominent use of two of his most resonant words: *aghast* and *doom*; Douglas writes: 'I cannot stand aghast // at whatever doom hovers in the background'. In 'Break of Day in the Trenches', Rosenberg asks the rat what it sees in the soldiers' eyes: 'What quaver – what heart *aghast*?' and in 'Daughters of War' the mythic daughters 'Beckon each soul *aghast* from its crimson corpse'. In 'Dead Man's Dump', at the moment of death, no one 'stood aside for the half used life to pass / Out of those *doomed* nostrils and the *doomed* mouth'; the soliloquising Daughter of War tells us that her sisters ' "force their males / From the *doomed* earth, from the *doomed* glee / And hankering of hearts" '.[74] Douglas has absorbed the power of these repeated words but here, in his inexperience, he light-heartedly rejects their tone and import: he tells his lover that, even if this summer is to be his last, he 'cannot stand aghast // at whatever doom hovers in the background'. And yet, this love-fuelled dismissal of Rosenberg's lexicon is undercut by the discordant influence of Owen, hinting at the poetic forces at work in Douglas in the first year of the war.

---

[74] 'Break of Day in the Trenches' in Rosenberg, *Isaac Rosenberg*, 106; 'Daughters of War' in ibid., 116; 'Dead Man's Dump' in ibid., 115; 'Daughters of War' in ibid., 118–19.

The same sense of internal conflict is evident in 'John Anderson', written in the same year. The form is terza rima but, again, full rhyme gives way to half-rhyme and the metre passes through various shifts and changes. These formal features suit the poem's doubleness. In the first four stanzas, Douglas emphasises the futility of the high rhetoric with which we traditionally honour the dead: the scholarly Anderson fails to conjure, in his last moments alive, an 'Apt epitaph' for himself that might counter the brutal facts of his death: 'Blood turned his tunic black // … he only eyed the sun'.[75] But then the poem turns: the poet imagines that Anderson, in his last moments, beheld the god Zeus giving orders to honour his corpse. At first, this is merely an affectionate imagining of Anderson's last thoughts: Anderson hears 'in his swoon' Zeus instructing Apollo to cleanse the corpse and pass it to Death and Sleep who will bear it to Lycia.[76] But, in a further turn which completes the poem's volte-face, the fantasy of the dying man becomes the poem's reality: 'the brothers, Sleep and Death / lift up John Anderson at his last breath'. The move here is from satire to elegy. The final couplet reasserts full rhyme and revives the strong sense of closure of the lyric form. The corpse is accorded its purifying rituals, erasing that glimpse of the abject in the black blood and the 'desperate final stare'.

Douglas may have had these poems in mind when confessing to Hall that, in his earlier work, he 'wrote lyrically, as an innocent', but the process of change is strongly evident in 'Simplify me when I'm dead', a self-elegy drastically different to 'Canoe', written after a year of army training though still in England. The iambic tetrameters of the opening couplet, which refer ironically to the patriotic rhythms of Henry Newbolt and his imitators, are immediately undercut as Douglas shifts into rhythms 'carefully chosen to enable the poems to be *read* as significant speech':

> As the processes of earth
> strip off the colour and the skin:
> take the brown hair and blue eye
>
> and leave me simpler than at birth[77]

Douglas again anticipates his own death but, here, in place of the ethereal transformation of 'Canoe', there are the 'processes of earth', breaking down

---

[75] 'John Anderson' in Douglas, *Collected Poems*, 70.
[76] Peter Lowe's interesting reading of the poem expands and emphasises the Homeric origin of these allusions (Lowe, 'Stripped Bodies and Looted Goods: Keith Douglas's *Iliad*', *The Cambridge Quarterly*, 43.4 (2014), 304–8).
[77] 'Simplify me when I'm dead' in Douglas, *Collected Poems*, 89.

the corpse and leaving remains that will become an object of academic curiosity:

> Of my skeleton perhaps,
> so stripped, a learned man will say
> 'He was of such a type and intelligence,' no more.

The poem is informed by Thomas Hardy's 'His Immortality', which is collected by Parsons in *The Progress of Poetry*. Hardy's speaker imagines that a dead friend lives on in the hearts of his peers, but as the years pass, their memories fade, then they die in their turn leaving only the speaker who faces his own oblivion.[78] But, in place of Hardy's lament, Douglas creates the matter-of-fact tone, one which he develops in his later poems. The title, repeated twice in the poem, is finely balanced: it is both an ironic statement about the inevitable simplifications of fading memory, and a piece of advice intended to lessen his lover's grief.

> Remember me when I am dead
> and simplify me when I'm dead.

These two linked injunctions contradict each other: to simplify is not meaningfully to remember. There is a recognition here of the separateness of the processes of memory and the fact of the corpse.

By the time of the Battle of El Alamein in October 1942, Douglas is alluding to the Romantic tradition with deep irony in 'The Offensive II'.[79] He begins 'The stars dead heroes in the sky', and we may anticipate a eulogy for those killed which imagines their spirits transmogrified into heavenly bodies.[80] We are thrown by the tone of the second line – the stars 'may well approve the way you die' – but may still hold on to the idea of stellar spirits welcoming just-killed soldiers into their panoply. However, the second stanza upends this idea with brutal comedy. Douglas addresses his fellow soldiers:

> when you are dead and the harm done
> the orators and clerks go on
> the rulers of interims and wars
> as effete and stable as stars.

The 'dead heroes' of the first line are not, it transpires, the dead soldiers but the politicians and bureaucrats who sent them to their deaths. The

---

[78] Thomas Hardy, 'His Immortality' in Parsons, *Progress of Poetry*, 9.
[79] Desmond Graham dates the poem thus: '*Wadi Natrun, October 1942 – Tripolitania, January 1943*' (Douglas, *Complete Poems*, 98). It may have been begun just before Douglas's direct involvement in the Battle of El Alamein on 28 October 1942.
[80] 'The Offensive II' in Douglas, *Collected Poems*, 103. (See the version in *Complete Poems*, ed. Graham, for significant variants.)

connotations of the metaphor are quite different to what we supposed: the stars are 'the heavenly symbols of a class / dead in their seats'. The poem's title, now, might be an adjectival epithet for the 'orators and clerks' as much as a noun describing military action. The dramatic rejection of Romantic elegy is assisted by Douglas's play with poetic form: as in 'Simplify me when I'm dead', the poem begins with ironic use of thumping Newboltian metre which then gives way to a formal looseness and unpredictability which recall both Owen's experiments with rhyme and metre and Rosenberg's cadences. All that said, the trick by which the reader is led from a misreading of the phrase 'dead heroes' to an understanding of its ironic usage necessarily elides the soldiers' corpses. In 'Mersa', however, Douglas seems to react against this omission. He focuses on the bodies of living soldiers, moving towards a sharp awareness of their potential to become corpses: 'the cherry skinned soldiers stroll down / to undress to idle on the white beach', but the poet, among them, stands in the sea looking down at his own feet:

> The logical little fish
> converge and nip the flesh
> imagining I am one of the dead.[81]

'Mersa' opens the way to the mature poems of 1943. Douglas was wounded by an exploding mine at Wadi Zem Zem on 15 January 1943.[82] With battle experience behind him, and recuperating from his injury, he wrote the major poem 'Dead Men'. The title alludes to those poems, by Brooke and others, titled 'The Dead'. Following Rosenberg, Douglas deletes the definite article and adds the missing noun, signalling that this poem is about not a coterie of spirits but the unburied bodies on the battlefield. However, the poem approaches those bodies with caution. It begins in the city where lovers court, moves to a hospital ward where the poet lies among the battle's survivors, and then makes an imagined journey 'to the west', to the battlefield itself. This takes mental effort: the poet urges his own heart to 'Come // to the west, out of that trance'.[83] The trance imposed on thought by the elegiac tradition is hard to dispel: the dead men are first called 'sleepers', before the poet achieves the simple, factual phrase, 'the dead men'. Their dead bodies have to be faced in stages. There are signs of retreat as he notes how the corpses are powdered by the

---

[81] 'Mersa' in Douglas, *Collected Poems*, 118.
[82] Graham, *Keith Douglas*, 179–82.
[83] 'Dead Men' in Douglas, *Collected Poems*, 116.

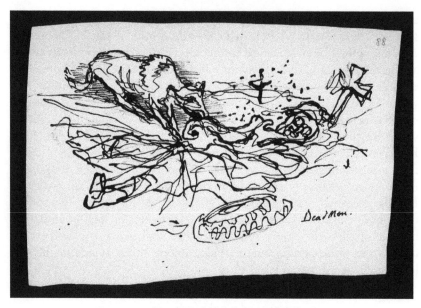

Figure 5.1 'Dead Man'. Sketch by Keith Douglas.
© The British Library Board, Add. 53775A No. 88.

wind 'till they are like dolls', but he pushes himself beyond this apparent artificiality.[84] In the third stanza, the bodies

> rest in the sanitary earth perhaps
> or where they died, no one has found them
> or in their shallow graves the wild dog
> discovered and exhumed a face or a leg
> for food: the human virtue round them
> is a vapour tasteless to a dog's chops.

Initially, he imagines the corpses safely buried in the 'sanitary' earth before conceding the likelihood that they either lie 'where they died' or, if hastily buried, have been disinterred by desert dogs. It is as if Douglas is forcing himself ever closer towards a full confrontation with the abject.[85]

The image of a wild dog unearthing, dragging and chomping a corpse was the subject of at least two sketches Douglas made in the desert. The

---

[84] Douglas further explores this sense of the artificiality of corpses in 'Landscape with Figures II' (Douglas, *Collected Poems*, 127).

[85] Note that Douglas writes 'where they *died*', not 'where they *fell*'. He scrupulously avoids the evasive diction so persistent in the poetry of the previous war.

one pictured here (Figure 5.1) is titled 'Dead Man' in the lower right hand corner. The image strongly recalls Rudyard Kipling's poem 'The Hyænas' in which the animals' teeth 'Take good hold in the army shirt, / And tug the corpse to light'.[86] Kipling was remembering the fate of corpses in the Boer War, though the poem was first published in *The Years Between* in 1919 alongside poems about the First World War. Kipling describes the hyaenas emerging 'After the burial parties leave', making a mockery of the human attempt to purify the corpse by putting it in the ground. They are 'wise' because they care not 'How he died and why he died'; they are only 'resolute they shall eat / That they and their mates may thrive'. The poem may be read as a response to the elegiac 'Drummer Hodge' in which Thomas Hardy imagines the corpse mingling eternally with 'that unknown plain': *this* corpse does not 'Grow to some Southern tree', it enters the gut of a wild animal.[87]

For Douglas, as for Kipling, the image of the wild dog eating a soldier's remains challenges the comforts of Romantic notions of rebirth through nature.[88] In both cases, the challenge is effected through an imaginative engagement with a Homeric tradition which insistently sees the defeated warrior's corpse as meat for carrion animals. Jasper Griffin notes 'the vital importance of the corpse and its treatment' in the *Odyssey* and the *Iliad*, explaining that 'the corpse of the dead man continued, in a sense, to be the man himself, the object of passionate hatred in his enemies, who desire to dishonour it and deprive it of burial.'[89] If the corpse is denied proper burial, the dead man's spirit cannot find its way to Hades. The distinction between the buried corpse and the unburied corpse (or purified and abject, in Kristeva's terms) is made clear in the second sentence of the *Iliad*: 'Many a brave soul did [Achilles's anger] send hurrying down to Hades, and many a hero did it yield a prey to dogs and vultures'.[90] The most appalling fate is for a warrior's corpse to be dishonoured and eaten by carrion animals, because 'To deprive the dead of a grave is to abolish his memory, to make him as if he had never been'.[91] At the end of book 16 of the *Iliad*, Hector tells Patroclus: ' "vultures shall devour you here" ' and book 17 focuses on Menelaus's fight to prevent that

---

[86] 'The Hyænas' in Rudyard Kipling, *The Years Between*, (London: Methuen, 1919), 69.
[87] Thomas Hardy, 'Drummer Hodge' in Parsons, *Progress of Poetry*, 1.
[88] Douglas will have seen 'Drummer Hodge' in *The Progress of Poetry*, where it appears as the first poem.
[89] Jasper Griffin, *Homer on Life and Death* (Oxford: Clarendon, 1980), 44, 160.
[90] Butler, *Iliad*, 1.
[91] Griffin, *Homer on Life and Death*, 46.

happening.⁹² Menelaus rescues Patroclus's body and, in book 18, the corpse is purified by various rituals. When Achilles takes his revenge on Hector, he tells the dying Trojan: ' "The Achæans [Greeks] shall give him [Patroclus] all due funeral rites, while dogs and vultures shall work their will upon yourself" '.⁹³ Hector begs him: ' "let not dogs devour me" ', Achilles replies ' "nothing shall save you from the dogs ... dogs and vultures shall eat you utterly up" '.⁹⁴ Achilles defiles Hector's body, dragging it behind his chariot, but relents when Priam, Hector's father, begs for the corpse so that it too may be given the proper rites.

Kipling and Douglas allude to these ideas but both make the point that, in modern warfare, it makes no difference whether the corpse is honourably buried or eaten by wild animals. The enemy makes no such threats – in the twentieth century, combatants do not *converse* before killing and these wild animals just happen along. Both poets focus on the shallowness of the soldier's grave, moving beyond Homeric ideas, and beyond Kristeva, seeing in such burials a provisionality which thus brings no comfort for the living. For Kipling's hyaenas, 'the dead are safer meat / Than the weakest thing alive' and for Douglas's wild dog, the corpse is no more than 'meat in a hole'. However, while Kipling's poem ends by making a strident political point, Douglas, under Rosenberg's influence, reaches for something more complex. Kipling concludes that the hyaenas,

> being soulless, are free from shame,
> Whatever meat they may find.
> Nor do they defile the dead man's name –
> That is reserved for his kind.

In notes on *The Years Between* prepared for his American publisher, Frank N. Doubleday, Kipling describes this poem as 'a parable of newspaper attacks on dead men who cannot defend themselves'.⁹⁵ The final stanza makes it apparent that Kipling's ironic engagement with Homeric tradition has been in the service of this polemic, which comes as a kind of punchline. Douglas's way of handling Homeric allusion is more closely reminiscent of Rosenberg's. Rosenberg shifted focus from the 'charioteer'

---

⁹² Butler, *Iliad*, 280.
⁹³ Ibid., 370.
⁹⁴ Ibid., 370–1.
⁹⁵ Letter to Frank N. Doubleday, 18 March 1919; *The Letters of Rudyard Kipling*, 5 vols, ed. Thomas Pinney (Iowa City: University of Iowa Press, 1990–2005), vol. IV, 543. Kipling was probably alluding to critics of the general conduct of the war.

to the soldier beneath his wheels; Douglas shifts focus from the defiled corpse to the hungry dog. The effect is not ironic, but rather forges a voice that is similarly dispassionate and curious, moving away from horror of abjection. Douglas, like Rosenberg, sees clearly that the body, once dead, is non-sentient and so no threat to the self (in distinction from Kristeva) – 'an organism / not capable of resurrection'.

Like 'Dead Man's Dump', 'Dead Men' draws on the *Iliad* to move beyond a mere graphic description of the corpse to consider in philosophical terms its meaning. When Douglas writes of the dead men: 'All that is good of them, the dog consumes', he plays grimly on the word *good*, forcing our attention onto the distinction between virtue and nourishment – and away from the Homeric idea that ingestion of the soldier's corpse by a dog denies honour and a peaceful afterlife. So much is clear but, in the rest of Douglas's fourth stanza, meaning is harder to pin down:

> You would not know now the mind's flame is gone,
> more than the dog knows: you would forget
> but that you see your own mind burning yet
> and till you stifle in the ground will go on
> burning the economical coal of your dreams.

The pronoun *you* may refer to the dead man whose 'mind's flame is gone', to the poet's heart (apostrophised in the second stanza) or to the reader whose own mind is 'burning yet'. The first of these lines seems to address the dead man and, in doing so, plays the double game we have seen in Owen ('if I wince, I shall not know I wince') where the deadness of the dead is simultaneously asserted and undermined. But *you* seems then to become the poet himself (or his heart): lying injured in a hospital bed, he tells himself 'you would forget' – that is, either, once dead he would have no memory, or, equally, while living he is in danger of losing the rational understanding he struggles to maintain. The following lines liken the mind to a fire, suggesting the Romantic trope in which the passionate imagination survives death, but the verb *burning* loses its connotation of passionate intensity when connected to 'economical coal'. This is just what the mind does: it cannot imagine its own cessation. Yet in addressing *you* thus, Douglas seeks to force that understanding on himself – and on that other *you,* his reader. In the struggle to make sense of these lines, we come away with a kind of mingling of their possibilities. Douglas, thus, reaches with difficulty towards a new tone and a response to the corpse not seen before in war poetry. In this, 'Dead Men' moves beyond 'Dead Man's Dump' while recalling Rosenberg's prescription (as quoted by Parsons) that '"complexity of thought"' must be '"kept in tone and right value to the dominating idea so that it is understandable and still ungraspable'", and that difficulty in poetry arises from '"the Herculean effort to enrich the world of ideas"'.

The final stanza sets out an opposition between 'the wise man' and 'the wild dog' (connected by their shared spondaic metre). The wise man 'is the lover', one of those described at the poem's opening who sustain a skilful obliviousness to the nearness of death, free from 'the traction of reason'; the wild dog on the other hand 'is a philosopher' because he does the only rational thing that can be done by a wild dog to a dead body. A more romantic poet would favour the wise man, a more satirical one the wild dog, but Douglas, recognising both the efficacy of the former and the rationalism of the latter, simply advises us to choose one position or the other and stick to it: 'The prudent mind resolves / on the lover's or the dog's attitude for ever'. However, he does no such thing himself, preferring to leave the poem in the moment of choice rather than dictating one option or excluding the other. Douglas thereby shifts, under Rosenberg's influence, and with appropriate difficulty, to a new representation of the soldier's corpse. He challenges the Homeric notion that honourable burial makes a difference: here the shallow-buried corpse is dragged from its hole.[96] But, if (philosophically) there is no harm in this, that is only because this is a world in which the soul and the afterlife have no meaning. Confronting the loss of both Homeric and Christian cosmologies, Douglas masters the abject by applying an intellectual curiosity to the disquieting matter of the dead body, so that it ceases to be disquieting.

In 'Desert Flowers', as we have noted, Douglas formally recognises his debt to Rosenberg:

> Living in a wide landscape are the flowers –
> Rosenberg I only repeat what you were saying –[97]

Douglas refers here specifically to the way the earlier poet reconfigured the elegiac notion of the dead entering the cycle of nature through a flower.

---

[96] He may also be recalling Eliot's lines about a corpse in *The Waste Land*: 'O keep the Dog far hence, that's friend to men, / Or with his nails he'll dig it up again!' (Eliot, *Complete Poems and Plays*, 63). Eliot, of course, alludes to John Webster's revenge tragedy *The White Devil*, where Cornelia laments that her son has been refused a proper burial. Eliot's 'dog ... that's friend to men' replaces Webster's 'wolf ... that's foe to men'.

[97] Douglas, *Collected Poems*, 129.

In a letter to his friend Margaret Stanley-Wrench, Douglas noted the flowers growing in the landscape of the Western Desert: 'There are indeed flowers of various indeterminate sorts and colours even on these bits of desert, mostly they are mauve and yellow. Occasional and quite veritable daisies and dandelions.'[98] In the poem, Douglas seeks obliquely to set these mauve and yellow blooms alongside the red poppy of the Western Front, recalling Rosenberg's recasting of the flower as an active, possibly malign agent. He foregrounds that agency in the inverted syntax of the first line, which brings *Living* to the front. The elegiac idea of a Nature which subsumes the dead through ill-defined processes is supplanted by a Nature with an *appetite* for corpses. Like Rosenberg, Douglas radically alters the feel of the idea; he intensifies the sense that 'the hungry flowers' have a malign agency and sets them alongside carrion animals – here, again, the wild dog – to question the difference. Thus, he equates 'the shell and the hawk' as agents of death, and the 'men and jerboas' as their respective victims.[99] Warfare, he suggests, is not different to other forms of predation in nature, and the preyed-upon man is not qualitatively different to the preyed-upon jerboa. However, this is not *simply* a bleak assertion of the insignificance of the dead men. Douglas's jerboa recalls Rosenberg's 'sardonic rat' (with which the speaker of 'Break of Day in the Trenches' both converses and identifies) and he may also be thinking of Marianne Moore's poem 'The Jerboa', which was included by Parsons in *The Progress of Poetry*.[100] For Moore, the jerboa is highly valued, a symbol of everything that is right about the natural world when it is left unmolested by powerful human elites. It is the antithesis of the Romans who 'put / baboons on the necks of giraffes to pick / fruit'.[101] Moore dwells on the fine details of the tiny creature's body while alive, as Douglas is preoccupied with the soldier's body when dead. Thus, in 'Desert Flowers' the equivalence suggested between 'men and jerboas' may not simply emphasise the insignificance of the dead men, but also connect them in a positive sense to this extraordinary creature. Even so, unlike Moore's jerboa, Douglas's jerboas have been killed as the men have been killed: this is a war and this is the cost of it. There is a lament

---

[98] Letter to Margaret Stanley-Wrench, 8 January 1943; Douglas, *Letters*, 256.
[99] The jerboa is a tiny desert rat with long feet and a high leap.
[100] Desmond Graham notes that Douglas also acquired Moore's *Selected Poems* at Port Said in 1943 (Graham, *Keith Douglas*, 274), in which the poem appears again.
[101] Marianne Moore, 'The Jerboa' in Parsons, *Progress of Poetry*, 132.

of sorts here, but one lacking all notes of elegiac grief or consolation – because such notes would be hypocrisy when the deaths have been deemed necessary.

Douglas turned an unflinching eye on the abject corpse in 'Dead Men' (he will do so again in '*Vergissmeinnicht*') but here he considers the impossibility of speaking knowledgeably about death and, nevertheless, persists in his continuing struggle to do so. He tells us:

> I see men as trees suffering
> or confound the detail and the horizon.
> Lay the coin on my tongue and I will sing
> of what the others never set eyes on.

Douglas alludes here to the incident in the Gospel of Mark where Jesus cures a blind man:

> And he took the blind man by the hand, and led him out of the town; and when he had spit on his eyes, and put his hands upon him, he asked him if he saw ought. And he looked up, and said, I see men as trees, walking. After that he put his hands again upon his eyes, and made him look up: and he was restored, and saw every man clearly.[102]

The blind man sees 'men as trees, walking' in a transitional state between blindness and clear sight. Douglas, too, describes an intermediary state and seeks the extra vision a journey to the underworld would provide.[103] The poem ends with the paradox that, with a coin to take him across the Styx he will be able to move beyond Rosenberg and the other First World War poets, to 'sing / of what the others never set eyes on' – but to achieve this, he will need to die. 'Lay the coin on my tongue', he urges, but Charon's fee is only laid on tongues that can no longer sing.

The development of tone and ideas in 'Desert Flowers' belies the statement in its second line. That self-dismissal is fuelled perhaps by modesty but also by a sense of the struggle Douglas is engaged in to create a form of expression equal to the experience. Yet, simply by writing 'I only repeat what you were saying', Douglas shows that he is self-consciously reflecting on previous attempts to express a response to the fact of the battlefield corpse, and this self-reflexivity *is* new, anticipating an aspect of the postmodern. In doing so, also, he implicitly argues for the value of Rosenberg's unique response to the dead body (he does not apostrophise Owen, Sassoon or Graves) and his

---

[102] Mark 8:22–5.
[103] See also Kendall, *Modern English War Poetry*, 166. Douglas's alteration of 'trees, walking' to 'trees suffering' recalls Paul Nash's First World War landscapes such as 'The Menin Road', 'The Mule

choice, which was by no means a likely one in 1943, indicates a discerning eye, an understanding of the poet's task as it was expressed by Rosenberg and passed on to Douglas via Parsons's Introduction to *The Progress of Poetry*. Finally, that understanding means that he does not 'only repeat'; he absorbs Rosenberg's dispassionate curiosity, his attention to the actuality of the corpse, in order to reshape his own voice.

If anything, Douglas discards the traces of tenderness in Rosenberg's work. As Goldensohn says, the savage title 'Dead Man's Dump' is countered by 'Rosenberg's caressive, pitying tone, and the evocative pastoral-elegiac, [which] find no match in Douglas, whose coverage of death always mutes pathos'.[104] There is a coldness to Douglas's developing thoughts about battlefield corpses and what it means, or does not mean, for the wild dogs to eat them. That coldness also owes something to W. H. Auden (whose influence is very clear in the lines of 'Dead Men', which mimic the phrasing of Auden's 'Spain': 'Tonight the white dresses and the jasmine scent / in the streets'). Several early critics reacted strongly against this voice. Ian Hamilton accused Douglas of 'reticence stiffening into the tight-lipped insensitivity of the officers' mess', John Carey asserted that 'in his war poems, the meticulously stiffened upper lip can cramp response' and Kevin Crossley-Holland, while acknowledging 'a distinctive voice – utterly unsentimental', averred that 'even his best work is flawed by inhibition'.[105] Rebutting these attacks, Kendall sees a 'fault line between Owen's pity and Douglas's dispassion', and suggests that Douglas was 'driven to acts of aggression against much of what Owen's work stands for'.[106] Ted Hughes, also, sees Owen and Douglas as polar opposites: for Owen, the suffering of war was 'all but an actualization of Christ's suffering and death', whereas, for Douglas, all the killing showed us only that we inhabit 'a purely material Creation in which man is one of the working parts ... and the living are hardly more than deluded variants of the dead'.[107]

Kendall observes that Douglas's reaction against Owenesque pity arises because he is 'suspicious of its motivations' and refuses 'to succumb to consolation'.[108] There is hypocrisy in the consolatory gestures of elegy when the deaths lamented have been deemed necessary. So, while Douglas draws

---

Track', 'Void of War', 'Wire' and 'We are making a new world', all of which are populated by blasted trees.
[104] Goldensohn, *Dismantling Glory*, 131.
[105] All quoted in William Scammell, *Keith Douglas: A Study* (London: Faber & Faber, 1988), 200, 208, 205.
[106] Kendall, *Modern English War Poetry*, 149, 150.
[107] Ted Hughes, 'Introduction' in Douglas, *Collected Poems*, xxiii.
[108] Kendall, *Modern English War Poetry*, 158.

on Owen's poetics as part of the process of awakening from the trance of the elegiac tradition, he finds in Rosenberg the raw materials he needs to forge a voice which can express 'the scrupulous dispassion … by which the full horror may be expressed'.[109]

This approach reaches a kind of apotheosis in 'Landscape with Figures I', in which Douglas offers an aerial view of the battlefield, but omits the corpses altogether describing only the 'vehicles / squashed dead'.[110] He ironically calls the wrecked vehicles 'monuments, and metal posies', as if they have been placed there to commemorate the dead:

> on each disordered tomb
> the steel is torn into fronds
> by the lunatic explosive.

This is a wry allusion to Owen's 'A Terre' (collected by Parsons in *The Progress of Poetry*), where the speaker comments 'Soldiers may grow a soul when turned to fronds'.[111] As we have noted, Owen's soldier suggests that the corpse's commingling into surrounding plant-life might be the process which *creates* a soul. Douglas alters 'turned' to 'torn', reminding us of the force of the lethal explosion and, in likening the resultant shreds of metal to flowers, indicates how far he has come from the Shelleyan notions which featured in 'Canoe'. While the battlefield's corpses are conspicuously absent in this poem, the ironic juxtaposition is implicit: if steel is thus torn, what has happened to flesh and bone? Douglas compares metal and flesh explicitly in 'Dead Men', where the corpses are 'less durable than the metal of a gun' and does so again in '*Vergissmeinnicht*' where the dead soldier is 'mocked at by his own equipment / that's hard and good when he's decayed'.[112] In the latter poem, Douglas returns to the experience of a direct confrontation with the unburied corpse, recalling Graves's 'A Dead Boche'. But where Graves shares his own traumatic sensory experience with the reader in order to provide 'A certain cure for lust of blood', Douglas sets his own experience aside to imagine the trauma of Steffi, the dead man's lover:

> But she would weep to see today
> how on his skin the swart flies move;
> the dust upon the paper eye
> and the burst stomach like a cave.[113]

---

[109] Ibid., 159.
[110] Douglas, *Collected Poems*, 127.
[111] Owen, 'A Terre' in Parsons, *Progress of Poetry*, 62.
[112] Douglas, *Collected Poems*, 116, 121.
[113] For an insightful analysis of Douglas's revision of these lines, see Vincent Sherry, 'Hectic Stasis: The War Poetry of Keith Douglas', *University of Toronto Quarterly* 58.2 (1989), 301–3.

We pity Steffi for the pain she will soon experience, but Douglas challenges the reader to separate utterly the living man from his corporeal remains, to banish sentimentality, and to accept that *this* is what war unavoidably means. *She* would weep. Douglas invites us to observe closely and attend to his own thoughtful response, which teases out the nature of the event with beautiful economy:

> For here the lover and killer are mingled
> who had one body and one heart.
> And death who had the soldier singled
> has done the lover mortal hurt.

In this final stanza, Douglas does not so much turn away from the actuality of the gruesome sight as accept it. He finds room for some pity – a softening of the tone achieved in 'Dead Men' – but the tears are Steffi's not his own. Like Rosenberg, he challenges Kristeva's psychological conception with a considered response to the physical reality of the battlefield corpse, but he also goes beyond Rosenberg – and beyond every other poet of the First World War – when he emphasises that the men who have been killed were themselves killers: 'the lover and killer are mingled'. The lover's death is unfortunate but unavoidable.[114] Rosenberg helps him to this clear-sightedness, which escapes heroic, ironic, satirical and polemical commonplaces and moves beyond Owenesque pity, but Douglas does more than 'only repeat', finding a new language with which to express his own experience of the corpsescape of the Western Desert in a war that began with too much foreknowledge for a poetry of disillusionment.

---

[114] In 'How to Kill' (Douglas, *Collected Poems*, 122), Douglas emphasises his *own* role as killer – this is virtually unheard of in the poetry of the First World War.

CHAPTER 6

'Horrors Here Smile'
The Poem, the Photograph and the Punctum

> Photography is an elegiac art, a twilight art. Most subjects photographed are, just by virtue of being photographed, touched with pathos ... All photographs are *memento mori*. To take a photograph is to participate in another person's (or thing's) mortality, vulnerability, mutability. Precisely by slicing out this moment and freezing it, all photographs testify to time's relentless melt.[1]

Susan Sontag's metaphor eloquently expresses that about the photograph which makes it both truthful and untruthful. Nothing in the flow of life freezes quite in the way that a moment in time is frozen in a photograph. But in this very representation of something that is not characteristic of life, the photograph enables, indeed forces the viewer to see both the captured moment and the passage of time from which the moment has been artificially isolated but which surrounds it and contextualises it. The viewer is inevitably led to interpret the image in terms of this surrounding knowledge, and so to see in the frozen image 'time's relentless melt'. Since its inception, photography has thus entered our sensibility and affected our consciousness. For Roland Barthes, in his moving investigation of its effects in *Camera Lucida*, the photograph can capture in the same moment of viewing '*This will be* and *this has been*'.[2] For Barthes, as we view (certain) photographs, we see both the moment when the image of the living body is captured, when death still lies ahead, and the moment after death, the moment of knowing that the photographic image is now all that remains of the once living body. It can thus provoke both a sense of dread of what will be lost, and a sense of what has been lost. The photograph can make us 'shudder ... *over a catastrophe which has already occurred*'.[3] Here Barthes goes beyond Sontag's simpler point in his understanding that the

---

[1] Susan Sontag, *On Photography* (London: Penguin, 1979), 15.
[2] Roland Barthes, *Camera Lucida: Reflections on Photography*, trans. Richard Howard (1981; London: Vintage, 2000), 96.
[3] Ibid.

photograph is not only an object arousing the viewer's compassion for the subject's mortality; it captures mortality itself in enabling us to understand in the one moment of viewing that we are alive and that we are always going to die.

For Barthes, this wrenching of consciousness is brought about by the '*punctum*' in the photograph. This may be a small, apparently inconsequential detail which 'rises from the scene, shoots out of it like an arrow, and pierces me'; but it may also arise from the way a photograph catches the passage of time itself, 'the lacerating emphasis of the *noeme* ("*that-has-been*"), its pure representation'.[4] We will argue that poems which take photographs as their starting point are able to re-present and sharpen the *punctum* which Barthes so elegantly analyses. Such poems both recreate the photograph they start from and act as an extended commentary upon it and upon the act of viewing. Our three examples, Ted Hughes's 'Six Young Men' (1957), Philip Larkin's 'MCMXIV' (1964) and Douglas Dunn's 'Portrait Photograph, 1915' (1979), all take as their subject photographs depicting men who (we either infer or are told) were to die in the First World War.[5]

These poems draw on a long tradition of ekphrasis, a classical mode which has been revivified in twentieth-century poetry. Ekphrasis is, at its simplest, '*the verbal representation of visual representation*',[6] but in both its rhetorical origins and in the poems we consider, the attendant dimension of 'out-speaking' (evident in the etymology – '*ek-phrasis*') is significant.[7] Hughes, Larkin and Dunn draw on some of the original classical elements of the mode, whilst also using it to extend their understanding and poetic expression of the human predicament in modernity. Ekphrasis, via the photograph, is for them not a device on which to turn a poem, but an instinctive mode for the mid- to late-twentieth-century poet in which to address the First World War – the defining catastrophe of modernity, whose growing historical distance the photograph promises to bridge.

That it is a photograph, rather than a painting (the classic visual representation), at the centre of these poems distinguishes them from most poetry in the ekphrastic tradition. The photograph has always had

---

[4] Ibid., 26–7, 96.
[5] We give the date of first publication in volume form. Ted Hughes, *The Hawk in the Rain* (London: Faber & Faber, 1957), 54; Philip Larkin, *The Whitsun Weddings* (London: Faber & Faber, 1964), 28; Douglas Dunn, *Barbarians* (London: Faber & Faber, 1979), 35.
[6] James A. W. Heffernan, *Museum of Words: The Poetics of Ekphrasis from Homer to Ashbery* (Chicago: University of Chicago Press, 1993), 3.
[7] Peter Barry, 'Contemporary Poetry and Ekphrasis', *The Cambridge Quarterly*, 31.2 (2002), 155.

an uneasy relationship with the gallery, and in accounts of modern poetic ekphrasis we see the same hierarchy at work: paintings are dominant, and poems about the photograph are marginalised. But it is in those margins that our poets work. The photographs that Hughes, Larkin and Dunn single out are part of a democratic tradition of art, both portrait and document, personal and public, and accessible in the way a painting cannot be precisely by lying outside rather than within the walls of the museum. Their poetic responses carry ekphrasis right back into the real world.

In using the popular technology of the camera, through which the twentieth century has characteristically been seen, these poets present us with an image both familiar and unfamiliar – ourselves, yet other. And at the simplest level, the photograph – whether it be the journalistic record or a 'snap', a well-preserved studio photo in a nice frame or a cracked and fading print curling up on the sideboard – is the democratic medium through which we are most likely to meet, directly and personally, images from the First World War.

The tension between the living subject captured in the photographic image, and the viewer's knowledge that the subject is now dead, is redoubled in these poems by the second order of representation they provide. In confronting these poetic recreations of the photographic image, we confront the human body at the moment of life and death, and also at a particular historical moment. Our own mortality is depicted there in the way defined by Barthes, but perhaps what we are most seized by is, simply, the fading depiction of men who died in the First World War. The mediation of the photograph and the remediation of the poem create a reflective distance but, also, these poems bring us face to face with those who died – historical distance is both acknowledged and set aside. They investigate rather than exploit the poignancy inherent in the photograph of someone who has died, moving us in precisely the way that the *punctum* of the photograph can move us – pierce us – by allowing us to be both in the moment of the photograph and outside it. These poems capture both that '*this will be*' and '*this has been*'.

Ted Hughes says of his poem 'Six Young Men':

> This is a meditation of a kind – on a photograph of six youths. And it's taken in a valley just below where I lived in Yorkshire and just before the outbreak of the First World War. These six youths were all friends of my father's. And the war came, and this photograph is just one among family photographs – so I've been hearing stories about these characters on this photograph for as long as I've been picking up the photograph and looking

at it ... They all trained together. They all went out together. They all fought together and so they tended to get killed together.[8]

This description of the 'photograph of six youths' has a deceptive surface normality and matter-of-factness. It is left to the poem to catch what is unbearable: 'Six months after this picture they were all dead'. At the heart of the horror is the photograph, capturing aliveness which persists after the death of the bodies it depicts. Walter Benjamin, looking at the nineteenth-century photographic portraits made by David Octavius Hill, notes how

> the viewer feels irresistibly compelled to seek out the tiniest spark of concurrence, a here and now, in such an image, with which actuality has seared, so to speak, the characters in the image. We are compelled to find the inconspicuous place in which, in the essence of that moment which passed long ago, the future nestles still today, so eloquently that we, looking back, are able to discover it.[9]

Hughes places us in the same relation to the photograph he represents. Central to that deeply felt irony of the apparent aliveness of those depicted is the fact that the natural features in the photograph – bank, tree, waterfall – are still there, and Hughes knows them. He cannot know the men in that actual sense. But he knows them through the photograph, and through his father's anecdotes about them.

A poem about a photograph re-presents the photograph whilst taking a position in relation to it. Hughes's poem shows a full awareness of the complications of perception, relayed feeling, unsettling of reality that the business of the photograph can engineer. These are all implied in the poem, indeed taken advantage of, yet somehow buried there. In the first stanza Hughes uses the photograph to home in on the six young men; closer and closer is the close-up, clearer and clearer the individuals (see lines 6–8). And this individualising of their happy present, captured in time, is matched by the specifics of their subsequent deaths (lines 19–21). The changing of tense from present to past in these two stanzas divides the two moments, of life in Yorkshire and death at the Front. But they are brought together by their syntactical echoes.

The photograph catches these young men at an iconic moment, innocently enjoying life just before the outbreak of the First World War. A photograph encapsulates a moment of being; but it is also a moment

---

[8] Ted Hughes at the Adelaide Festival Writers' Week, March 1976, talking about the poem before reading it. Transcript at: http:/ann.skea.com/Adelaide.htm.
[9] Walter Benjamin, *On Photography*, ed. and trans. Esther Leslie (London: Reaktion Books, 2015), 66–7.

of seeing. We are brought into an intimacy with the young men's lives and deaths through the poet's drawing us into the similarly intimate act of looking at the photograph with him. Hughes beautifully reproduces the act of seeing in the mechanics of the poem, drawing attention to physical and psychological detail – then he adds a further layer of seeing, one available only in retrospect but here married to the moment of time of the photograph. Through his historical sight we see the fates of the six men. Hughes's use of tenses conjures the complication of this relationship of present to future (though both 'now' in the past). The photograph, of course, pre-dates the young men's deaths: its natural tense is the present, and Hughes catches the illusion of the men's also remaining in some way always in the present. '[T]heir expressions listen yet' to the sounds of the valley that can indeed still be heard. But while, at the moment of the photograph, the deaths of the men lie in the future, those deaths are activated in the poem by the past tense, in the last line of the first stanza: 'Six months after this picture they were all dead'. Apart from this line, the past tense and its implication are saved up for the account of the men's deadly fate in the third stanza, where the young lives caught in the printed image of the photograph – young men clearly, shiningly alive – are reduced implacably to the past, to what is gone.

But Hughes goes further than the particular, or even the historical. He wants to understand the way that a photograph can capture both life in death and death in life. The last two stanzas of the poem move us into this more fugitive area. There is a rhetorical shift at this structural volta in the poem; Hughes apostrophises the reader, bringing him into the poem:

> Here see a man's photograph ...
> And on this one place which keeps him alive
> (In his Sunday best) see fall war's worst
> Thinkable flash and rending

The repeated injunction to the reader to 'see' makes us feel also the full weight of the poet's gaze on us, demanding that we take notice of the horror caught here. It is notable that Hughes, in his first published version of the poem (in *Delta*, Summer 1957), has a far less arresting opening line for this fourth stanza: 'It is fearful seeing a man's photograph'.[10] For its publication in *The Hawk in the Rain* (Hughes's first collection), it is revised strikingly to what we have now: 'Here see a man's photograph'. The line thus becomes the pivot on which the poem balances. There is an

---

[10] Variant noted in Ted Hughes, *Collected Poems*, ed. Paul Keegan (London: Faber & Faber, 2003), 1243.

accompanying change of focus, even of subject, as Hughes moves from 'six young men' to the more generalised yet more particular 'man'. And it is 'on this one place that keeps him alive' (i.e. the photograph) that 'war's worst thinkable flash' falls, and which the poet enjoins us to 'see'. We see the image rent, and the body depicted in the image also rent; the smile on the photographic paper is also the smile 'Forty years rotting into soil'. Photograph and body become one.

Elizabeth Bergmann Loizeaux argues that 'ekphrasis is an emphatically deictic mode: ... "see," "look" are frequent imperatives of the pointing poet'.[11] She attributes this trope to the poet's anxiety that 'works of art [have] an immediacy, a presence, a "hereness" that they have wanted for words, but that they suspect words can only gesture toward'.[12] The photograph may have even greater 'hereness' than the work of art in that it is, as Barthes says, 'literally an emanation of the referent'.[13] However, it is not envy of the other medium which motivates Hughes. We are caught by the arm in this way, made to take notice, because Hughes has a larger truth to tell about our own mortality (lines 37–40), and it is the poetry itself which here does double duty, making us 'see' the photographic image *and* the bodies it represents. 'Six Young Men' poetically enacts Barthes's view that the photograph can make us 'shudder ... *over a catastrophe that has already occurred*'. In this way, both the photograph which is the poem's subject, and the poem itself, express more than simple loss; they enable us as mortal humans to understand in the moment of (imagined) viewing both that we – as they – are alive and that we – as they – are always going to die. In Keith Sagar's words about the six young men depicted:

> we know that they are as dead as dinosaur or dodo, dead and rotten. If I have my photograph taken today, someone will look at it forty years hence and be looking at the photograph of a dead man. It is like seeing one's own tombstone, like becoming aware of one's own skeleton which will one day shrug off its flesh.[14]

But this we could not understand without the way the technology of the photograph 'snaps' that moment.

Only rarely do photographs have this powerful effect on us, but here Hughes reproduces the effect by both presenting us with the photographic

---

[11] Elizabeth Bergmann Loizeaux, *Twentieth-Century Poetry and the Visual Arts* (Cambridge: Cambridge University Press, 2008), 4.
[12] Ibid., 4.
[13] Barthes, *Camera Lucida*, 80.
[14] Keith Sagar, *The Art of Ted Hughes* (Cambridge: Cambridge University Press, 1975), 31.

image and drawing our attention forcibly to what it really means. He ends the poem thus:

> To regard this photograph might well dement,
> Such contradictory permanent horrors here
> Smile from the single exposure and shoulder out
> One's own body from its instant and heat.

The horrors smile; they are both contradictory and permanent – '*this will be* and *this has been*'. The 'single exposure' is deceptively simple and singular; what it reveals to us is a whole history of individual lives before this moment's capture, and a whole expunged history after it. It is not the specifics of the men's deaths that move us in the end; it is that they died before their time. For the aspect of this particular photograph which makes its *punctum* so aggressively piercing is that the men's deaths were not natural, and might have been avoided. They might have had at least the same distance of time spreading ahead of the photograph as spreads behind it. The 'single exposure' thus concertinas past and present into the one image, rendering the six young men both alive and dead. In recognising that, we as viewers are shouldered out from our own 'instant and heat' and realise our own incipient deaths just as we are shouldered out of the poem. As readers/viewers we thus have some understanding of what it must have felt like when the men experienced each other's deaths. For, as Hughes points out in his Adelaide remarks, these were friends who signed up together and fought alongside each other, as in many of the 'Pals' battalions. And – what is unspoken in the poem – Hughes's father, who survived, experienced the loss of each and all of them, and would be left to remember them.

Geoffrey Batchen, writing on photographs which have been individually embellished, customised, to create a memorial object for display, notes that such photographs represent not so much their subjects, but the desire we have as humans to be always remembered. The viewer, recognising this, sees also that it is impossible: 'For these photographs remind us that memorialization has little to do with recalling the past; it is always about looking ahead toward that terrible, imagined, vacant future in which we ourselves have been forgotten'.[15] Yet for Hughes, and for us as readers, this remains a moment of compassion even while it is inherently self-reflective, and this makes the ending of the poem curiously comforting. The act of

---

[15] Geoffrey Batchen, *Forget Me Not: Photography and Remembrance* (New York: Princeton Architectural Press, 2004), 98.

seeing properly what the photograph depicts leads us to inhabit it, to feel 'war's worst / Thinkable flash and rending' of the bodies depicted. We may be shouldered out from the benign solidity of our own bodies into the consciousness of the void which awaits, but that happens because the poem shoulders us *into* the bodies of the young men. We truly remember them.

Hughes's understanding of humanity and identity remains then, at its core, Romantic in that it is underpinned by this essential sense of solidarity and unity with other human beings, placed firmly in a natural world which sustains. But, because he uses here the technology of the photograph as the medium for this, he is also able to catch the isolation of the human condition in modernity. The piercing insight of the *punctum* can bring us as viewers together with the viewed. The photograph allows us as viewers to believe briefly that we have crossed time to a point in the past; or that the people represented there have crossed to our present. It allows, in the act of seeing, the illusion of a moment of coincidence with those seen. The poem propels the reader into the same present tense occupied by the young men (see lines 12–15). But while we look into the smile of this young man, or try to catch the eyes of that one, none of them is looking back at us. The great strength of Hughes's poem is that he elucidates the power of the illusion whilst also taking us into the horror at its heart – their deaths – without ever losing the sense of communion we can feel even with a mere image of another human being. That he is representing a photograph rather than a painting is surely crucial here. Stephen Burt, writing on C. D. Wright's poetic collaborations with the photographer Deborah Luster, places their work in the context of the history of the portrait photograph as a medium that speaks to the viewer, revealing the inner self of the subject, and attesting to the shared humanity of both viewer and subject.[16] In this respect, Burt sees a clear continuity between the portrait photograph tradition and that tradition of poetry which speaks for the human subject. In Hughes's poem the two traditions coalesce.

In 'MCMXIV', Larkin also meditates on a photograph of men pictured just before they go to war. He begins with an ekphrastic description of the 'long uneven lines' of men waiting to enlist. They stand as if queuing for a cricket match or football game (lines 1–8). Larkin does not mention the physical fact of the photograph in his description. We infer that it is a press photograph – taken to illustrate, and presumably to encourage, enlistment

---

[16] Stephen Burt, 'Lightsource, Aperture, Face: C. D. Wright and Photography', *In the Frame: Women's Ekphrastic Poetry from Marianne Moore to Susan Wheeler*, ed. Jane Hedley, Nick Halpern and Willard Spiegelman (Newark: University of Delaware Press, 2009), 227–44.

in 1914 – which the poet has seen reproduced in some new context, perhaps in a historical account where it signifies differently, illustrating the naivety of early enthusiasm for the war. The irony of Hughes's poem, whereby the ageing print shows unlined faces, is here replaced by the irony of a reproduction signifying differently in a new time and place.

Larkin, in his earlier poem 'Lines on a Young Lady's Photograph Album' (1955), gives a similar account of the experience of looking at old photographs, in this case photographs of a loved one taken before he met her. Trying to tease out what it is that he finds so unsettling about the photographs, he addresses the art of photography:

> But o, photography! as no art is,
> Faithful and disappointing! that records
> Dull days as dull, and hold-it smiles as frauds …
>
> How overwhelmingly persuades
> That this is a real girl in a real place[17]

The element of unfalsifiability in the snapshot sharpens his sense of the actuality of the woman's past existence. He then modifies this position, focusing on the sadness of the *pastness* of the past:

> These misty parks and motors, lacerate
> Simply by being over; you
> Contract my heart by looking out of date.

As we have noted, Barthes finds in photography 'the lacerating emphasis of the *noeme* ("*that has been*")' and Larkin, here, uses the same word to describe this pain – it *lacerates*.[18] '[W]e yowl across // The gap from eye to page', says the poet. He is left contemplating 'a past that no one now can share'. This is the pain of the *punctum* – an acute sensitivity to the simultaneous nowness and pastness of the captured moment. The unusually visceral nature of Larkin's verbs here – 'lacerate', 'yowl' – helps us to feel that pain. Sontag's view that photographs thus testify to 'time's relentless melt' is felt all the more keenly when viewing a photograph of men who do not know how soon they will be killed. In 'MCMXIV', Larkin evokes this *punctum*, this awareness of the simultaneous *nowness* and *pastness* of the image: the split second of the captured moment has 'changed itself to past / Without a word'. The wordless image remains, unnaturally, *still*.

---

[17] 'Lines on a Young Lady's Photograph Album' in Philip Larkin, *The Less Deceived* (Hessle: Marvell Press, 1955), 13.
[18] Barthes, *Camera Lucida*, 96.

Barthes began his enquiries into the nature of photography, at about the same time that Larkin wrote this poem, with the essay 'The Photographic Message' (1961), in which he suggests that any attempt to describe a photograph will unavoidably 'signify something different to what is shown', introducing connotations unique to the viewer.[19] This is evident in 'MCMXIV'. The poet's sense of irony, there in the word 'patiently', shades into scorn with the image of the foolish 'grinning' volunteers. The idea that they queue as if for a cricket or football match reminds us of Henry Newbolt's notorious poem, 'Vitaï Lampada' (1897), in which the English schoolboy-turned-soldier is urged to 'Play up! play up! and play the game!'[20] None of this is self-evidently in the photograph: the poet cannot really tell if they queued with patience or boredom. Not everyone in the photograph can be grinning, and those who are may do so specifically because they know they are being photographed – performing the expected response and, perhaps, overriding inner feelings of anxiety about warfare, or resentment at the societal pressure which brought them to the recruiting office that day. So, in the first stanza, Larkin re-reads the image, imposing certain connotations. However, the poem goes on to do something more complex in relation to the photograph.

Barthes says that written text works in relation to press photographs in a unique way:

> the text constitutes a parasitic message designed to connote the image, to 'quicken' it with one or more second-order signifieds. In other words, and this is an important historical reversal, the image no longer *illustrates* the words; it is now the words which, structurally, are parasitic on the image … Formerly, the image illustrated the text (made it clearer); today, the text loads the image, burdening it with a culture, a moral, an imagination.[21]

We might consider Larkin's poem as just such a piece of text, a kind of extended caption – except that, as the poem is an ekphrasis, the photograph itself is absent from the page. The text re-produces the photograph for us and thereby regains primacy – and becomes a supplement, or a challenge, to the captions previously appended to such images. But this is not simply a repudiation of the captions of 1914. While the first stanza seems to express a view commonly held in 1960s Britain about the naivety of early enthusiasm for the war, that response to the photograph is itself interrogated and modified in the following stanzas as the poet reflects

---

[19] Roland Barthes, *Image Music Text*, trans. Stephen Heath (London: Fontana, 1977), 19.
[20] Henry Newbolt, *Collected Poems 1897–1907* (London: Thomas Nelson & Sons, 1910), 131–3.
[21] 'The Photographic Message' in Barthes, *Image Music Text*, 25–6.

critically upon it. The poem achieves a moving ambivalence towards the past, founded on an awareness that the poet's response is a response to a photograph whose meanings are layered.

Only the first stanza describes what is within the frame of the photograph. The second moves beyond that frame to the surrounding streets and the third moves further afield into the surrounding countryside. Here Larkin interrogates his response (and the *punctum* effect) by imagining the impossible: he steps, Alice-like, inside the frame and moves beyond its limits.[22] What he finds there is a series of images of a lost England which recall the Georgian poetry of 1914. The second stanza emphasises that this world is changeless and bound by tradition: the shop owners' names are 'Established', the coinage is ancient (farthings, legal tender from the thirteenth century, were withdrawn the year this poem was written), the naming of children is deferential to royalty (lines 9–13). The pub – that ancient institution – was free to stay open all day (a tradition that ended in 1915, when restrictions were imposed to assist the war effort and, specifically, to prevent munitions workers from making fatal errors after drinking). The third stanza extends the Georgian aesthetic in relation to the English countryside. Its eight lines recall another eight, from Edward Thomas's 'Adlestrop' (1917):

> And willows, willow-herb, and grass,
> And meadowsweet, and haycocks dry,
> No whit less still and lonely fair
> Than the high cloudlets in the sky.
>
> And for that minute a blackbird sang
> Close by, and round him, mistier,
> Farther and farther, all the birds
> Of Oxfordshire and Gloucestershire.[23]

Andrew Motion reads Larkin's lines as straight Georgian nostalgia: 'In "MCMXIV" the countryside forms part of a vanished ideal, a better world than ours, marooned on the wrong side of a colossal war'.[24] However, as James Booth argues, this is not simply a naive lament for a lost England: 'the poet shows himself quite aware of the mediated quality of this image … he is dramatising a particularly potent cultural myth'.[25] The photograph, as it

---

[22] Grant F. Scott notes that, in antiquity, the ekphrastic description could 'move *into* the artwork, taking up an imaginative position within the depicted world' (Scott, 'Copied with a Difference: *Ekphrasis* in William Carlos Williams' *Pictures from Brueghel*', *Word & Image*, 15.1 (1999), 64.
[23] Edward Thomas, *The Annotated Collected Poems*, ed. Edna Longley (Tarset: Bloodaxe, 2008), 51.
[24] Andrew Motion, *Philip Larkin: A Writer's Life* (London: Faber & Faber, 1994), 419.
[25] James Booth, *Philip Larkin: Writer* (Hemel Hempstead: Harvester, 1992), 72.

signifies in 1964, is an encapsulation of that myth, but one in which Larkin tries to move around, seeking something. The ambivalent relationship to a Georgian aesthetic is there in the form. Thomas's *abcb* quatrain is replaced by an eight-line stanza in which the single rhyme is not immediately visible to the eye; in the first two stanzas, one comes upon the experience of rhyme unexpectedly and searches back to find the source ('Villa Park'; 'children at play'). In this third stanza, the rhyme is very faint, recalling the para-rhymes and half rhymes of Wilfred Owen, expressing an appropriate anxiety about the neatness and closure of full rhyme.

Larkin's faux-Georgianism is double-edged. It seems to mourn a loss of the sense of certainty that belonged with innocence, but the last stanza can also be read as a rebuke to the discourses called to mind by the photograph: the naive patriotism, the Georgian sentimentalism *and* the post-1945 myth of 1914. That final stanza is often misrepresented: it does not unequivocally present 1914 as the moment at which a state of innocence came to an end. Larkin's triptych of *never*s reads:

> Never such innocence,
> Never before or since,
> ...
> Never such innocence again.

August 1914, then was no watershed of modernity, but a unique moment of innocence in history – 'Never *before* or since' – and the sense of that innocence only increases for the reader as time passes. That movingly ambiguous last line *can* be read as a lament for lost innocence, but it might equally be read as a warning to the self: 'Never such innocence again'.

Whereas Hughes apostrophises the reader, buttonholing her with a vocative command ('Here see a man's photograph'), trying to evoke in her something of his own sense of grief, Larkin's poem is grammatically reticent – its one long sentence is made up of a series of clauses which lacks a main verb. It addresses no one, and the final, reflective stanza has the form of internal contemplation. This reinforces the poem's quality of being like an epitaph, or tombstone inscription as suggested by the Roman numerals of the title.[26] This in turn calls up that epigrammatic poetry which was one of the original forms of ekphrasis in the classical world.[27]

---

[26] In Larkin's own words: 'It is called "1914", but written in roman numerals, as you might see it on a monument. It would be beyond me to write a poem called "1914" in Arabic numerals' ('The Living Poet' in Philip Larkin, *Further Requirements*, ed. Anthony Thwaite (London: Faber & Faber, 2001), 85).

[27] 'From the third century B.C.E. onwards for the next four hundred years and more, the epigram is one of the prime exemplars of ekphrastic writing. It takes its cue from epigrams inscribed on graves

Larkin's photograph, unlike Hughes's, is public; a piece of reportage rather than a memento of friends – he has no personal connection with the people pictured and the image is representative rather than specific – and this leads the poet to consider not personal tragedies or private griefs, but rather the functioning of cultural mythologies through the photographic image. In this, it takes us further away from the individuals who died; but it places those men before us both as once they were, and also as we see them from a historical standpoint, thus prompting us to understand what lies in the distance between. We thus think of them – especially those among them who will have died – in a more complex way. While Larkin notes their innocence, the image itself can't remain innocent.

Douglas Dunn, in 'Portrait Photograph, 1915', focuses on a third kind of photo – the memento, taken in a High Street studio and given as a gift by the subject to his loved ones. Dunn, rather than apostrophising the reader as Hughes does, or ruminating over the image like Larkin, chooses to give a voice to the man captured by the camera in a dramatic monologue. As we noted in our first chapter, this ventriloquising of the dead, a form of prosopopoeia, was a common strategy in First World War poetry – most famously in John McCrae's 'In Flanders Fields' – used most often to lend authority to the poet's position in relation to the war. McCrae's dead urge the reader:

> Take up our quarrel with the foe:
> To you from failing hands we throw
>   The torch; be yours to hold it high.
>   If ye break faith with us who die
> We shall not sleep, though poppies grow
>   In Flanders fields.[28]

The allusion to Newbolt's 'Vitaï Lampada' (whose title means 'Torch of Life')[29] places the dead on the side of those who believed in the continued prosecution of the war and, rather cruelly, attempts to convince those mourning a soldier's death that to hold an alternative view would be to 'break faith' with their loved one and prevent him from 'sleeping' soundly.[30]

---

and other monuments' (Simon Goldhill, 'What is Ekphrasis For?', *Classical Philology*, 102.1 (2007), 1–2). See also Jas Elsner, 'Introduction: The Genres of Ekphrasis', *The Verbal and the Visual: Cultures of Ekphrasis in Antiquity*, ed. Jas Elsner, special edition of *Ramus*, 31.1–2 (2002), 9–13.

[28] John McCrae, 'In Flanders Fields' in Hibberd and Onions (eds), *Winter of the World*, 56.

[29] 'This they all with a joyful mind / Bear through life like a torch in flame, / And falling fling to the host behind – / "Play up! play up! and play the game!"' (Newbolt, *Collected Poems*, 133).

[30] For an attack on this poem, see Fussell, *Great War*, 248–50: 'words like *vicious* and *stupid* would not seem to go too far' (ibid., 250).

Making the dead say this, rather than saying it himself, lends the poet's view a spurious authority and excuses him from the need to present an argument.[31]

Dunn takes this inherently conservative tradition and makes very different use of it. In 'Portrait Photograph, 1915', the dead man speaks from a photograph, which occasions perhaps the only instance where a soldier ponders from beyond the grave the meaning of being photographed, and this changes everything. In this new context, prosopopoeia becomes the companion to ekphrasis: hearing the dead soldier speak is akin to seeing the dead soldier smile intimately (Hughes), stand patiently (Larkin) or pose for posterity (Dunn).[32] This individualises the soldier, just as having his photograph taken has done. He describes the experience as a rare moment of dignity – notwithstanding the fact that he struck his pose only when it was his 'turn in the queue'.[33] He ascribes that feeling of worth not to the attention momentarily given to him as a man, or to the resulting image in itself, but to his sense of the ways that the portrait will signify for others in future years. Initially, he tells us, he imagined the effect of the photo 'in the eyes of descendants' – at this point he may still have been imagining that he would survive the war and be remembered by subsequent generations as one who did his duty – but then he tells us he had a sense,

> Of my own face in a frame on a small table
> Over which her eyes would go, and my sons',
> And that I would persist

From the grave, he now remembers having imagined his future death in action, a thought which prompted him to imagine the *punctum* effect that the portrait would then have. The grammatical shift evident in those *would*s suggests simultaneously the subjunctive (this *may* come to pass) and the future continuous (this *will* be so).

Implicitly, that imagined *punctum* is set alongside, and indeed illustrates, the *punctum* effect which the photograph has had on the poet (who speaks

---

[31] See also the poetic inscription on Canterbury's Buttermarket memorial (discussed in Chapter 4), where the dead urge the reader: 'Live thou for England / We for England died'.

[32] These two rhetorical forms are closely connected. Valentine Cunningham suggests that ekphrasis recalls prosopopoeia by 'putting a face on, granting presence, the presence of the made object, where there was none'; in this, it 'grants a demonstration of literature's persistent resurrectionist desires – the craving to have the past return livingly, to live again, to speak again … out of the silence of the historical and textual past come these voices, heard again, voices granted to the silent, voiceless object, in the act of *ek-phrasis*, literally a speaking-out, an audible *speaking-out* now in the present text, a speaking made *out of* the silence of the past' (Cunningham, 'Why Ekphrasis?' *Classical Philology*, 102.1 (2007), 63–4).

[33] Dunn, *Barbarians*, 35.

only through the soldier). There is an extraordinary circularity here: the photograph has so moved the poet that he is prompted to voice the dead soldier, who in turn imagines the way the photograph will move his loved ones and, so, the poet.[34]

The source of the *punctum* – which has moved the poet and, though we cannot see the photo, moves us in turn – is the same contrast between the unageing face and the ageing surface of the print which we saw in Hughes's poem:

> I had a sense …
> That I would persist, in day and night,
> Fading a little as they say they do.

The ageing of the print emphasises the relationship between *nowness* and *pastness*, juxtaposing youth with death. What makes this doubly moving is that the dead soldier, who has shown sophisticated understanding in imagining the effects of the photograph, adopts in the final line the naive voice of that self whose poverty makes having his photograph taken so meaningful. He knows so little of photography that he can only pass on hearsay about the way photographic images fade: that last line is in the present tense, taking us back to Anderson's Photographic Arcade and Salon in 1915.

Jane Hedley suggests that 'To attribute speech to the work of art or someone depicted within it is the most radical move an ekphrastic poet can make: a generous gift or a more or less hostile takeover, depending on the spirit in which it is used'.[35] From Dunn it is certainly 'a generous gift', the more so in that it acknowledges, in the shifts of tone and tense he gives to the dead soldier, the poignant ironies involved in giving him speech. Here again, that it is a photograph at the heart of the ekphrasis is crucial. Speech can, of course, be given to a character in a painting too; Bergmann Loizeaux writes movingly about Adrienne Rich's prosopopoeia of the dead child Effie, figured in her father's painting.[36] But Bergmann Loizeaux sees Rich as working outside the 'male' museum tradition by allowing Effie to question her own representation, her being fixed in amber in the memorial picture. Dunn's soldier, by contrast, can affirm the medium by which he is

---

[34] The title invites us to assume that an actual photograph has prompted the poem.
[35] Jane Hedley, 'Introduction: The Subject of Ekphrasis', *In the Frame*, ed. Hedley, Halpern and Spiegelman, 32. On ekphrastic prosopopeia, see also Bergmann Loizeaux, *Twentieth-Century Poetry*, 23–4. It is one of six 'tropes or practices' which Bergmann Loizeaux identifies in poetic ekphrasis.
[36] Elizabeth Bergmann Loizeaux, 'Women Looking: The Feminist Ekphrasis of Marianne Moore and Adrienne Rich', *In the Frame*, ed. Hedley, Halpern and Spiegelman, 136–9.

represented since it grants him a place in history, and thus in itself allows him to speak.

By convention, dead soldiers speak in the first person plural ('We are the dead' etc.); Dunn's soldier begins in this way ('We too have our place') but quickly abandons it for the singular. It is photography, and not the more advanced technology of the newsreel, which confers this individuality upon him:

> We too have our place, who were not photographed
> So much and then only in multitudes
> Rising from holes in the ground to fall into smoke
> Or is it newsreel beyond newsreel

The technologically more sophisticated art of film is here seen to fail beside the specificity and materiality of the photograph. Dunn is the only poet of those discussed here to set photography in opposition to the moving image and this serves to emphasise photography's unique effect as the moving image lacks the very thing that creates the *punctum*, the impossible capturing and freezing of a moment. 'Newsreel beyond newsreel' – these spool into anonymity, swallowing up the individual like the smoke of No Man's Land. But the photograph can sit on a table carrying a dead man's image into the heart of his family.

The photograph, then, lends itself to the poet of the twentieth century, as the Grecian urn lent itself to Keats. It is singular and material; it is familiar to all as a medium and as a form of technology; and it relays images of humanity on which the poet, and alongside him the reader, can dwell. At the same time, for the poet wanting to find a new way of addressing the First World War, the photograph inherently creates a distance which can be manipulated ironically, or which can allow the sorts of interrogation we have discussed. Thus Hughes can both identify with the men depicted, and see and reveal the power of the captured image to help us to understand our own mortality: 'Here see a man's photograph … see fall war's worst/ Thinkable flash and rending'. Both involvement and distance are possible. For Larkin, the less personal image allows a questioning exploration of the nostalgia evoked by a world which seems more innocent than our own. Larkin evades the lure of that nostalgia, but draws us with him into the photograph, ignoring its limits and building a world not actually depicted there. Hughes keeps more strictly to the specifics of the photograph but blurs the edges between the depictions of natural reality and what still remains of that (lines 11–12). Rather than taking us into the photograph, he dissolves its edges and makes it continuous with what still exists.

Those imagined extended worlds don't interest Dunn, who leaps over the distance inherent in the photograph and boldly enters the mind of the soldier shown there, and, in the most powerful form of 'out-speaking', prosopopoeia, gives the dead man a voice. Dunn perhaps benefits from the years of poetic development which separate him first from Hughes's poem and then from Larkin's. The voice of the poem moves freely between hesitant inarticulacy and a knowing awareness of how the speaker's own history will be mediated through time and by technology; he is allowed this very human hesitancy whilst still being granted by the poet the power of his own voice.

It would be wrong, however, to see the photograph, or ekphrasis itself, as a mere device for the post-war poet engaging with an overwritten but also over-simplified cataclysm. In this respect, the poets and poems we consider are in sharp distinction to what some have seen as a trend driven by the institutions of art and academia. The post-war 'boom' in ekphrastic poetry was, according to Hedley, partly led by American 'university writing programs where, from the 1950s onward, would-be poets increasingly went to learn their craft'; here 'ekphrasis became a standard writing exercise' and 'during the 1980s and 1990s museums themselves contributed to the boom in ekphrastic writing by commissioning anthologies from poets with established reputations.'[37] We can see the shadow of the writing exercise in Glyn Maxwell's 'My Grandfather at the Pool', which, like Hughes's poem, contemplates a family photograph, here of his grandfather and four friends about to dive into the water at a swimming baths. Just as Hughes's father (an absent presence in the photograph Hughes writes about) survived the war when his six friends did not, Maxwell's grandfather was the only one of the group pictured to live through the war. Coincidentally he is the only one of the five photographed not to be looking directly at the camera. These are great circumstances for a poem; and Maxwell is not shy of printing the very photograph on the front cover of his collection *The Breakage*.[38] But circumstances are not themselves sufficient for a good poem. Perhaps 'My Grandfather at the Pool' suffers by comparison with the linguistic intensity and complex thought and feeling of 'Six Young Men'; but suffer it does. Maxwell pulls too far back from the feeling engendered by the image, and the carefully laconic couplets withdraw us even further. It is clear what the poet is doing poetically, catching the not-knowingness of

---

[37] Hedley, 'Introduction', 28.
[38] Glyn Maxwell, *The Breakage* (London: Faber & Faber), 1998.

the image, its conceptual innocence, but he is over-careful, and the poem strikes coldly. The ekphrastic poem has its dangers.

The writing classroom and the museum could not be further from the impetus that drives the poems of Hughes, Larkin and Dunn considered here. If the First World War has been widely seen as the rupture which led to a modern consciousness different from that which existed before it, the photographs catching men at that moment of change are uniquely rich in meaning for poets finding a voice for the later twentieth century. The recreation of the photograph in the poem becomes also a re-reading of it, an extension of it and even a voice for it. But the ekphrasis also allows the poet to bring the reader with him in a re-viewing of the image thus created in the poem. We see, and in Dunn's case hear, alongside the poet, and negotiate the multiple meanings that both image and poem generate. In its most potent form, this can bring before us those who have died long years before; it can even allow them to speak, and we can hear them. In these poems of Hughes, Larkin and Dunn, it does this not deceptively but in a way that forces the reader/viewer/listener to understand – '*This will be* and *this has been*'.

Peter Barry avers: 'ekphrastic poetry seems to embody an acknowledgement of the unbridgeable hermeneutic gap between poetry and the real... Writing a poem about (say) a photograph seems to involve tacitly accepting that poetry can only deal with *representations* of reality, never reality itself'.[39] However, quite the opposite is the case in these poems, since the photographs they describe, and the verbal representations they give of those photographs, both refer to the real world. For all the philosophical complications inherent in viewing the photograph as capturing reality, it stands in relation to a particular historical actuality as the painting or sculpture does not. As Barthes points out:

> the photograph is literally an emanation of the referent. From a real body, which was there, proceed radiations which ultimately touch me, who am here; the duration of the transmission is insignificant; the photograph of the missing being, as Sontag says, will touch me like the delayed rays of a star. A sort of umbilical cord links the body of the photographed thing to my gaze: light, though impalpable, is here a carnal medium, a skin I share with anyone who has been photographed.[40]

These poems are not post-structuralist or post-modernist in intent – they affirm rather than question the ability of the poem to represent reality.

---

[39] Barry, 'Contemporary Poetry and Ekphrasis', 157.
[40] Barthes, *Camera Lucida*, 80–1.

Far from taking us back into the museum, with its implications of the deadness of the art object, these poems 'shoulder' us into bodies like our own, whose very deadness is what brings them to life.

Yet these poems are not *simply* realist; if they were, they would not employ the layers of meaning and seeing which ekphrasis allows, indeed insists upon. The use of a photograph at the heart of the ekphrasis is what allows both the referential dimension in them, and the interrogation of meaning generated by the act of using a verbal medium to recreate a visual representation. As Barry himself goes on to say, 'The ekphrastic object is the intermediary [between poetry and the real], whose very presence is a reminder of the gulf between the two sides'.[41] Barthes has shown that we see the truth about ourselves not by seeing the image as a simple reflection but by means of that in the image, the *punctum*, which pierces us. This is the strength, ultimately, of these ekphrastic poems, that the photographs depicted there cannot actually be *seen*. For us, they exist only in the mind's eye. It is no surprise that Barthes, who reproduces many photographs in *Camera Lucida* to illustrate his argument, does not reproduce the one at the heart of what is essentially a work of mourning, the photograph of his mother in the Winter Garden: 'I cannot reproduce the Winter Garden Photograph. It exists only for me. For you, it would be nothing but an indifferent picture, one of the thousand manifestations of the "ordinary"… but in it, for you, no wound.'[42] Our three poets recreate the photograph through language just as Barthes does. In this they make us, paradoxically, more truly aware of the 'contradictory permanent horrors' involved in remembering those alive-but-dead faces. In these poems there is, for all of us, a wound.

---

[41] Barry, 'Contemporary Poetry and Ekphrasis', 157.
[42] Barthes, *Camera Lucida*, 73.

CHAPTER 7

Dulce et Decorum Est

In the middle of the Bois-l'Évêque, close to the village of Ors, one finds an extraordinary structure: *La Maison Forestière Wilfred Owen*, a 2011 work by Simon Patterson. The artist's design has transformed the small forester's house, in which Owen spent the last four nights of his life, into a space where his writing is carved, etched, projected, animated and spoken. The red-brick exterior has been rendered and painted white; the windows are shuttered; the tiled roof has been removed and its corrugated replacement is lifted at the back, suggesting an open book that has been laid print-side down.[1] At the back of the house, there is a circular garden with curved benches forming a kind of miniature amphitheatre.[2] Along one side of this space, a curving ramp with high walls on either side leads down to the cellar where Owen wrote his final letter to his mother on Thursday, 31 October 1918 (three nights before the engagement in which he was killed). Sentences from that letter are sunk into the left-hand wall of the ramp. The cellar itself is unaltered and unadorned. Worn and pitted bricks form the low, arched ceiling and the ground underfoot. A tiny, unglazed window lets in some light from the road. One stands in the gloom, listening to a recording of the final letter in two languages.

The interior of the house has been emptied to create a single white space – there are no dividing walls, floors or stairs – and the internal walls are clad in translucent glass sheets onto which has been etched a facsimile of one of Owen's drafts of the poem 'Dulce et Decorum Est'.[3] The only

---

[1] This is Patterson's own description, in an interview for a BBC Radio 4 documentary, *Bleached Bone and Living Wood*, aired 10 November 2011, to mark the opening of *La Maison Forestière*. He was interviewed by Christine Finn. Programme available at: www.bbc.co.uk/programmes/b016x2jy. See also Raymond Balau, 'Bleached Bone', *La Maison Forestière Wilfred Owen: Une Œuvre de Simon Patterson* (Lille: artconnexion, 2011), 15.

[2] In an interview, Patterson said that this space was inspired by the Odeon in Athens and the amphitheatre at Epidaurus; Simon Patterson, 'Conversation' [with Amanda Crabtree and Bruno Dupont], *La Maison Forestière Wilfred Owen: Une Œuvre de Simon Patterson*, 24.

[3] Four drafts survive. The one chosen here is undated, but seems likely to be the last. The facsimile was provided by the British Library.

light comes from the opalescent eave-windows created on the south side by the lifted roof. In this space, visitors stand or sit (there are two small benches) while Owen's poems and 'fragments' are successively projected onto the four walls. Two voices, one English, the other French, speak the poems.[4] The fragments – incomplete or not fully revised pieces – appear in silence. The synchronised projections and recordings are on a loop which lasts for one hour. In this closing chapter we want to explore this unique attempt to commemorate a soldier killed in the First World War, one who was also a poet, and to use it as a lens through which to look at Owen's poetic explorations of the representing and remembering of the dead.

La Maison Forestière was commissioned in 2004 by the *mairie* of Ors, led by the mayor, Jacky Duminy, who was motivated by the number of literary pilgrims to the house and the various nearby sites relating to Owen's last days, which had alerted him to Owen's significance.[5] M. Duminy was the original driving force in this project; as soon as he realised that Wilfred Owen, an important English poet, was buried in the Ors village cemetery, he saw that a properly considered response was required from the community. At this point, Lille-based consultancy artconnexion was enlisted as a mediating agency, through whom Simon Patterson was appointed as the artist. Patterson has commented that the project's sponsors 'were very specific what they didn't want … They didn't want a memorial, they didn't want a museum, they didn't want a … statue or something conventional that way, or something too didactic.'[6] Perhaps it took non-English enthusiasts, free from the heavy freight of British cultural memory, to make these stipulations. In M. Duminy's recent words, 'to transform the *Maison Forestière* into a contemporary work of art would signify that Owen's poetry was still relevant, and had lost none of its authenticity'.[7]

This commission took place in the wider context of Owen-memorialising. Of the millions of soldiers killed in the First World War, Owen was already one of the most commemorated. Physical memorials to him include a sculpture in the grounds of Shrewsbury Abbey; a stained glass window in

---

[4] The voices are those of actors Kenneth Branagh and Philippe Capelle, respectively. Several, though not all, poems are read in both languages. Branagh's recording of the poems and the letter existed already; Capelle's recordings were made specifically for *La Maison Forestière* (see Patterson, 'Conversation').

[5] These include the Sambre-Oise canal where Owen was killed, the military cemetery at Ors containing (among others) the graves of soldiers killed in the same action, and the Ors communal cemetery, at the back of which lies another group of soldiers' graves, including Owen's.

[6] *Bleached Bone and Living Wood.*

[7] In an email exchange with Sally Minogue, 21 September 2016, trans. Damian Grant.

Birkenhead Central Library; a stone bench in Oswestry; several plaques in England to mark places where he lived, wrote and trained; further plaques in France in the places where he fought; a plinth at Gailly where he recuperated from an injury. He is one of sixteen First World War poets whose name is engraved on a memorial stone in Poets' Corner, Westminster Abbey.[8] These memorials constitute one element of an evolving cultural memory of Owen. That process began with Sassoon's brief Introduction to *Poems* (1920), and developed in a hagiographic 'Memoir' included in *The Poems of Wilfred Owen* (1931) by its editor, Edmund Blunden. A series of publications in the 1960s led to his iconic status – and the subsequent creation of all the sculptures, plaques and markers mentioned. Dennis Welland published the first book-length critical study in 1960; in 1962 Benjamin Britten's *War Requiem*, which included nine Owen poems and fragments, was performed at the consecration of Coventry Cathedral. Public enthusiasm for this work prompted Chatto & Windus to commission a new, expanded edition of the poems, edited by Cecil Day Lewis and published in 1963.[9] Owen's brother Harold published his memoir *Journey from Obscurity* in three parts between 1963 and 1965 and then co-edited the *Collected Letters*, which appeared in 1967. Harold's censorship was powerful in both. The combined apparatus provided by Welland, Britten, Day Lewis, Harold Owen and others created in Owen a powerful and ubiquitous figure on the curriculum of British schools, where his work was used selectively to educate children about the horrors of war.

We noted in our Introduction Mark Rawlinson's complaint that this process of cultural memory formation 'threatens to reduce his poems to convergent paraphrases'.[10] Former Poet Laureate Andrew Motion notes a general problem about approaching the poetry of the First World War which applies particularly to Owen's work: 'The poems risk becoming less and less intimate *as poems*, as they are more and more widely accepted as state furniture. Their fame makes them glassy, so we slip off their surfaces when we want to penetrate their depths. What is indispensable about them can also make them seem ossified.'[11] As 'state furniture', Owen risks disappearing under as many layers of varnish as Rupert Brooke. The

---

[8] For further details of these memorials, see the website of the Wilfred Owen Association: www.wilfredowen.org.uk/memorials. In addition, several British streets are named after him, as well as a school, a pub and a beer.
[9] See 'Owen and his editors', Appendix D in Owen, *Complete Poems and Fragments*, 554.
[10] Rawlinson, 'Wilfred Owen', 114–15.
[11] Andrew Motion, 'Introduction', *First World War Poems*, ed. Andrew Motion (London: Faber & Faber, 2004), xi–xii.

Figure 7.1 'Ever Wilfred x', *La Maison Forestière Wilfred Owen* (under renovation). Photograph © Nina Carrington.

cultural politics behind his canonisation is of a different stamp, but the process is the same.

In this context, and in response to the commission, Patterson decided against any reverent presentation of Owen's image or engraved name, instead focusing our attention on the sensory experience of his writing and, simultaneously, on the space associated with Owen's presence. In fact, Owen's surname does not appear anywhere on, or inside, the work itself; nor do any of the familiar images of his face.[12] These absences sharply distinguish *La Maison Forestière* from earlier memorials. In place of 'Wilfred Owen', we have only his self-representation at the end of his final letter to his mother, now engraved: 'Ever Wilfred x' (see Figure 7.1).

As we approach *La Maison Forestière* from outside, the work reverses the usual language of the stone memorial – in place of high verticals, it offers curving lines which incorporate our movement, and when we look at its exterior, it always remains a domestic object – a house – even though a ghostly and other-worldly one. The walls down to the cellar stand reachably alongside us; for Patterson, their curve replaces the direct path: 'Why does everything have to be in a straight line? It's very masculine to have that sort

---

[12] Owen's name does appear on an adjacent marker which gives the title of the work. There are also nearby information boards, put up by bodies promoting regional tourism, headed 'Sur les pas de Wilfred Owen'.

of direct route. Also I thought a curve was a protective way of enclosing the space at the south of the building.'[13]

As we pass the sentences of Owen's last letter, inscribed in the white surface of the wall leading down to the cellar they describe, we are moved that we are reading his own words, and homely ones at that, and not a Latin proverb or a quotation from Ecclesiastes. We are moved by the disparity between the personal letter, scribbled with a blunt pencil in semi-darkness, and the white memorial lettering; we are moved by the way this reminds us of conventional memorial practice, while being something else. The sentences on the white wall recall memorial convention but, though both Patterson and the project's architect, Jean-Christophe Denise use the term 'engraved', they are in fact 'shot-blasted into the concrete'.[14] Shot-blasting is an altogether more modern, and more forceful, process than engraving; it produces letters that, on close inspection, are ragged around the edges rather than finely chiselled. Again, Patterson alludes to memorial convention but also raises questions about it (see Figure 7.2).

The sweeping curve of the wall leads us down towards the cellar, while the walls at each side of us 'rise in inverse proportion to the ramp's descent'.[15] We are not placed statically in front of an inscription; as we move along it we glimpse the sentences. We walk down alongside Owen's last written words to enter the doorway through which he too passed. There is something dynamic here which is not achieved by a monument. We go down to the cellar as if to a tomb, but emerge into poetry.[16]

It is the cellar which, initially, gives meaning to this place and this building, but Patterson then turns us away from that meaning to concentrate solely on the poetry, so that when we move up from the cellar and into the house, Owen's lines are placed so centrally and powerfully that they seem more important than his individual death. Eschewing any sentimentalisation or even representation of the individual, it locks us up with, and thus locks us into, the poetry. And this brings us into close contact with one of Owen's own abiding poetic concerns: how to represent and remember the dead. This is a new way of leading us into questions of

---

[13] Patterson also notes that he had already thought of a ramp; amongst other considerations, it would give disabled access (Patterson, 'Conversation', 24).
[14] *Bleached Bone and Living Wood.* Patterson's use of pre-stressed concrete also necessitated shot-blasting as this material, unlike stone, could not be chiselled without falling apart (Patterson, in conversation with the authors, 6 September 2016).
[15] Patterson, 'Conversation', 24.
[16] Patterson notes that 'the shape of the ramp may have been influenced by the so-called tomb of Agamemnon at Mycaenae' (ibid.).

Figure 7.2 Shot-blasted letters, *La Maison Forestière Wilfred Owen* (under renovation). Photograph © Nina Carrington.

remembrance, dependent on our participation and response, unlike the standard monolithic monument or memorial.

War memorials such as those at Ypres and Thiepval offer panels of names, but show nothing of the experience; *La Maison Forestière* omits the full name but has the experience etched onto its panels in the form of Owen's handwriting. We are reminded of the scribbling man, crossing out, adding in, seeking ways to express and represent. Superimposed onto this surface, the projected, animated text of each poem or fragment emerges and fades, transient and insubstantial (see Figure 7.3).[17]

La Maison Forestière is also unlike a memorial in the way it encourages visitors to move: at Thiepval, we stand still and then pass slowly along panels of names; inside *La Maison* we turn our head and our body around in the space, constantly moving, searching for the whereabouts of the next projected poem or fragment. In these features, and in its general modesty, *La Maison Forestière* refuses to monumentalise and therefore provides a notable addition to the ways in which the dead of the First World War are remembered.

[17] Patterson experiments with different kinds of fade, such as the imitation of a 'drawing down of blinds' at the end of 'Anthem for Doomed Youth', and the D. W. Griffith-influenced opening/closing eye, as for 'Exposure' (ibid., 23).

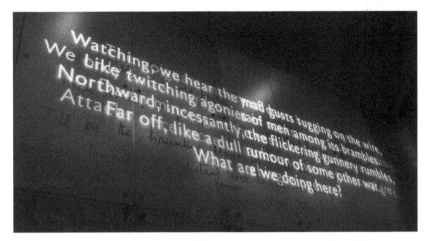

Figure 7.3 Transitioning stanzas of 'Exposure', over etched facsimile of 'Dulce et Decorum Est', *La Maison Forestière Wilfred Owen*.
Photograph © Nina Carrington.

However, that said, *La Maison Forestière* is not simply an *anti*-memorial. It does not refuse or reject the desire to commemorate. Indeed Patterson has referred to it as 'a commemoration of someone's work' and expressed his desire 'to create one small chapel-like space'.[18] Certainly, the many visitors who have left comments in the visitors' book clearly experience it in the context of remembrance.[19] The very ambiguity of the work's relationship to memorials is part of its broader identity as a *meta*-memorial, foregrounding the ways it reflects on its own form, and so on the business of commemoration. Its interior literally reflects itself (see Figure 7.4).

This glass surface recalls the polished black granite of the Vietnam Veterans Memorial (discussed in Chapter 4), but here the reflection includes, alongside the visitor's image, the opposite wall of *La Maison*, foregrounding the work's own radical form, drawing our attention to all the ways in which it challenges memorial conventions.

This self-reflexive quality, involving an ambivalent stance in relation to memorial, has its source in Owen's work. Jahan Ramazani has characterised Owen's poetry as 'anti-elegiac' – he reminds us that Owen declared in his draft Preface that 'these elegies are to this generation in no

---

[18] Patterson, conversation with the authors, 6 September 2016.
[19] Many refer to it as a 'memorial', though one calls it a 'poetry-house in the forest' – which seems more accurate to us.

Figure 7.4 Reflective interior, *La Maison Forestière Wilfred Owen*.
Photograph © Nina Carrington.

sense consolatory' – and this category is certainly illuminating, not least in foregrounding the extent to which Owen's poems are *some sort* of elegy (a fact often overlooked).[20] However, not all of Owen is so resolutely anti-elegiac. Ramazani concedes that elements of consolation remain in 'Anthem for Doomed Youth', but his suggestion is that such false notes are part of a process of development which reaches its apotheosis in the out-and-out anti-elegy of 'Futility', a poem which angrily rejects the conventions of pastoral elegy. Ramazani's reading of 'Futility' is very convincing but, in trying to fit 'Asleep' and 'Mental Cases' into this schema, he tends to elide counter-voices and iron out the ambiguities in those poems. For example, he asserts that, in the second half of 'Asleep', Owen rejects the notion of a heavenly afterlife in favour of the stark reality of the body's decomposition.[21] In fact, the 'Whether ... Or whether' construction in which Owen sets out

---

[20] See Ramazani, *Poetry of Mourning*, 69, 73–5. Dominic Hibberd, too, has argued that Owen developed the elegiac tradition 'in a way that was both radical and comfortless' (Hibberd, *Wilfred Owen: A New Biography* (London: Weidenfeld & Nicolson, 2002), 291), while Douglas Kerr suggests that he 'is in grim, covert, antagonistic dialogue with the genre' (Kerr, *Wilfred Owen's Voices: Language and Community* (Oxford: Oxford University Press, 1993), 290).

[21] Ramazani, *Poetry of Mourning*, 75–6.

these two alternatives is not so decisive: he does not choose between them, but concludes: 'Who knows?'[22] This ambivalence is inherent in the poem's ambiguous title: the reader may initially assume that 'Asleep' is an elegiac euphemism for 'Dead', but it becomes apparent that the soldier is in fact sleeping when he is killed. The effect is anti-elegiac in that the title thus draws our attention to the brutal difference between the two states and seems to reject elegy's habit of conflating them, but the poem also reasserts an elegiac note: there is consolation in the fact that the soldier is killed 'in the happy no-time of his sleeping'. Owen also reasserts the notion that death is a kind of sleep: after he is shot, the soldier's 'sleepy arms once more fell slack', as if returning to the former state.[23]

Just as *La Maison Forestière* reflects upon memorial conventions, so Owen's poetry reflects upon elegiac conventions rather than simply rejecting them. It is not so much anti-elegy as meta-elegy – it does not simply speak honestly of the dead, but also speaks insistently about *how* to speak of them. And as *La Maison Forestière* shows strong awareness of the monumental conventions to which it alludes and from which it departs, so the poems show a strong awareness of the elegiac conventions they deploy, test and resist. This reflexivity is evident in the self-elegy 'With an Identity Disc'. In the octave of this Shakespearean sonnet, the poet, considering how he wishes to be commemorated, rejects two hallowed forms of memorial: the engraving of his name 'High in the heart of London' (an earlier draft makes clear that he has in mind Poets' Corner at Westminster Abbey) and, also, the romantically shaded marker of Keats's grave in Rome.[24] Instead, he chooses the identity disc which will be returned to his family following his death.

> But let my death be memoried on this disc.
> Wear it, sweet friend. Inscribe no date nor deed.
> But let thy heart-beat kiss it night and day,
> Until the name grow vague and wear away.[25]

The rejections of the octave are anti-elegiac, but the mournful idea to which they lead cannot be so characterised. There is consolation for the

---

[22] 'Asleep' in Owen, *Complete Poems and Fragments*, 152.
[23] Owen expressed a similar ambivalence, being torn between the religious and the scientific notions of death, in the fragment beginning 'Science has looked, and sees no life but this', written in 1912 (ibid., 35).
[24] The description of Keats's grave recalls also Rupert Brooke's grave on Skyros. Stallworthy records that Owen kept a magazine photograph of Brooke's grave in his copy of *1914 & Other Poems* (Jon Stallworthy, *Wilfred Owen*, (London: Pimlico, 2013), 140n).
[25] 'With an Identity Disc' in Owen, *Complete Poems and Fragments*, 96.

'sweet friend' in that it is his love which the poet values rather than literary recognition, that a hidden memorial known only to himself is preferable to some public 'florid screed'. There is also consolation in the final line's suggestion that grief will fade with the wearing away of the poet's name; and that it is the beating of the friend's heart which will cause the fading – that is to say, his grief will be overcome by his continuing to live. This is a moving set of ideas, strongly connected to the elegiac tradition of foretelling consolation while suffering loss. The counterpoint of octave and sestet is part of the poem's larger project, to meditate upon forms of remembrance: the poet rejects first one, then another, before devising something more fitting to the times.[26]

That Owen was writing *about* elegy (rather than simply writing elegy) is underlined by the poem's history. Stallworthy identifies a page of 'preliminary rough working' and six further drafts, three of which are 'heavily corrected'.[27] Owen enclosed a fair copy in a letter to his brother Colin on 24 March 1918 – but the letter's chief subject is his plan to become a pig farmer after the war. Although the letter is comedic in tone, Owen goes into some detail, suggesting that pig-farming would be a useful way to subsidise his poetry-writing: 'I should like to take a cottage or orchard in Kent Surrey or Sussex, and give my afternoons to the care of pigs. The hired labour would be very cheap, 2 boys could tend 50 pigs. And it would be the abruptest possible change from my morning's work.'[28] This practical imagining of a future life strongly suggests that the sonnet is not an expression of a sense of impending death. It is not a prophecy but an exercise in poetic craft by a poet who envisages more years of poetry-writing.[29]

Similarly, 'Anthem for Doomed Youth', widely read in schools as a powerful statement about the horrors of war is, in fact, primarily a

---

[26] When he wrote 'With an Identity Disc', Owen could not of course have imagined that, a century later, his name would indeed be engraved in Poets' Corner, and that his quiet grave, shaded by a hedge at the back of the communal cemetery in Ors, would, like Keats's, be a site of literary pilgrimage.

[27] Owen, *Complete Poems and Fragments*, 241.

[28] Wilfred Owen, *Collected Letters*, ed. Harold Owen and John Bell (London: Oxford University Press, 1967), 446. Owen may have been influenced here by the initiation at Craiglockhart by his own doctor, Dr Brock, of a small poultry farm, part of the general intent to instigate useful, practical, productive work (Stallworthy, *Wilfred Owen*, 193).

[29] Owen was writing from a Casualty Clearing Station, where he had been sent after suffering concussion. In case Colin should think his pig-farm plan a sign of madness, he offers the poem as evidence that, if not completely sane, his 'old form of madness has in no way changed'. After the

meta-elegy. Rather than commemorating, Owen wonders about the nature of commemoration. Following the same pattern as 'With an Identity Disc', the octave is anti-elegiac, the sestet consolatory (as Ramazani notes), but each part offers an answer to the question in its opening line about how to commemorate the dead: 'What passing bells for these who die as cattle?', and 'What candles may be held to speed them all?'[30] Owen's answers to the first question are bitterly ironic, his answers to the second more conventionally elegiac, but both parts reflect on how to mourn. 'Spring Offensive', also, ends with a meta-elegiac thought about those who have just been killed: while 'Some say God caught them even before they fell', the survivors of the attack 'speak not … of comrades that went under'.[31] The reader is left to wonder about the relative merits of these two responses while being aware that the poem itself does not choose. Again, Owen speaks not of the dead but of the difficulty of speaking honestly about them.

While it is true that Owen wrote in his draft Preface that 'these elegies are to this generation in no way consolatory', he added in the following sentence: 'They may be to the next.' His poems take issue with consolation in its standard poetic forms. But that very engagement with conventional forms of remembering the dead – coupled with the power and sensitivity of his poetic attention on the dying, the dead and those who have had to witness the death of others and imagine their own deaths – force us as readers to pay the same careful attention to his representation. That we are still reading these poems means that some trace of the momentous event of the First World War continues beyond the span of communicative memory. This may be the one consolation Owen could imagine his poems carrying.

In keeping with the self-reflective aspect of Owen's poems, *La Maison Forestière* resists the simplifying force of our cultural memory of Owen. The decision to offer a broad selection of poems and fragments is crucial: the handful of poems which will be familiar to most visitors appears in the midst of an extensive cycle that runs on an hour-long loop. Fifteen complete poems appear on the longer, north and south walls, all in English and eight in French translation, accompanied by an actor's reading. These are interspersed with ten fragments which appear on the shorter, east

---

poem, he adds: 'This is private. I stickle that a sonnet must contain at least 3 clever turns to be good. This has only two' (Owen, *Collected Letters*, 446).

[30] 'Anthem for Doomed Youth' in Owen, *Complete Poems and Fragments*, 99.
[31] 'Spring Offensive' in ibid., 193.

and west gable walls – in English only and in silence.³² A distinction is made, then, between poems and fragments, but the way they interweave recalls the poet's processes and overrides the absolute separation imposed by editorial policy in *The Complete Poems and Fragments*. The unfamiliar fragments appear for just long enough to be read – provided the visitor spots them as soon as they appear and remains focused in the reading of them. As our eyes near the end of a fragment, negotiating its various gaps and confusions, the words start to fade and soon, perhaps before we have finished reading, they are gone. Powerful but rarely seen lines of poetry appear and then vanish, their bracketed gaps marking a blank where Owen had not yet found the right words to complete a line. The visitor thereby gathers a broader sense of Owen's poetic work, the graft behind the more familiar lines. At the same time, some 'big' Owen poems are placed centrally; while fragments punctuate the early and late sections of the hour-long loop, there is a twenty-four-minute central section in which only finished poems appear, some projected and read only in English (for example, 'Mental Cases', 'The Parable of the Old Man and the Young' and 'The Show'), some in both English and French (for example, 'Exposure', 'Spring Offensive' and 'Dulce et Decorum Est').

The full sequence begins with lines from the fragment '[Full springs of thought]', written in 1911, and ends, aptly, with the most pregnant fragment of all, the prose Preface, written probably in May 1918, when Owen was stationed at Ripon prior to being sent back to France. There he rented an attic room in a cottage near to the military camp, escaping to it every evening to work on his poems. With encouragement from the literary grandee Robert Ross (whom he met via Sassoon), he began to prepare a collection for publication and in the process produced the Preface which, as Stallworthy says, 'he left not as a finished and final statement but as a single rough draft'.³³ It is often quoted as if it clearly expresses profound truths; two of its famous sentences are engraved around the names of the sixteen First World War poets commemorated on a stone in Poets' Corner, Westminster Abbey: 'My subject is War, and the pity of War. The poetry is in the Pity'.³⁴ Patterson too lends it significance by placing it at the end but, as the sequence is on a loop, it is also amidst the poems, appearing as one of several fragments on the gable walls. Thus, it appears in interplay

---

³² Patterson comments: 'The breakthrough for me was deciding to project the poetry fragments without sound to create a breathing space', (Patterson, 'Conversation', 23).
³³ Stallworthy, *Wilfred Owen*, 266.
³⁴ 'Preface' in Owen, *Complete Poems and Fragments*, 535.

with the fragments and poems we have just experienced, placed in dialogue with Owen's work rather than presented as a finished statement. As was the artist's intention in using the fragments, this one again reminds us of 'the poet's potential – of what might have happened'.[35]

In *La Maison Forestière*, then, Owen's oeuvre is reopened, our mental image of him complicated and refreshed. One of the significant ways in which Patterson does this is by giving Owen a voice. If, on the ramp leading to the cellar, you read the engraved lines from his last letter out loud, you are surprised by an extraordinary, resonant echo in the high-walled space of the ramp. The visitor's own voice becomes part of the work and, in a way, part of Owen's voice – we inhabit him. In the poetic space of the house itself, there are no other sound effects: no music or noise of rifles firing or shells exploding, just the sound of spoken words accompanying the projected text. There is an emanation of Owen, but it is fragile, as the projected words are fragile, emerging on the inner glass walls then fading almost before we can grasp them. At the same time there is a powerful feeling of words expanding outwards – a great swelling of poetry in a constricted space, an expansion of the imagination – and the sense that the upraised roof is being lifted by the huge charge of the poetry.

The combination of evanescence and intensity is accentuated by the fact that Patterson gives Owen not one but two voices, one French and one English. This bilingual element is more than simply practical. Each actor's intonation and way of expressing is different from the other, in part because of the different nature of each language.[36] The hearer is placed in relation both to her own language and another's. For English-speakers, the French defamiliarises the poems and this promotes a sense of their plurality of meaning. This determinedly bilingual and bi-artistic project – proposed and sponsored by French enthusiasts who commissioned an English artist – reflects the complicated cultural geography of Owen as poet, nurtured and sustained by an English poetic tradition which was hurled into otherness by his time at the Western Front. Wartime France became, for him and others, the accidental site of extremities of experience which had a profound effect on his work and on the formation of the poetic voice we hear resounding in *La Maison Forestière*.

---

[35] Patterson, conversation with the authors, 6 September 2016.
[36] Patterson wanted a French voice distinctively different from Branagh's, and the two styles of reading are also different (ibid.).

The importance of voice to the artwork has its foundation in Owen's own understanding of the power of the poet's voice, an article of faith developed long before the war, through his immersion in Romantic poetry. In 'On My Songs', written in 1913, he describes how, when the words of other poets which once brought comfort now fail to succour him, so he must 'voice mine own weird reveries' and concludes that, as other poets once expressed his own 'soul's cry', *his* poetic voice 'may haply lend thee ease'.[37] By 1917, he was much struck by passages in Elizabeth Barrett Browning's *Aurora Leigh* (1856) about the role and voice of the poet, as he reconsidered his relationship to the Romantic tropes which had influenced him so far.[38]

Owen's faith in the power of the poet's voice never fades; his mission to be a poet is founded on it and he reiterates that mission constantly in his letters. But in his early, pre-war sense of himself the poet's voice is simply that: it has little to say. In uniform, he came to see himself as a poet who could give voice to the experience of common soldiers who were themselves unable or unwilling use their voices. As a result, his poetry is able to take a new turn, under the influence of both a new mission and a new set of experiences. Owen's considering his role as a poet now becomes bound up in reflecting on the ways in which he might speak of the unspeakable things he has seen. Time and again in his letters he questions the manner in which the horrific things he has experienced should, or even could, be represented, often comparing poetry favourably with other possible modes of artistic representation as a means to convey what seems beyond expression. In one of his most powerful evocations of his experiences at the Front, he recalls in his 1917 New Year's Eve letter to his mother, written in Scarborough, how he had spent his previous New Year's Eve:

> Last year, at this time ... I lay awake in a windy tent in the middle of a vast, dreadful encampment. It seemed neither France nor England, but a kind of paddock where the beasts are kept a few days before the shambles ...
> But chiefly I thought of the very strange look on all faces in that camp; an incomprehensible look ...
> It was not despair, or terror, it was more terrible than terror, for it was a blindfold look, and without expression, like a dead rabbit's.
> It will never be painted, and no actor will ever seize it. And to describe it, I think I must go back and be with them.[39]

---

[37] Owen, *Complete Poems and Fragments*, 113.
[38] Letter to Mary Owen, 22 March 1917; Owen, *Collected Letters*, 497, and see Stallworthy, *Wilfred Owen*, 173.
[39] Letter to Susan Owen, 31 December 1917; Owen, *Collected Letters*, 520.

This is the point at which Owen links his mission to be a poet with his soldierly duty to his men. He has a duty to 'describe' because he feels that poetry can capture what other representational arts (here painting and theatre) cannot.

A few months later, it is photography to which he compares poetry as a means of representation. Working on the first draft of 'A Terre', he describes the process, in a letter to his mother, as 'retouching a "photographic representation" of an officer dying of wounds'.[40] But words remain prime as means of representation against the inadequacy of photographic representations, to which he returns, in a famous passage, about the experience of having a young soldier lie on top of him with bleeding head on his shoulder: 'Catalogue? Photograph? Can you photograph the crimson-hot iron as it cools from the smelting?'[41] The implication is that neither catalogue nor photograph will do. Underlying these scepticisms about other means of representation is the undimmed belief in the word – 'to describe it'. Crucial to this belief is that to describe it, he must once again be part of it, and speak for his men.

Owen's sense that he must speak *for* such soldiers has a paternalistic dimension which we can't ignore – and which is never present in the poetry of Rosenberg, Gurney or Jones, all in the ranks, who speak not for but *as* ordinary soldiers. In a letter to his mother, Owen puts it thus: 'I came out in order to help these boys – directly by leading them as well as an officer can; indirectly, by watching their sufferings that I may speak of them as well as a pleader can'.[42] Nonetheless, war gave him the ambition and opportunity to speak about and for the soldier who *didn't* have a public voice, and it also gave him a plenitude of voices as a poet. When he allows these various voices to chime against each other, then he produces the complex, ambiguous meta-elegies which are a distinctive dimension of his poetry, one which is elided in standard readings of his work.

In *La Maison Forestière*, the actual voicing of Owen's poems by two actors draws our attention to 'voice' in the literary sense. About seven minutes into the sequence, Philippe Capelle reads a French version of 'Anthem for Doomed Youth', followed by Kenneth Branagh's rendition of the original. This is immediately followed by two fragments: 'I know the music' and 'But I was looking at the permanent stars', both of which contain elements of the finished poem we have just heard. The first fragment contains 'slow bells'

---

[40] Letter to Susan Owen, April 1918; ibid., 545.
[41] Letter to Siegfried Sassoon, 10 October 1918; ibid., 581.
[42] 4 (or 5) October, 1918; ibid., 580.

and 'country bells', 'Bugles that sadden' and 'evening prayer'; the second has 'Bugles sang, saddening', 'The wailing of the high far-travelling shells' and, closest of all, 'The monstrous anger of our taciturn guns'.[43] These fragments are unfinished work – in both, Owen has left several gaps to be filled. Both suffer from some of the plangent vocabulary and conventional associations of Owen's earlier, archaic mode: the first has 'The warbling drawl of flutes and shepherds' reeds', 'Thrilling of throstles' and 'sainfoin-fields'; the second 'sorrowful to hear', 'Sleep mothered them' and 'The shadow of the morrow'. They are projected onto the west gable wall in silence. Moving from the *son et lumière* of the famous, fully realised poem to its mute predecessors in this way makes a particular point about 'voice': voice is only fully realised after the graft of revision, of working through. In those fragments we see that working.

Furthermore, 'But I was looking at the permanent stars' is specifically concerned with the problem of 'voice' in wartime.[44] Owen sets the voices of innocent boys, despondent adults and bugles (which are sounded by human breath) against the more powerful 'wailing' and 'cursing' of the shells and the 'monstrous anger of our taciturn guns'. In the last four lines of the fragment, Owen's voice suddenly shifts from Romantic archaisms into its later register as he connects the human voices with 'the wailing of the high far-travelling shells' and 'the monstrous anger of our taciturn guns'. Though this fragment is far removed from the fully formed 'Anthem for Doomed Youth', here we see Owen trying out ideas, expanding the metaphors that he would later trim down. The 'mouths' of the guns are 'deep cursing', issuing 'insults'. The guns, with their 'monstrous anger', 'insults' and 'mouths' replace the human voice – and would do so utterly, were it not for the poet's voice.

By the time 'The Last Laugh' appears, towards the end of the sequence, Owen's 'voice', powerfully *voiced*, is secure. Owen effectively interlaces the words of dying soldiers (with none of the awkward ventriloquism of 'The Chances') with his own mature register. The voices of the guns and shells have become crueller still, overtly mocking the human predicament: there's no weighing up or irony; the voices of dying men, appealing to God, parents or a lover, are shown to be risible, as 'the Big Gun guffawed', 'the splinters spat, and tittered', 'And the Bayonets' long teeth grinned'.[45] And yet, facing

---

[43] Owen, *Complete Poems and Fragments*, 485, 487–8. Stallworthy's notes point out the extent to which these fragments anticipate 'Anthem for Doomed Youth', which was written about a month later.

[44] Edmund Blunden later gave to this fragment the title 'Voices', in the 1931 edition of Owen's poetry which he edited.

[45] 'The Last Laugh' in Owen, *Complete Poems and Fragments*, 168. In redrafting this poem, Owen moved from the full rhymes and identical rhymes of February 1918 to para-rhymes and non-rhyming lines by March.

down those overbearing mechanical voices is the poet's voice. The last line – 'And the Gas hissed' – simultaneously expresses the overwhelming malevolence of the instruments of slaughter and – in Branagh's powerful reading – demonstrates the power of the poet to express.

On the page, this particularly bitter poem may seem devoid of any note of meta-elegy, or even anti-elegy, as human language is rendered empty. But, projected and spoken out loud in *La Maison Forestière*, as we stand in this unique white space, surrounded by the etched glass, our feet inches away from the place where, beneath, Owen's head bent over the last sheet of his last letter, we are reminded, movingly and powerfully, of the man, the muscles of his writing hand gripping the pencil, the synapses of his brain sparking as he shapes his sentences. And all this only amplifies our awareness of that sense of mission Owen felt, best exemplified in the last stanza of 'The Calls', revised in May 1918, only a few months before his final return to the Front:

> For leaning out last midnight on my sill,
> I heard the sighs of men, that have no skill
> To speak of their distress, no, nor the will!
> A voice I know. And this time I must go.[46]

* * *

In this final chapter, we close with Owen, in part because of the power of the collective cultural memory. We would also like to shift the way in which he is seen – not so much as the superlative (anti-) war poet but, rather, as a poet experimenting with language and form to answer to a unique, extreme experience. We do not forget here that he was still making his way as a poet at the time of his death, that his experiments can be tentative, his diction archaic and his sensibility over-freighted with romanticism and/or paternalism. As Owen felt his way through the complications and contradictions of speaking about and for soldiers who had been killed, Gurney, Rosenberg and Jones had, in their most powerful writing, leapt ahead to a whole different understanding, and a different voice – as we have discussed in the preceding chapters. If there is something still-conventional about Owen's voice, he remains the war poet of whose poetry readers are most aware. Fifty years on from Britten's *War Requiem*, *La Maison Forestière* provides a powerful intervention in that awareness,

---

[46] Owen, *Complete Poems and Fragments*, 162.

drawing on his status while defamiliarising his writing and, in doing so, pointing to its greater strengths, some of which have been underplayed or neglected in the narrowing process of his canonisation. To explore this, we will end by looking closely at Owen's most fetishised poem, 'Dulce et Decorum Est', and at the ways *La Maison Forestière* has revivified it, and brought it freshly to a fresh audience.

Simon Patterson's original idea for the interior of *La Maison Forestière* was for an internal blank space upon which the animations of chosen Owen texts would be projected; he subsequently decided to have one poem etched permanently on the walls, partly to ensure that there would be something to see if the projections were not in play (for example, if *La Maison* were being used for another purpose such as a poetry reading). He chose 'Dulce et Decorum Est' as the one permanent poem because it was 'the most angry' of Owen's poems, and 'probably one of the most famous'.[47] The poem also figures as one of the animated projections and readings, entering at just under thirty minutes into the hour-long running time. The centrality of this poem in Owen's work is thus doubly acknowledged and dramatised in the installation.

This likewise reflects its placing in the public imagination. However, the poem's very popularity has led to a reductive effect on our understanding both of the poem and of the rest of Owen's oeuvre, and some notable critics have criticised the poem itself in strong terms.[48] Tim Kendall, for example, has suggested that 'It meets one kind of propaganda with an equal and opposite kind', reiterating this charge by calling Owen here 'more the propagandist' than the reporter, and then attacking the whole of the fourth section of the poem for its 'slack writing'.[49] Ramazani, following Desmond Graham, sees the poem as primarily confronting the civilian reader, who, by being placed via the direct address alongside the proponents of 'the old Lie', has no opportunity of escaping that position.[50] Conversely, in schools the poem has regularly been taught as an anti-war poem in the context of Owen's 'pacifism' (even though he never was a pacifist); it is doubtful whether modern schoolchildren understand themselves to be addressed as adherents of 'the old Lie' – rather they

---

[47] Patterson, conversation with the authors, 6 September 2016.
[48] 'Dulce et Decorum Est' was probably the poem W. B. Yeats referred to as '[Owen's] worst and most famous poem', writing to Dorothy Wellesley on 21 December 1936 (*Letters on Poetry from W. B. Yeats to Dorothy Wellesley* (Oxford: Oxford University Press, 1940), 124).
[49] Kendall, 'Wilfred Owen: "Dulce et Decorum Est"', *War Poetry* blog, 28 October 2010, http://war-poets.blogspot.co.uk/2010/10/wilfred-owen-dulce-et-decorum-est.html.
[50] Ramazani, *Poetry of Mourning*, 80–2; Graham, *Truth of War*, 60.

will put themselves in Owen's position, sharing what they see simply as his contradiction of that 'Lie'.[51] Seamus Heaney raises a different issue, derived from teaching Owen's poetry in the 1960s: that of the 'immense disparity between the nit-picking criticism I was conducting on ['Dulce et Decorum Est'] and the heavy price, in terms of emotional and physical suffering, the poet paid in order to bring it into being'. Nonetheless, Heaney records, he felt it important to 'make pejorative critical remarks about the excessively vehement adjectives and nouns' in the final section of the poem, since 'I was also concerned with what was artistically good as well as what was generally true'.[52]

Heaney was better placed than most, as a poet, and one who found himself in a highly charged political situation, to understand the complexities he outlines. Yet even he makes an over-simple opposition between art and truth, with critical approaches to 'Dulce et Decorum Est' reduced to a 'nit-picking' role concerned with 'excessively vehement adjectives and nouns'. In our discussion of Owen's – we'll argue, deservedly iconic – poem, we want to look freshly at his lines, in the spirit of *La Maison Forestière*. At the same time, as in our discussions throughout this book, we will keep firmly in mind that this is a poem about how the dead are to be best remembered. If we keep that before us, there need be no false opposition between the requirements of art and the requirements of what it represents.

Lorrie Goldensohn notes acutely that 'Owen takes a good look at all the different ways to die; he lets his poems visit hospitals, listen to soldiers' nightmares, and play the whole keyboard of wartime injury, mental and physical'.[53] This she sees as part of his attentive tenderness to the sufferings that those alongside him endured in the circumstances of modern warfare, where such tenderness is all there is to replace the consolations of religion or heroism which have been blown to bits like the bodies themselves. If we see his account of the man dying (as we presume) of the effects of gas inhalation as part of this poetic project, the one thing he can do is to pay scrupulous attention to it.

What we find in the poem, then, is a creative engagement with a new and particularly horrible form of dying, and with the way this might be represented in poetry. The horrors of the gas attack are represented in acute form in its peculiarly nasty effects on one individual and, in delayed form, in the representation of the traumatic effects of experiencing war, including

---

[51] See Rawlinson, 'Wilfred Owen', 116.
[52] Seamus Heaney, *The Government of the Tongue* (London: Faber & Faber, 1988), xv–xvi.
[53] Goldensohn, *Dismantling Glory*, 76.

the effect on one man of observing the dying of his fellow man. Running below this is the question of how these things should be represented in poetry. We don't get fully to this subject till part way through the poem. It begins, in classical style, *in medias res*, though in a past tense which asserts a distance that is soon to be exploded. This first section is aggressively bodily, but in relation to the normal unpleasantness of war – 'Bent double', 'Knock-kneed', 'blood-shod' – the stuff of many a GCSE account.[54] But let's not mock; this sensuous dimension of the poem, which sets a norm of soldierly exhaustion and physical privation, is there to provide a foil for what is to come. The panic of the next section shoots us from weary past to galvanised present and the terror of 'Gas! GAS!' Suddenly being 'Bent double' and 'blood-shod' seems petty stuff compared with 'flound'ring like a man in fire or lime'. The third, two-line section takes us into 'all my dreams', in which the image of the dying man is endlessly replicated.

The progress of the poem to this point, through various modes of time and perception, is reflected in the subtly changing tenses and moods of the verbs. The simple, descriptive past of the first eight lines is interrupted violently at the start of the second, six-line section by the present tense of speech (made more direct by the lack of speech punctuation). This then modulates into the past continuous, the constant participles ('yelling', 'stumbling', 'flound'ring' and finally 'drowning') leading the reader to feel they are sharing a still-continuing action, though it is caught in the past of memory. This leads naturally but frighteningly into the dreamworld where the ever-dying man repeatedly 'plunges at me'. There is no past but only, for the span of the dream, an inescapable and hellish present. Finally, the poem turns on the reader/addressee, in the section most questioned by critics.

Now the poet posits a counter-factual, though again one which forms a natural progression from the poet's dreams to those we as readers might have, by using the conditional: '*If* in some smothering dreams …'. The whole weight of that 'If' is that the reader cannot 'pace / Behind the wagon that we flung him in', except through Owen's words. And in those words he lets us have it: 'white eyes writhing', 'hanging face', 'the blood / Come gargling', 'froth-corrupted lungs', 'Obscene as cancer', 'vile, incurable sores'. These words are the only means, as readers, that we have to understand the particularity of what a gas attack might do. *If*, then, we could see the dying man thus 'in some smothering dreams' – the 'smothering' adds a further

---

[54] Owen, *Complete Poems and Fragments*, 140. In talking about the sections of the poem, we refer to what Stallworthy presents as Owen's final text. Some drafts of this much-revised poem reflect divisions, via line gaps, while these are less clear in other drafts.

dreadful and helpless element – then of course we could not subscribe to any simple, emollient axiom. By the time we get to the final four lines, they have been framed in such a way that we see that the Horatian tag is utterly discredited and that it is the dynamic of the traumatically imagined experience of a horrible death by gas that leads us there. Far from being monolithic, the last four lines become the final point in the drama.

Of the first importance in its engagement with Horace, and with the way in which death in war should be articulated in poetry, is that this is a poem about a *gas* attack. While endless attention has been given to the way Owen describes the attack and its effect on the dying man, little notice has been taken of his originality in choosing this as a subject in the first place. He seems to indicate a sort of category of poem when, in his letter to his mother, he laconically writes 'Here is a gas poem, done yesterday'.[55] Yet, just as the use of gas was innovative as a means of assault in the early stages of the First World War, so Owen's use of it as a subject for a poem is highly innovative. In the much-widened canon of First World War poetry that we now have available, there is a small number of brief mentions of gas and its effects; but Owen's is the only canonical poem that can be said to make a gas attack its central subject.[56] It charts in grotesque detail the effect of gas on an unprotected soldier ('someone still was yelling out and stumbling', unable to get his gas mask on in time). The lines which do this, the first eight lines of the final section of the poem, are the very ones that cause Kendall and, in his different way, Heaney some unease. But is there any poetic model with which we can compare these lines? Just as 'Mental Cases' required a phantasmagoric vocabulary to capture the strange hells of those whose mental state is affected ineradicably by what they have experienced, so something verbally extraordinary and shocking is required to represent an entirely new way of dying in warfare – and the experience of someone watching that dying.

Only one description of Owen's actual experience of gas pre-dates the first draft of the poem, that in his letter to his mother, 19 January 1917.[57]

---

[55] Letter to Susan Owen, ?16 October 1917; Owen, *Collected Letters*, 499.
[56] Of canonical poems, Kipling's 'Gethsemane' takes a sideways look at gas. Gilbert Frankau's 'How Rifleman Brown Came to Valhalla' can claim to be a full-on 'gas poem' but is little-known; it is a ballad in the style of Robert Service, showing the heroism of a Rifleman who chooses to warn his fellow soldiers of a gas attack rather than taking time to don his protective helmet. Frankau's poem, published in his collection *The Other Side* (New York: Alfred A. Knopf, 1918), deserves to be made available to a larger audience, but it has somehow missed being anthologised even in collections intended to widen the First World War canon.
[57] Owen, *Collected Letters*, 428–9. There are three slight mentions in the letters when Owen resumes his last period of engagement in France, all of which post-date March 1918, the last suggested date of revision of the poem. None of these reflect the drama of the poem itself.

> I went on ahead to scout – foolishly alone – and when, half a mile away from the party, got overtaken by
> GAS
> It was only tear-gas from a shell, and I got safely back (to the party) in my helmet, with nothing worse than a severe fright! And a few tears, some natural, some unnatural.

The capitalisation he uses strikingly here, emphasised further by this one word being placed alone on a separate line, is echoed in Patterson's massive animated 'GAS!' (repeated in the French 'GAZ!'), which assaults us from the glass walls of *La Maison*.

Later in this same letter he talks about the fact that the powers-that-be want to call No Man's Land 'England' to reflect the Allied supremacy there: 'To call it England! I would as soon call my House (!) Krupp Villa, or my child Chlorina-Phosgena.' The latter is a reference to phosgene gas, which replaced or was sometimes combined with the original chlorine gas. Owen was, then, fully acquainted with the use of gas on the Western Front, but his own experience of it seems to have been limited (tear gas was used intermittently but was relatively ineffective). What makes him use it as the central subject of a poem in the highly creative period at Craiglockhart War Hospital?

Siegfried Sassoon, in the barely fictionalised *Sherston's Progress*, describes the night-time at Craiglockhart thus:

> Around me was that underworld of dreams haunted by submerged memories of warfare and its intolerable shocks and self-lacerating failures to achieve the impossible ... by night each man was back in his doomed sector of a horror-stricken front line where the panic and stampede of some ghastly experience was re-enacted among the livid faces of the dead.[58]

Famously contained and distanced as he was, Sassoon here uses the guise of fictional memoir to admit to quotidian nightmare horror. Again, though much has been made of Craiglockhart as meeting ground for the two poets, the damaged mental states which led them there have generally been normalised or minimised; but neither Sassoon nor Owen were there for the good of their poetry. Certainly, politics played a part in Sassoon's being sent there, to allow his protest against the war to be seen, literally, as madness. But his writing about this period, in letters as well as fictionally, makes it clear that he did suffer from the same traumas as other inmates.[59] Owen's is an even clearer case of mental stress: the

---

[58] Siegfried Sassoon, *Sherston's Progress* (London: Faber & Faber, 1936), 87–8. Craiglockhart is renamed Slateford War Hospital.
[59] See his letter to Bertrand Russell, quoted on pp. 74–5 (Sassoon, *Diaries 1915–1918*, 161).

trigger seems to have been his being blown in the air by a shell (mid-April 1917), then lying in a shell-hole for days, surrounded by the body parts of a brother officer. Soon afterwards, his Commanding Officer observed him to be 'behaving strangely'. The Battalion Medical Officer confirmed a diagnosis of neurasthenia, which, over a period of several weeks, led him eventually to Craiglockhart.[60] Cheerful as his letters are from there, even before his momentous encounter with Sassoon, odd remarks reveal the darkness beneath. In an otherwise sunny letter to Mrs Bulman (1 July 1917), thanking her for sending some strawberries, he writes 'I have endured unnameable tortures in France'. And to his mother he mentions 'having had some rather bellicose dreams' (15 August 1917), and then 'I still have disastrous dreams, but they are taking on a more civilian character' (2 September 1917), and then 'I had one horrid night since last I wrote' (25 September 1917). On that same day, he appears before a medical board, to assess his state of fitness for service, and is found not yet fit.[61]

Goldensohn interprets 'Dulce et Decorum Est' squarely in this context, seeing it as 'a combat nightmare' with 'the piercing recall of a moment when the brotherhood of war leaves behind one of its members to a death made hideous to reader and complicit speaker alike' and locates the poem as a whole in post-traumatic 'uncontrollable' dreaming.[62] Goldensohn's sensitive study is highly influenced by late twentieth-century conflicts, and most notably Vietnam, but her insights into Owen's poem are enabled by this, and open it to an understanding not available in his own time. Nonetheless, current understanding of post-traumatic stress does not seem to align quite with First World War experience, and to see the poem only as the product of trauma is again to reduce it unnecessarily. What is certain is that Owen's poem is informed by the sort of experiences and reflections on past experience that he was allowed at Craiglockhart – where the admission of mental stress could be separated from the anxiety (which Owen certainly felt) that being taken out of the front line might be interpreted as cowardice. And in this environment he had time and mental and creative space in which to mine his mass of experiential material within the constraints of considered and at the same time experimental

---

[60] Stallworthy, *Wilfred Owen*, 183. According to Douglas Kerr, in February 1917, GHQ issued instructions that patients should be distinguished as either 'shell-shock wounded' (if in contact with an explosion) or 'neurasthenic' if not. The former diagnosis qualified for a 'wounded' stripe – the latter not (Kerr, *Wilfred Owen's Voices*, 192). The awarding of the stripe shows that diagnosis was a sensitive area, with neurasthenia sometimes seen as closer to an attribution of moral failure.
[61] Owen, *Collected Letters*, 473, 484, 490, 496.
[62] Goldensohn, *Dismantling Glory*, 53.

poetic form. Sassoon was on hand as an expert reader – both as poet and as combatant.

As we have noted, other than his reference to a tear-gas attack, there is nothing in the letters referring to Owen's having observed a gas attack or its consequences. But, even when, in Bordeaux in 1914, he was well removed from the war emotionally as well as physically, he was writing to his brother Colin, carefully delineating in words and drawings the wounds he had observed at the local hospital.[63] The story of his carrying photographs of the horrors he had witnessed at the Front chimes with this close concern to observe and give a proper account.[64] 'Dulce et Decorum Est' gives similarly proper attention to a weapon that, even by the standards of the Front, meted out cruel and unusual punishment. If Owen did not experience it, he felt it incumbent on himself to imagine it. As he imagines it, he also wants the reader to imagine it. In imagining the gas attack from these different points of view, Owen is also dramatising the difficulty of knowing how to react as a poet to the particular horrors of modern warfare. Making the gas attack his subject is key to Owen's challenge to Horace, as a poet whose approach to war was based on classical models of heroism.

Though the Germans introduced the use of gas in April 1915 (in Ypres) and the British quickly followed suit in the Battle of Loos, September 1915, both sides felt uncomfortable initially about this new weapon, seeing it as contrary to the 'normal' rules of combat (and its use did in fact contravene the Hague Convention, 1907, to which both were signatories). As a silent weapon, it seemed underhand; it was also notoriously unpredictable, since gas once released could be sent by a changed wind direction towards the lines that had released it. At the same time, it was a powerful psychological weapon, precisely because of its immateriality. Physically it affected the lungs and thus the capacity to breathe – an especially distressing effect, which seems to have been more frightening than a shrapnel wound. Certainly Owen's 'ecstasy of fumbling' reflects the scramble to get on the gas mask or smoke helmet. Seconds were vital, as the fate of the man in 'Dulce et Decorum Est' signifies. The fear of gas seems to have been pervasive, along with the sense that it was a weapon that contradicted notions of heroism. This is surely central to Owen's poem: the gas attack breaks the rules. Horatian rhetoric no longer applies. That Horace's tag was still widely used, and widely known, made Owen's engagement with

---

[63] Owen, *Collected Letters*, 284–5.
[64] The source of this anecdote is Frank Nicholson's reminiscences of Owen, published as an appendix to *The Poems of Wilfred Owen*, ed. Edmund Blunden (1931; London, Chatto & Windus, 1969), 134.

it more powerful.[65] Here was a modern poetic voice showing precisely why classically heroic modes of representation in poetry (and indeed any former modes of representation) would not fit a new kind of warfare – a new kind of dying. In writing that is neither 'slack' nor 'excessively vehement', the poem forces us to see that new kind of dying, so that we can't turn away from it.

'Dulce et Decorum Est' is, then, in that line of meta-elegy that we have suggested is central to Owen's poetry. It ends by taking issue with the way in which others will seek to commemorate those who died. It is a commentary on Horace's third ode, and on the much-used elegiac inscription deriving from that.[66] But, rather than simply opposing Horatian elegy, it engages with it by offering a new form of writing to match circumstances that Horace could not have known. In showing us the way that Horace's complex poem has been reduced to a seven-word Latin tag, it is a reminder of the way poetry can be used, by the poet but also by others who borrow the power of his words, to inscribe a moral purpose on to war. In 'Dulce et Decorum Est', Owen seeks to destabilise any such possibility, and it is a sad irony that the poem has been reduced, as Horace's was, to its final seven words.

Patterson's representation of 'Dulce et Decorum Est', both delicate and tough where it is etched into *La Maison*'s glass walls, places the viewer close enough to reach out and touch Owen's pencil strokes, his crossings out – his hand writ large.[67] This tactile element of the experience recalls the touching of names at the Vietnam Veterans Memorial, but here we touch a permanent, non-fading facsimile of a fragile, faded draft and our attention is drawn to the provisionality of the poem. We are reminded of the creative processes which began with a blank sheet of paper; through all the projecting of printer's font onto the surface of the script, we see the marks of a blunt pencil, miraculously preserved. This sense of provisionality can be felt most keenly when the 'print' version of 'Dulce et Decorum Est' is projected on to the etched holograph, midway through the

---

[65] Kerr tells us that the Commandant of the 2nd Artists' Rifles OTC, Lieutenant-Colonel W. Shirley, gave a lecture on the importance of morale (then called 'moral') to officers in training which drew on Horace's words as a central tenet (Kerr, *Wilfred Owen's Voices*, 183). The lecture was published as *Moral: The Most Important Factor in the War* (London: Sifton, Praed, 1916). Kerr can't demonstrate that Owen heard this lecture, but the circumstantial evidence makes it likely, and Kerr suggests that Owen may be referring to the lecture in his letter to Susan Owen, 14 January 1916; Owen, *Collected Letters*, 376.

[66] Horace, *Odes*, 3.2.

[67] The experience recalls the way that Owen himself was deeply affected when seeing Keats's manuscripts in the British Museum (where his own would later be displayed).

immersive poetry experience. The paradox of Owen's original manuscript (its workings all this poem consisted of in his lifetime) standing as the permanent etched form, while the 'fixed' print version is superimposed fleetingly onto it, brings us forcibly to understand what was lost with this man's life, but what also was left to us. This, in the end, is what *La Maison Forestière* achieves: reminding us of the evanescence of mere words scribbled on paper, it presents us also with the beautiful and permanent forms of art, but the two are kept in constant, carefully modulated balance. It remains a living thing, both because of the voices which always remind us of the human, and because as viewers and participants, we are part of the experience. And always we are brought back to the poetry: Owen is everywhere, and nowhere, and the poetry floats free.

Coda

In *La Maison Forestière Wilfred Owen*, when the projected texts have disappeared and the actors' voices have fallen silent, it is the heavily worked-on autograph manuscript of 'Dulce et Decorum Est' that remains, etched on the glass wall: Owen's thinking, revising, reflecting poetic imagination expressed in the traces of his handwriting. In writing this book, we have aspired, similarly, to draw attention to the power and creativity of poets struggling to represent and to remember, with honesty, truthfulness and a proper respect, soldiers killed in battle. Through re-reading as openly as possible their words, we in turn pay proper but clear-eyed regard to those who died, and to how they died.

Standing in the ruins of Thiepval in 1918, the botanist Reginald Farrer saw a naked soldier washing:

> A little way off a naked Tommy was standing under a spout of water ... And the beauty of that tiny frail fair thing, vividly white in the sunshine upon that enormous background of emptiness and dun-coloured monotony of moorland was something so enormous in itself, that it went straight through me like a violent lance of pain. So minute a little naked frog, hairless and helpless, to have made the earth such a place of horror, and itself, incidentally, in the making, a thing so infinitely great ... He is supremely pitiful and also supremely august, in his contrast of utter feebleness and immeasurable power, and all the boundless wonder of his endurances and heroisms, bounded physically in that strange, small engine of lusts ... All those complicated bedevilments of iron and dynamite, got together at so vast an expense of thought and money and labour, to destroy just – *that*.[1]

Farrer puts into ordinary words the sheer frailty of the individual man in relation to the forces of destruction brought down upon him in the First World War (and of which he was also, however undeliberately, an agent).

---

[1] Reginald Farrer, *The Void of War: Letters from Three Fronts* (Boston: Houghton Mifflin, 1918), 99–100. Quoted, in part, by Fussell in *The Great War and Modern Memory*, 301.

Farrer, in describing what he sees, voices a sense of existential vertigo which more celebrated modernist writers would struggle to express. He echoes Mary Borden's acute gaze on the individual soldier about to die, in 'Unidentified'; he catches something of the sense of the vulnerable beauty of the male body exposed to threat that we find in Owen, Monro and Gurney; he anticipates Barthes in the way the vignette pierces his spirit. What he sees is a man and, in the exposed body, that man's projected death; he sees the grief and mourning to come even as the man is still alive and enjoying the brief pleasure of the water spout. If in this account we have emphasised the poetry that resists consolation, while exposing the limits of the consolatory poem, it is because our readings have brought us face to face with all the implications of Farrer's passage.

On 11 November 2016, Remembrance Day, Rupert Brooke's 'The Soldier' was still the poem of choice to be read by Prince Harry at the UK's National Memorial Arboretum. We can't ignore the fact that this would answer to many people's feelings about how to remember those who died in the First World War. But in this centenary period, instead of reaching back atavistically to a monolithic way of remembering the dead, we need to be alive to the many different ways in which the poets of the time, and poets since, have represented those who died. Most of all, we need to engage with the very process of remembering, mourning, representing – as David Jones does here:

> The First Field Dressing is futile as frantic seaman's shift bunged to stoved bulwark, so soon the darking flood percolates and he dies in your arms.
> And get back to that digging can't yer –
> This aint a bloody Wake
> for these dead, who soon will have their dead
> for burial clods heaped over.
> Nor time for halsing
> nor to clip green wounds
> nor weeping Maries bringing anointments
> neither any word spoken
> nor no decent nor appropriate sowing of this seed
> nor remembrance of the harvesting
> of the renascent cycle …
> No one sings: Lully lully
> For the mate whose blood runs down.[2]

---

[2] Jones, *In Parenthesis*, 174.

In this passage from the brutal final section of *In Parenthesis*, Jones's insistent repetition of 'nor', varied only by 'neither' and 'no-one', allows the reader no leeway, no place of cover or redemption, no room for a softer interpretation. Here is the brute fact of death at the Front, as Jones brings before us the possible ways a man's death in battle might be mourned, only to negate them all: 'This aint a bloody Wake'. This passage rejects in turn the mourning of fellow soldiers, the covering of the dead body with earth, the post-mortem rituals of care for the corpse, notions of regeneration in the cycle of birth and death or the return to nature, and lyric itself. It is a sharp rebuke to any reader who imagines that some comfort might be had. Finally, Jones robs us even of the power of his own, and any, poet's voice: 'No one sings'. Between Jones's bleak vision and Patterson's re-invigoration of Owen's voice, there is not one right place to stand. In the space of *La Maison Forestière*, we want more; we want to see it again; we don't want to leave, as the poet speaks to us again through the power of the word. The same power gives to us Jones's 'darking flood' percolating, Gurney's 'red wet / Thing', Rosenberg's 'sprawled dead' whose 'bones crunched' under the limber wheels, Borden's 'mass of matter, horrid slime – and little brittle bits –', Blunden's 'eye under the duckboard', Sassoon's Dick 'flapping along the firestep like a fish' and Sorley's 'mouthless dead'. Confronted with these images we may want to turn away, but we don't. Instead the poets' words impel us to look: these are 'the remembered dead'.

Bibliography

Primary Sources

Aldington, Richard, *Images of War* (London: Beaumont Press, 1919).
Barbusse, Henri, *Under Fire*, trans. W. Fitzwater Wray (1917; London: Dent, 1965). Originally published as *Le Feu (Journal d'une Escouade)* (Paris: Ernest Flammarion, 1916).
Barker, Pat, *Regeneration* (London: Viking, 1991).
Bennett, Alan, *The History Boys* (London: Faber & Faber, 2004).
Blake, William, *Selected Poetry*, ed. Michael Mason (Oxford: Oxford University Press, 1996).
Blunden, Edmund, *Poems 1914–30* (London: Cobden-Sanderson, 1930).
  Undertones of War (1928; Harmondsworth: Penguin, 1982).
Borden, Mary, *The Forbidden Zone* (1929; London: Hesperus, 2008).
Brittain, Vera, *Chronicle of Friendship: Vera Brittain's Diary of the Thirties 1932–1939*, ed. Alan Bishop (London: Gollancz, 1986).
  Testament of Youth (1933; London: Virago, 2004).
Brooke, Rupert, *1914 and Other Poems*, ed. Edward Marsh (London: Sidgwick & Jackson, 1915).
  The Collected Poems, with a memoir by Edward Marsh (1918; London: Sidgwick & Jackson, 1989).
  The Letters of Rupert Brooke, ed. G. Keynes (London: Faber & Faber, 1968).
Butler, Samuel, *The Iliad of Homer* (Longmans: New York, 1898).
Conrad, Joseph, *Heart of Darkness* (1902; Harmondsworth: Penguin, 1973).
Douglas, Keith, *Collected Poems*, ed. John Waller, G. S. Fraser and J. C. Hall (London: Faber & Faber, 1966).
  Complete Poems, ed. Desmond Graham, 3rd edition (London: Faber & Faber, 2000).
  The Letters, ed. Desmond Graham (Manchester: Carcanet, 2000).
Dunmore, Helen, *The Lie* (London: Hutchinson, 2014).
Dunn, Douglas, *Barbarians* (London: Faber & Faber, 1979).
Ehrhart, W. D., *The Madness of It All: Essays on War, Literature and American Life* (Jefferson, NC: MacFarland, 2002).

Eliot, T. S., *The Complete Poems and Plays of T. S. Eliot* (London: Faber & Faber, 1969).
  Selected Prose of T. S. Eliot, ed. Frank Kermode (London: Faber & Faber, 1975).
  The Waste Land: A Facsimile and Transcript of the Original Drafts Including the Annotations of Ezra Pound, ed. Valerie Eliot (London: Faber & Faber, 1971).
Farrer, Reginald, *The Void of War: Letters from Three Fronts* (Boston: Houghton Mifflin, 1918).
Ford, Ford Madox, *Parade's End* (1924–8; New York: Alfred A. Knopf, 1992).
Frankau, Gilbert, *The Other Side* (New York: Alfred A. Knopf, 1918).
Gardner, Brian, ed., *Up the Line to Death: The War Poets 1914–1918*, revised edition (London: Methuen, 1976).
Gibson, Wilfrid, *Battle* (London: Elkin Mathews, 1915).
Gurney, Ivor, *Collected Poems*, ed. P. J. Kavanagh (Manchester: Fyfield Books/Carcanet, 2004).
Heaney, Seamus, *Field Work* (London: Faber & Faber, 1979).
Hibberd, Dominic, and John Onions, eds, *The Winter of the World: Poems of the Great War* (London: Constable, 2008).
Hughes, Ted, *Collected Poems*, ed. Paul Keegan (London: Faber & Faber, 2003).
  The Hawk in the Rain (London: Faber & Faber, 1957).
Jones, David, *The Anathemata* (London: Faber & Faber, 1952).
  Epoch and Artist (London: Faber & Faber, 1959).
  In Parenthesis (1937; London: Faber, 1978).
Kendall, Tim, ed., *Poetry of the First World War: An Anthology* (Oxford: Oxford University Press, 2013).
Kipling, Rudyard, *The Collected Poems of Rudyard Kipling* (Ware: Wordsworth, 2001).
  The Letters of Rudyard Kipling, 5 vols, ed. Thomas Pinney (Iowa City: University of Iowa Press, 1990–2005).
  The Years Between (London: Methuen, 1919).
Komunyakaa, Yusef, *Dien Cai Dau* (Middletown, CT: Wesleyan University Press, 1988).
Kyle, Galloway, ed., *More Songs by the Fighting Men* (London: Erskine MacDonald, 1917).
  ed., *Soldier Poets: Songs of the Fighting Men* (London: Erskine MacDonald, 1916).
Larkin, Philip, *Further Requirements*, ed. Anthony Thwaite (London: Faber & Faber, 2001).
  The Less Deceived (Hessle: Marvell Press, 1955).
  The Whitsun Weddings (London: Faber & Faber, 1964).
Lawrence, D. H., *Lady Chatterley's Lover* (1928; Harmondsworth: Penguin, 1960).
  Sons and Lovers, ed. Helen Baron and Carl Baron (1913; Cambridge: Cambridge University Press, 1992).
Lloyd, Bertram, ed., *The Paths of Glory: A Collection of Poems Written during the War 1914–1919* (London: Allen & Unwin, 1919).
Lowell, Robert, *For the Union Dead* (London: Faber & Faber, 1965).
Maxwell, Glyn, *The Breakage* (London: Faber & Faber), 1998.

Milton, John, *The Poems of John Milton*, ed. John Carey and Alastair Fowler (London: Longmans, 1968).
Monro, Harold, *Children of Love* (London: Poetry Bookshop, 1914).
Newbolt, Henry, *Collected Poems 1897–1907* (London: Thomas Nelson & Sons, 1910).
Nichols, Robert, *Ardours and Endurances* (London: Chatto & Windus, 1917).
Osborn, E. B., ed., *The Muse in Arms* (London: John Murray, 1917).
Owen, Wilfred, *Collected Letters*, ed. Harold Owen and John Bell (London, Oxford University Press, 1967).
  The Complete Poems and Fragments, 2 vols, ed. Jon Stallworthy, (London: Chatto & Windus, 2013).
  The Poems of Wilfred Owen, ed. Edmund Blunden (1931; London: Chatto & Windus, 1969).
Parsons, I. M., ed., *The Progress of Poetry* (London: Chatto & Windus, 1936).
Plowman, Max, *A Lap Full of Seed* (Orford: Blackwell, 1917).
Reilly, Catherine, ed., *Scars upon My Heart: Women's Poetry and Verse of the First World War* (London: Virago, 1981).
Rosenberg, Isaac, *The Collected Works of Isaac Rosenberg*, ed. Ian Parsons (London: Chatto & Windus, 1979).
  Isaac Rosenberg, ed. Vivien Noakes (Oxford: Oxford University Press, 2008).
  Poetry out of My Head and Heart: Unpublished Letters and Poem Versions, ed. Jean Liddiard (London: Enitharmon, 2007).
Sassoon, Siegfried, *Collected Poems 1908–1956* (London: Faber & Faber, 1961).
  Diaries 1915–1918, ed. Rupert Hart-Davis (London: Faber & Faber, 1983).
  Sherston's Progress (London: Faber & Faber, 1936).
  The War Poems (London: Faber & Faber, 1983).
Shelley, P. B., *Selected Poems of Percy Bysshe Shelley* (London: Oxford University Press, 1960).
Shirley, W., *Moral: The Most Important Factor in the War* (London: Sifton, Praed, 1916).
Sorley, Charles Hamilton, *The Collected Poems*, ed. Jean Moorcroft Wilson (London: Cecil Woolf, 1985).
  The Letters of Charles Sorley, ed. W. R. Sorley (Cambridge: Cambridge University Press, 1919).
Stallworthy, Jon, ed., *The New Oxford Book of War Poetry* (Oxford: Oxford University Press, 2014).
Taylor, Martin, ed., *Lads: Love Poetry of the Trenches* (London: Constable, 1989).
Thomas, Edward, *The Annotated Collected Poems*, ed. Edna Longley (Tarset: Bloodaxe, 2008).
Walter, George, ed., *The Penguin Book of First World War Poetry* (London: Penguin, 2006).
West, Arthur Graeme, *The Diary of a Dead Officer* (London: George Allen & Unwin, 1919).
Whitman, Walt, *Leaves of Grass: Comprehensive Reader's Edition*, ed. Harold W. Blodgett and Sculley Bradley (New York: New York University Press, 1965).

Williams, Reese, ed., *Unwinding the Vietnam War: From War into Peace* (Seattle: Real Comet, 1987).
Woolf, Virginia, *The Diary of Virginia Woolf*, 5 vols, ed. Anne Olivier Bell (Orlando: Harcourt, 1977–84).
    The Essays of Virginia Woolf, vol. 2, ed. Andrew McNeillie (San Diego: Harcourt Brace Jovanovich, 1990).
    The Letters of Virginia Woolf, 6 vols, ed. Nigel Nicolson (London: Hogarth Press, 1975–80).
    Mrs Dalloway (1925; London: Penguin, 1992).
Wordsworth, William, *The Poetical Works*, ed. Thomas Hutchinson, rev. Ernest de Selincourt (London: Oxford University Press, 1961).
Yeats, W. B., *Letters on Poetry from W. B. Yeats to Dorothy Wellesley* (Oxford: Oxford University Press, 1940).

Secondary Sources

Assmann, Jan, 'Collective Memory and Cultural Identity', trans. John Czaplicka, *New German Critique*, 65 (1995), 125–33.
    Cultural Memory and Early Civilisation: Writing, Remembrance and Political Imagination (Cambridge: Cambridge University Press, 2011).
Baird, Neil P., 'Virtual Vietnam Veterans Memorials as Image Events: Exorcising the Specter of Vietnam', *Enculturation*, 6.2 (2009), n.p., http://enculturation.net/6.2/baird. Accessed 5 April 2017.
Balau, Raymond, 'Bleached Bone', *La Maison Forestière Wilfred Owen: Une Œuvre de Simon Patterson* (Lille: artconnexion, 2011), 13–15.
Baldick, Chris, *Literature of the 1920s: Writers among the Ruins* (Edinburgh: Edinburgh University Press, 2012).
Barry, Peter, 'Contemporary Poetry and Ekphrasis', *The Cambridge Quarterly*, 31.2 (2002), 155–65.
Barthes, Roland, *Camera Lucida: Reflections on Photography*, trans. Richard Howard (London: Vintage, 2000).
    Image Music Text, trans. Stephen Heath (London: Fontana, 1977).
    Mourning Diary, text established and annotated by Nathalie Léger, trans. Richard Howard (2010; London: Notting Hill Editions, 2011).
Batchen, Geoffrey, *Forget Me Not: Photography and Remembrance* (New York: Princeton Architectural Press, 2004).
Bell, Michael, *Literature, Modernism and Myth* (Cambridge: Cambridge University Press, 1997).
    'Myths and Texts', *A History of Modernist Poetry*, ed. Alex Davis and Lee M. Jenkins (Cambridge: Cambridge University Press, 2015), 46–67.
Benjamin, Walter, *Illuminations*, ed. Hannah Arendt, trans. Harry Zorn (London: Pimlico, 1999).
    On Photography, ed. and trans. Esther Leslie (London: Reaktion Books, 2015).
Bergmann Loizeaux, Elizabeth, *Twentieth-Century Poetry and the Visual Arts* (Cambridge: Cambridge University Press, 2008).

'Women Looking: The Feminist Ekphrasis of Marianne Moore and Adrienne Rich', *In the Frame: Women's Ekphrastic Poetry from Marianne Moore to Susan Wheeler*, ed. Jane Hedley, Nick Halpern and Willard Spiegelman (Newark: University of Delaware Press, 2009), 121–44.
Berry, Paul, and Mark Bostridge, *Vera Brittain: A Life* (London: Chatto & Windus, 1995).
Booth, Allyson, *Postcards from the Trenches: Negotiating the Space between Modernism and the First World War* (Oxford: Oxford University Press, 1996).
Booth, James, *Philip Larkin: Writer* (Hemel Hempstead: Harvester, 1992).
Bradbury, Malcolm, 'The Denuded Place: War and Form in *Parade's End* and *USA*', *The First World War in Fiction: A Collection of Critical Essays*, ed. Holger Klein (London: Macmillan, 1976), 193–209.
Burt, Stephen, 'Lightsource, Aperture, Face: C. D. Wright and Photography', *In the Frame: Women's Ekphrastic Poetry from Marianne Moore to Susan Wheeler*, ed. Jane Hedley, Nick Halpern and Willard Spiegelman (Newark: University of Delaware Press, 2009), 227–44.
Caesar, Adrian, *Taking it Like a Man: Suffering, Sexuality and the War Poets* (Manchester: Manchester University Press, 1993).
Clark, T. J., 'Living Death', *London Review of Books*, 7 January 2010, 10–12.
Clausson, Nils, '"Perpetuating the Language": Romantic Tradition, the Genre Function, and the Origins of the Trench Lyric', *Journal of Modern Literature*, 30.1 (2006), 104–28.
Compagnon, Antoine, 'Marcel Proust's *Remembrance of Things Past*', *Realms of Memory: The Construction of the French Past* vol. 2: *Traditions*, under the direction of Pierre Nora, English-language edition ed. Lawrence D. Kritzman and trans. Arthur Goldhammer (New York: Columbia University Press, 1997), 211–47.
Crane, David, *Empires of the Dead: How One Man's Vision Led to the Creation of WWI's War Graves* (William Collins: London, 2013).
Cunningham, Valentine, 'Why Ekphrasis?', *Classical Philology*, 102.1 (2007), 57–71.
Das, Santanu, *Touch and Intimacy in First World War Literature* (Cambridge: Cambridge University Press, 2005).
  'War Poetry and the Realm of the Senses: Owen and Rosenberg', *The Oxford Handbook of British and Irish War Poetry*, ed. Tim Kendall (Oxford: Oxford University Press, 2007), 73–99.
Dilworth, Thomas, *David Jones: Engraver, Soldier, Painter, Poet* (London: Jonathan Cape, 2017).
  The Shape of Meaning in the Poetry of David Jones (Toronto: University of Toronto Press, 1988).
Donoghue, Denis, 'Yeats, Eliot, and the Mythical Method', *The Sewanee Review*, 105.2 (1997), 206–26.
Dowson, Jane, *Women, Modernism and British Poetry, 1910–1939: Resisting Femininity* (Aldershot: Ashgate, 2002).
Egremont, Max, *Siegfried Sassoon: A Biography* (London: Picador, 2005).
  Some Desperate Glory: The First World War the Poets Knew (London: Picador, 2014).

Elsner, Jas, 'Introduction: The Genres of Ekphrasis', *The Verbal and the Visual: Cultures of Ekphrasis in Antiquity*, ed. Jas Elsner, special edition of *Ramus* 31.1–2 (2002), 9–13.

Erll, Astrid, *Memory in Culture*, trans. Sara B. Young (Basingstoke: Palgrave Macmillan, 2011).

Eysteinsson, Astradur, *The Concept of Modernism* (Ithaca: Cornell University Press, 1990).

Friedman, Alan Warren, *Fictional Death and the Modernist Enterprise* (Cambridge: Cambridge University Press, 1995).

Fussell, Paul, *The Great War and Modern Memory* (Oxford: Oxford University Press, 1975).

Gilbert, Sandra M., '"Rats' Alley": The Great War, Modernism, and the (Anti) Pastoral Elegy', *New Literary History*, 30.1 (1999), 179–201.

Goldensohn, Lorrie, *Dismantling Glory: Twentieth Century Soldier Poetry* (New York: Columbia University Press, 2003).

Goldhill, Simon, 'What is Ekphrasis For?', *Classical Philology*, 102.1 (2007), 1–19.

Graham, Desmond, *Keith Douglas 1920–1944: A Biography* (London: Oxford University Press, 1974).

The Truth of War: Owen, Blunden, Rosenberg (Manchester: Carcanet Press, 1984).

Griffin, Jasper, *Homer on Life and Death* (Oxford: Clarendon, 1980).

Griswold, Charles L., 'The Vietnam Veterans Memorial and the Washington Mall: Philosophical Thoughts on Political Iconography', *Critical Inquiry*, 12.4 (1986), 688–719.

Halbwachs, Maurice, *The Collective Memory*, trans. F. I. and V. Y. Ditter (1950; New York: Harper and Row, 1980).

On Collective Memory, ed. and trans. Lewis A. Coser (Chicago: University of Chicago Press, 1992).

Harington, Charles, *Plumer of Messines* (London: John Murray, 1935).

Hass, Kristin Ann, *Carried to the Wall: American Memory and the Vietnam Veterans Memorial* (Berkeley: University of California Press, 1998).

Hassall, Christopher, *Rupert Brooke: A Biography* (London: Faber & Faber, 1964).

Haughey, Jim, *The First World War in Irish Poetry* (London: Associated University Presses, 2002).

Haughton, Hugh, 'Anthologizing War', *The Oxford Handbook of British and Irish War Poetry*, ed. Tim Kendall (Oxford: Oxford University Press, 2007), 421–44.

Heaney, Seamus, *The Government of the Tongue* (London: Faber & Faber, 1988).

Hedley, Jane, 'Introduction: The Subject of Ekphrasis', *In the Frame: Women's Ekphrastic Poetry from Marianne Moore to Susan Wheeler*, ed. Jane Hedley, Nick Halpern and Willard Spiegelman (Newark: University of Delaware Press, 2009), 15–40.

Heffernan, James A. W., *Museum of Words: The Poetics of Ekphrasis from Homer to Ashbery* (Chicago: University of Chicago Press, 1993).

Hess, Elizabeth, 'Vietnam: Memorials of Misfortune', *Unwinding the Vietnam War: From War into Peace*, ed. Reese Williams (Seattle: Real Comet, 1987), 262–70.

Hibberd, Dominic, *Wilfred Owen: A New Biography* (London: Weidenfeld & Nicolson, 2002).
Hynes, Samuel, *A War Imagined: The First World War and English Culture* (London: Pimlico, 1992).
Karlin, Daniel, 'Kipling and the Limits of Healing', *Essays in Criticism*, 48.4 (1998), 331–56.
Kazantzis, Judith, 'Preface', *Scars upon My Heart: Women's Poetry and Verse of the First World War*, ed. Catherine Reilly (London: Virago: 1981), xv–xxiv.
Kendall, Tim, *Modern English War Poetry* (Oxford: Oxford University Press, 2006).
— ed., *The Oxford Handbook of British and Irish War Poetry*, (Oxford: Oxford University Press, 2007).
Kerr, Douglas, *Wilfred Owen's Voices: Language and Community* (Oxford: Oxford University Press, 1993).
Kiberd, Declan, 'Introduction', *Ulysses*, by James Joyce, annotated students' edition (London: Penguin, 1992), ix–lxxx.
Kristeva, Julia, *Powers of Horror: An Essay on Abjection*, trans. Leon S. Roudiez (New York: Columbia University Press, 1982).
Leed, Eric, *No Man's Land: Combat and Identity in World War I* (Cambridge: Cambridge University Press, 1979).
Levenson, Michael H., *A Genealogy of Modernism: A Study of English Literary Doctrine 1908–1922* (Cambridge: Cambridge University Press, 1984).
Longley, Edna, *Poetry in the Wars* (Newcastle-upon-Tyne: Bloodaxe, 1986).
Lowe, Peter, 'Stripped Bodies and Looted Goods: Keith Douglas's *Iliad*', *The Cambridge Quarterly*, 43.4 (2014), 301–24.
Lukács, Georg, *The Meaning of Contemporary Realism*, trans. John and Necke Mander (1958; London: Merlin Press, 1963).
Maccoby, Deborah, *God Made Blind: Isaac Rosenberg, His Life and Poetry* (London: Symposium, 1998).
Messinger, Gary S., *British Propaganda and the State in the First World War* (Manchester: Manchester University Press, 1992).
Miller, J. Hillis, *Tropes, Parables and Performatives: Essays on Twentieth Century Literature* (Hemel Hempstead: Harvester Wheatsheaf, 1991).
Minogue, Sally, 'Portrait of the Artist: Ivor Gurney as Modern Maker', *The Ivor Gurney Society Journal*, 11 (2005), 25–42.
— '"That Awkward Squad": Ivor Gurney and John Clare', *The Ivor Gurney Society Journal*, 13 (2007), 19–32.
Moffett, Alex, '"We Will Remember Them": The Poetic Rewritings of Lutyens' Cenotaph', *War, Literature & the Arts*, 19.1–2 (2007), 228–46.
Moorcroft Wilson, Jean, *Isaac Rosenberg: The Making of a Great War Poet* (London: Phoenix, 2009).
Motion, Andrew, 'Introduction', *First World War Poems*, ed. Andrew Motion (London: Faber & Faber, 2004), xi–xv.
— *Philip Larkin: A Writer's Life* (London: Faber & Faber, 1994).
Nicholls, Peter, *Modernisms: A Literary Guide* (Basingstoke: Macmillan, 1995).
Nora, Pierre, 'Note', *Representations*, 26 (1989), 25.

Realms of Memory: The Construction of the French Past, vol. 1: *Conflicts and Divisions*, English-language edition ed. Lawrence D. Kritzman and trans. Arthur Goldhammer (New York: Columbia University Press, 1992).

Realms of Memory: The Construction of the French Past, vol. 2: *Traditions*, English-language edition ed. Lawrence D. Kritzman and trans. Arthur Goldhammer (New York: Columbia University Press, 1997).

Norris, Margot, *Writing War in the Twentieth Century* (Charlottesville and London: University Press of Virginia, 2000).

Palmer, Andrew, '"Friend with the Musing Eye": Persuasion and Dissonance in "Call to Arms" Poems of the First World War', *Writings of Persuasion and Dissonance in the Great War: That Better Whiles May Follow Worse*, ed. David Owen and Cristina Pividori (Leiden: Brill Rodopi, 2016), 138–51.

Palmer, Andrew, and Sally Minogue, 'Modernism and First World War Poetry: Alternative Lines', *A History of Modernist Poetry*, ed. Alex Davis and Lee M. Jenkins (Cambridge: Cambridge University Press, 2015), 227–51.

Parsons, I. M., 'Introduction', *The Progress of Poetry*, ed. I. M. Parsons (London: Chatto & Windus, 1936), xi–xl.

Patterson, Simon, 'Conversation' [with Amanda Crabtree and Bruno Dupont], *La Maison Forestière Wilfred Owen: Une Œuvre de Simon Patterson* (Lille: artconnexion, 2011), 22–5.

Poole, Adrian, 'David Jones', *The Cambridge Companion to the First World War*, ed. Santanu Das (Cambridge: Cambridge University Press, 2013), 144–55.

Press, John, *Charles Hamilton Sorley* (London: Cecil Woolf, 2006).

Prost, Antoine, 'Monuments to the Dead', *Realms of Memory: The Construction of the French Past*, vol. 2: *Traditions*, under the direction of Pierre Nora, English-language edition ed. Lawrence D. Kritzman and trans. Arthur Goldhammer (New York: Columbia University Press, 1997), 307–32.

Ramazani, Jahan, *Poetry of Mourning: The Modern Elegy from Hardy to Heaney* (Chicago: University of Chicago Press, 1994).

Ramsey, William M., 'Knowing Their Place: Three Black Writers and the Postmodern South', *The Southern Literary Journal*, 37.2 (2005), 119–39.

Rawlinson, Mark, 'Wilfred Owen', *The Oxford Handbook of British and Irish War Poetry*, ed. Tim Kendall (Oxford: Oxford University Press, 2007), 114–33.

Ringnalda, Donald, *Fighting and Writing the Vietnam War* (Jackson: University Press of Mississippi, 1994).

Roberts, Beth Ellen, 'The Female God of Isaac Rosenberg: A Muse for Wartime', *English Literature in Transition 1880–1920*, 39.3 (1996), 319–32.

Roberts, John Stuart, *Siegfried Sassoon* (London: Richard Cohen Books, 1999).

Robichaud, Paul, *Making the Past Present: David Jones, the Middle Ages, & Modernism* (Washington, DC: Catholic University of America Press, 2007).

Sagar, Keith, *The Art of Ted Hughes* (Cambridge: Cambridge University Press, 1975).

Sanders, M. L., and Philip M. Taylor, *British Propaganda during the First World War, 1914–18* (Macmillan: London, 1982).

Saunders, Nicholas J., 'Crucifix, Calvary, and Cross: Materiality and Spirituality in Great War Landscapes', *World Archaeology*, 35.1 (2003), 7–21.

Scammell, William, *Keith Douglas: A Study* (London: Faber & Faber, 1988).
Scannell, Vernon, *Not Without Glory: Poets of the Second World War* (London: Woburn Press, 1976).
Scott, Grant F., 'Copied with a Difference: *Ekphrasis* in William Carlos Williams' *Pictures from Brueghel*', *Word & Image*, 15.1 (1999), 63–75.
——— 'Meditations in Black: The Vietnam Veterans Memorial', *Journal of American Culture*, 13.3 (1990), 37–40.
Sherry, Vincent, 'Hectic Stasis: The War Poetry of Keith Douglas', *University of Toronto Quarterly*, 58.2 (1989), 295–305.
——— 'A New Boast for *In Parenthesis*: The Dramatic Monologue of David Jones', *Notre Dame English Journal*, 14.2 (1982), 113–28.
Simmons, James, 'The Trouble with Seamus', *Seamus Heaney: A Collection of Critical Essays*, ed. Elmer Andrews (London: Macmillan, 1992), 39–66.
Smith, Angela K., *The Second Battlefield: Women, Modernism and the First World War* (Manchester: Manchester University Press, 2000).
Sontag, Susan, *On Photography* (London: Penguin, 1979).
Stallworthy, Jon, *Wilfred Owen* (London: Pimlico, 2013).
Staudt, Kathleen Henderson, *At the Turn of a Civilization: David Jones and Modern Poetics* (Ann Arbor: University of Michigan Press, 1994).
Stein, Kevin, 'Vietnam and the "Voice Within": Public and Private History in Yusef Komunyakaa's *Dien Cai Dau*', *Massachusetts Review*, 36.4 (1995–6), 541–61.
Stevenson, Randall, *Literature and the Great War 1914–1918* (Oxford: Oxford University Press, 2013).
Tate, Trudi, *Modernism, History and the First World War* (Manchester: Manchester University Press, 1998).
Vandiver, Elizabeth, *Stand in the Trench, Achilles: Classical Receptions in British Poetry of the Great War* (Oxford: Oxford University Press, 2010).
Winter, Denis, *Death's Men: Soldiers of the Great War* (London: Penguin, 1979).
Winter, Jay, *Sites of Memory, Sites of Mourning: The Great War in European Cultural History* (Cambridge: Cambridge University Press, 1995).

Online Sources

Bleached Bone and Living Wood, Radio 4, 10 November 2011. Programme available at www.bbc.co.uk/programmes/b016x2jy. Accessed 26 July 2017.
First World War Poetry Digital Archive, University of Oxford, http://ww1lit.nsms.ox.ac.uk/ww1lit/. Accessed 26 July 2017.
Great War Forum, http://1914-1918.invisionzone.com/forums. Accessed 26 July 2017.
Rupert Brooke Society, www.rupertbrooke.com. Accessed 26 July 2017.
Ted Hughes at the Adelaide Festival Writers' Week, March 1976, http://ann.skea.com/Adelaide.htm. Accessed 26 July 2017.
War Poetry (Tim Kendall's blog), http://war-poets.blogspot.co.uk. Accessed 26 July 2017.
The Wilfred Owen Association, www.wilfredowen.org.uk. Accessed 26 July 2017.

Index

Aldington, Richard
  'Apathy', 144
  'An earth goddess: after the advance 1917', 99n79
anthologies
  and canon formation, 12
  co-option of poets into *lieu de mémoire*, 14–15
  More Songs by the Fighting Men (Kyle), 138, 140
  The Muse in Arms (Osborn), 138, 140
  The Paths of Glory (Lloyd), 140
  Poetry of the First World War: An Anthology (Kendall), 13n31
  The Progress of Poetry (Parsons), 149, 150–1
  Soldier Poets: Songs of the Fighting Men (Kyle), 138, 139–42
  Up The Line to Death (Gardner), 12–13, 14
Assmann, Aleida, 10, 28–9, 49
Assmann, Jan, 10, 19, 23, 28–9, 49
Auden, W. H., 165

Baird, Neil P., 128
Baldick, Chris, 57, 70
Bannerot, Georges
  'As Ye Have Sown', 140
Barbusse, Henri
  Under Fire, 3, 6–7
Barrett Browning, Elizabeth
  Aurora Leigh, 200
Barry, Peter, 185, 186
Barthes, Roland
  Camera Lucida, 168–9, 173, 176, 185, 186
  the Irremediable, 49–50
  Mourning Diary, 11–12, 49–50
  'The Photographic Message', 177
Batchen, Geoffrey, 174
bathos
  'Comrades: An Episode' (Nichols), 67–9
  as modernist technique, 60–1
  'Pillbox' (Blunden), 65–6, 69, 72
Bell, Michael, 89, 102

Benjamin, Walter, 79, 171
Bennett, Alan
  The History Boys, 115
Bergmann Loizeaux, Elizabeth, 173, 182
Blake, William, 102, 107, 146
Blomfield, Sir Reginald, 114
Blunden, Edmund
  'Memoir' of Owen, 189
  'Pillbox', 65–6, 69, 72
  'Third Ypres', 19
  Undertones of War, 62, 64
  'Vlamertinghe: Passing the Chateau, July 1917', 143–4
Booth, Alysson, 57–8, 70
Booth, James, 178
Borden, Mary
  literary style, 41
  modernism of, 46, 76
  as non-combatant poet, 4
  'Unidentified', 41–2, 77–9, 80, 214
Bradbury, Malcolm, 53
Branagh, Kenneth, 201, 203
Brittain, Vera
  emotional response to war memorials, 118–19
  Leighton's response to Brooke's sonnets, 34–5
  Testament of Youth, 34
  on the Thiepval Memorial, 118
  'To My Brother', 48
  'Violets' (Leighton), 35–6
Britten, Benjamin, 189
Brooke, Rupert
  classical tradition and, 28–9, 31
  cultural determination of the sonnets, 28–9
  'The Dead', 27, 36, 119, 157
  death as peace, 27
  epic poetic tradition and, 25, 29
  eulogy for, 29–30
  final letter writing of, 25–6
  'Fragment', 26
  images of bodies, 27
  Leighton's criticism of, 34–5

227

Brooke, Rupert (*cont.*)
  as *lieu de mémoire*, 29
  'Peace', 26–7
  Rosenberg's criticism of, 37
  'The Soldier', 27, 29, 140, 214
  sonnets of, 24, 25, 119–20
  Sorley's criticism of, 33–4
  as tradition bearer of cultural memory, 28
  values in the sonnets, 26–8
  Virginia Woolf on, 30–1
Burt, Stephen, 175

Capelle, Philip, 201
Carey, John, 165
Carhart, Tom, 128, 129
Carroll, Lewis, 85
Churchill, Winston, 28, 29–30
Civil War, USA
  'As Toilsome I Wander'd Virginia's Woods' (Whitman), 1–2, 4–5, 12
  'For the Union Dead' (Lowell), 123–4, 134
Clark, T. J., 134
classical tradition
  Charles Sorley and, 31, 32, 33
  within elegiac poetry, 25
  heroic values of, 20
  influence on the First World War poets, 5, 24–5
  proving of self through battle, 25, 26–7
  Rupert Brooke and, 28–9, 31
collective memory
  concept of, 9–10, 12, 23
  formation of, 21
  resuscitation of the dead, 22–3
communicative memory, 10, 197
Compagnon, Antoine, 14
Conrad, Joseph, 54
corpses
  as abject, 136
  absence from the elegiac poetry, 139–42
  'Dead Man's Dump' (Rosenberg), 20fn.1, 37–41, 83, 99–102, 145–8, 154, 161–2, 165
  'Dead Men' (Douglas), 157–8, 160–2
  'The Dead Soldiers' (Plowman), 8–9
  depictions of as expressions of anger, 137–8
  as ever present, 53–5
  lack of ritual for, 142
  'The Night Patrol' (West), 6–8, 58–9, 60
  problems of representation, 144–5
  and the rejection of the elegiac tradition, 142–4
  self-elegy form for, 140–2
  and traumatic remembrance, 144–5
  tropes of nature and, 139–40, 159
Crossley-Holland, Kevin, 165

cultural memory
  and communicative memory, 10
  defined, 10
  role of First World War poetry, 12, 13
  through writing, 11–12
  tradition bearers, 28
  Wilfred Owen as, 49, 188–90

danse macabre genre, 73–4
Danto, Arthur C., 129
Das, Santanu, 4, 42–3, 61, 63, 79–80, 101–2, 145
Day Lewis, Cecil, 189
Dilworth, Thomas, 92–3
displacement, aesthetic of, 63–4
Donoghue, Denis, 88
Douglas, Keith
  'Canoe', 153–4
  contrasted with Owen, 165
  the corpse in his poetry, 149–50, 165
  'Dead Men', 157–8, 160–2, 166
  'Desert Flowers', 150, 162–5
  Homeric allusion, 160–1, 162
  'How to Kill', 152
  influence of Rosenberg on, 149–50, 154, 160–5, 167
  influence of *The Progress of Poetry* (Parsons), 149, 150–1
  'John Anderson', 155
  'Landscape with Figures I', 166
  letter to J. C. Hall, 153, 155
  letter to Margaret Stanley-Wrench, 162–3
  'Mersa', 157
  modification of the tradition of war poetry, 150, 152–3, 161–2
  'The Offensive II', 156–7
  Owenesque elements, 154
  'Poets in this War', 152
  self-elegiac poetry, 153–4, 155–6
  'Simplify me when I'm dead', 155–6
  sketches, 158–9
  '*Vergissmeinnicht*', 152, 163, 166–7
Dowson, Jane, 57
Dunn, Douglas
  'Portrait Photograph, 1915', 181–3, 184

Egremont, Max, 30
Ehrhart, W. D.
  'The Invasion of Grenada', 127–8
ekphrasis
  attribution of speech to the subject, 182–3
  concept of, 169
  as deictic mode, 173
  and epigrammatic poetry, 179
  in 'MCMXIV' (Larkin), 175, 177
  and photographs, 169–70, 185–6

Index

post-war boom in, 184–5
and prosopopoeia, 181, 184
elegy
  anti-elegiac poetry, 33, 193–4
  classical tradition within, 25
  influence on the First World War poets, 5, 8–9, 24
  Owen's poetry as anti-elegiac, 193–4
  Owen's poetry as meta-elegy, 193–7
  rebirth through nature, tropes of, 9, 25, 44, 47, 138–9, 159
  redemptive attitude to death, 29
  sacrificial themes of death, 81–3
  in wartime anthologies, 139–42
Eliot, T. S.
  mythical method, 88, 89
  The Waste Land, 54, 56, 88, 89
epic poetry
  and the classical tradition, 24–5, 29
  heroic values of, 20
  martial epics, 25
  use by Brooke, 25, 29
Erll, Astrid, 28–9
existential anxieties
  depictions of dying, 36–7
  the Irremediable (Barthes), 49–50
  life/death distinctions, 54–5
  over future death, 26
  role of remembrance, 49
Eysteinsson, Astradur, 55

Farjeon, Eleanor
  'Easter Monday', 47–8
Farrer, Reginald, 213–14
First World War prose
  the corpse in, 136
  realism of, 70
Fussell, Paul, 82, 86, 87, 88

Gardner, Brian, 12–13, 14
Garstin, E. J. L.
  'Lines written between 1 and 2.30 a.m. in a German dug-out', 141–2
gas attacks, 207–8
Gibson, Wilfrid
  'Between the Lines', 61–3, 64–5, 73
  as non-combatant poet, 4
  non-combatant status of, 25
Gilbert, Sandra M., 81, 92
Goldensohn, Lorrie, 137, 152, 165, 205, 209
Graham, Desmond, 15, 204
Graves, Robert
  'A Dead Boche', 137
  'To his Dead Body' (Sassoon), 22

grief
  consolation for the living, 196
  and the dead, 45
  role of poetry and, 12, 21, 48, 52, 82
  suffering and, 11
  war memorials and expressions of, 12, 114–16, 119, 122
Griffin, Jasper, 159
Gurney, Ivor
  'Butchers and Tombs', 135
  exclusion from Gardner's anthology, 13
  'Farewell', 22, 77
  use of juxtaposition, 76–7
  modernism of, 75–6
  'On Somme', 76
  'Swift and Slow', 76–7
  'To His Love', 50–2, 144–5

Halbwachs, Maurice, 9–10, 28, 42
Hamilton, Ian, 165
haptic, 63
Hardy, Thomas
  'Drummer Hodge', 159
  'His Immortality', 156
Hass, Kristin Ann, 134
Heaney, Seamus
  on 'Dulce et Decorum Est' (Owen), 205, 207
  'In Memoriam Francis Ledwidge', 124–6, 134–5
Hedley, Jane, 182, 184
Home Front
  knowledge of realities of war, 34
  memories of the Front in the domestic sphere, 74
  representations of the war to, 21
Homer
  Douglas's Homeric allusions, 160–1, 162
  Homeric antecedents in Rosenberg, 41, 146–9
  treatment of corpses in, 159–60
Horace, 211
Hughes, Ted
  on Owen and Douglas, 165
  'Six Young Men', 170–5, 179, 182, 183, 184
Hussey, Dyneley
  'The Dead', 139–40
  'Ode to a Young Man Who Died of Wounds in Flanders, January 1915', 138
Hynes, Samuel, 115

Jones, David
  The Anathemata, 90
  consolatory mythology, 98
  female mythical figures, 96, 97
  In Parenthesis, 83, 84–7, 89, 91–8, 214–15
  Le Morte Darthur (Malory) references, 85, 87, 93
  mother earth mythology, 93–4

Jones, David (cont.)
    mythopoeia in the work of, 83–8, 89, 90–3, 98, 108–9
    Queen of the Woods mythology, 94, 95–7
    The Song of Roland references, 92–3
    sweet sister death mythology, 94, 95, 96, 97
    Y Gododdin references, 87, 88, 90–2
Joyce, James
    mythical method, 90
    Ulysses, 88–9

Karlin, Daniel, 116
katabasis, 45
Kazantzis, Judith, 82
Keats, John
    grave of, 195
    Keatsian vocabulary, 43
    'Ode on a Grecian Urn', 183
    Shelley's elegy for 'Adonais', 9, 44, 138–9
Kendall, Tim
    criticism of 'Dulce et Decorum Est' (Owen), 204, 207
    criticism of *Up the Line to Death* (Gardner), 13
    on Douglas, 149, 165
    on Gurney, 51, 77
    on Mew, 119, 121
    Poetry of the First World War: An Anthology, 13n31
    self-elegy, 140
    trench songs, 15
Kipling, Rudyard
    'Gethsemane', 82
    'The Hyænas', 159, 160
    'London Stone', 115–16
    'My Boy Jack', 116
    role in consoling rituals, 116, 118–19
Komunyakaa, Yusef
    'Facing It', 128, 130–4
Kristeva, Julia, 136, 142, 145
Kyle, Galloway, 138, 139–42

La Maison Forestière Wilfred Owen (Patterson)
    commission of, 188
    description of, 187–8, 190–1
    'Dulce et Decorum Est', 204, 208, 211–12
    as meta-memorial, 191–3, 195
    poems and fragments selections, 188, 197–9, 201–3
    representations of Owen in, 190
    voice of Owen in, 199, 201–3
Larkin, Philip
    'Lines on a Young Lady's Photograph Album', 176
    'MCMXIV', 175–6, 177–80, 183
Lawrence, D. H.
    Lady Chatterley's Lover, 53
    Sons and Lovers, 78

Leed, Eric, 54–5, 60, 69, 77, 79
Leighton, Roland
    pre-war ideals, 34
    and Rupert Brooke, 34–5
    'Violets', 35–6
Levenson, Michael, 55–6
lieu de mémoire
    Brooke as, 29
    First World War poetry as, 13–15
    term defined, 13
    writing as, 13–14
Lin, Maya, 129
Lloyd, Bertram, 140
Lowell, Robert
    'For the Union Dead', 123–4, 134
Lukács, Georg, 79

Maccoby, Deborah, 106
Mackintosh, Ewart Alan
    'In Memoriam Private D. Sutherland', 5
Malory, Thomas
    Le Morte Darthur, 85, 87, 93
Marsh, Edward, 24, 28, 30
Maxwell, Glynn
    'My Grandfather at the Pool', 184–5
McCrae, John
    'In Flanders Fields', 22, 180–1
Mew, Charlotte
    'The Cenotaph', 119–22, 134
modernism
    bathos in, 60–1
    depictions of dying, 36–7
    examinations of war memorials, 122–3
    expressions of existential darkness, 54–5
    of First World War poetry, 55, 56–7, 58, 70, 75–6, 79–80
    frailty of life/void beneath, 70
    language and representation of reality, 55–6
    metaphors for, 53
    realism of, 55
    realist/modernist split, 75–6
    revisionism within, 57–8
modernism*s*, 57
Monro, Harold
    'Carrion', 47
    as non-combatant poet, 4
    non-combatant status of, 25
    Poetry Bookshop, 46
Moorcroft Wilson, Jean, 100–1
Moore, Marianne
    'The Jerboa', 163
Motion, Andrew, 178, 189–90
myth
    consolatory mythology, 81
    consolatory mythology (Jones), 98
    of masculine sacrifice (Brooke), 29–31, 34–5, 37

mother earth, 93
mythical method, 88–9
  in *In Parenthesis* (Jones), 83–8, 89, 98
  sacrificial themes of death, 81–3
mythical method
  Eliot, T. S., 88, 89
  Joyce, James, 90
mythopoeia
  concept of, 89–90
  consolatory mythology (Jones), 98
  'Daughters of War' (Rosenberg), 102, 104–9, 154
  in David Jones's work, 83–8, 89, 90–3, 98, 108–9
  Earth personification (Rosenberg), 99–100, 101–2
  female mythical figures (Jones), 96, 97
  in Isaac Rosenberg's work, 83–4, 108–9
  the moon (Jones), 94–5
  mother earth (Jones), 93–4
  of William Blake, 102, 107, 146
  Queen of the Woods mythology (Jones), 95–7
  sweet sister death mythology (Jones), 95, 96, 97
  terrible goddess figures (Rosenberg), 103–8

names/naming
  in 'Farewell' (Gurney), 77
  inscriptions on the Menin Gate, Ypres, 114, 117
  as representative of individual lives, 115, 117
  Thiepval Memorial, 118
  on the Vietnam Veterans Memorial, 127, 129–30
Newbolt, Henry
  'Vitaï Lampada', 177, 180–1
Nicholls, Peter, 57
Nichols, Robert
  'Battery moving up to a New Position from Rest Camp: Dawn', 82
  'Comrades: An Episode', 67–9
non-combatants' poetry
  imaginative understanding of, 25
  memorialisation in the works of, 48–9
  temporal distance of, 47
Nora, Pierre, 13–14
Norris, Margot, 75

Osborn, E. B., 138, 140
Osborne, David Cox McEwen
  'Private Claye', 140, 141
Owen, Harold, 189
Owen, Wilfred, *see also La Maison Forestière*
  Wilfred Owen (Patterson)
  'Anthem for Doomed Youth', 142, 194, 197, 201
  as anti-elegiac, 193–4
  'Asleep', 144, 194–5
  'A Terre', 44–5, 139, 142–3, 166, 201
  'But I was looking at the permanent stars', 201–2
  'The Calls', 203

  at Craiglockhart, 208–10
  as cultural memory, 49, 188–90
  depictions of death, 18
  depictions of dying, 43–4, 205–7
  'Dulce et Decorum Est', 187, 193f7.3, 204–12
  'Exposure', 154, 193f7.3
  'Futility', 194
  gas attacks and, 207–8, 210–11
  'Greater Love', 46
  hopes for a career as a pig-farmer, 196
  'I know the music', 47, 201–2
  I. M. Parsons on, 151
  importance of the poetic voice, 200
  influence on Keith Douglas, 154
  'Insensibility', 142
  Keith Douglas contrasted with, 165
  'The Last Laugh', 202–3
  'Mental Cases', 18, 19, 23, 52, 144, 194, 198, 207
  normative status of, 14–15
  'On My Songs', 200
  poetry of as meta-elegy, 193–7, 211
  Preface (draft), 193–4, 197, 198–9
  Sassoon's introduction to *Poems*, 189
  socio-cultural status, 43
  'Spring Offensive', 43–4, 154, 197
  'Strange Meeting', 45–6
  use of Shelleyan tropes, 44, 142–3
  as the voice of the soldiers, 200–1, 203–4
  'With an Identity Disc', 195–6

Parsons, I. M. (Ian), 102, 149, 150–1
Patterson, Simon, 187–8, 190–3, 204, 211–12
photographs, *see also* ekphrasis
  Camera Lucida (Barthes), 168–9, 173, 176, 185, 186
  function within poetry, 183–4
  'Lines on a Young Lady's Photograph Album' (Larkin), 176
  'MCMXIV' (Larkin), 175, 176, 177–80, 183
  and mortality, 168–9, 170
  'The Photographic Message' (Barthes), 177
  'Portrait Photograph, 1915' (Dunn), 181–3
  punctum in, 169, 170, 174–6, 181–2, 183, 186
  'Six Young Men' (Hughes), 170–5, 179, 182, 183
  viewer's interpretations of, 168
Pickthall, Marjorie
  'Marching Men', 82
Plowman, Max
  'The Dead Soldiers', 8–9
  use of Shelleyan tropes, 9, 141
  use of the elegiac tradition, 8–9
  'When It's Over', 141
Plumer, Field Marshal Herbert, 114, 117, 119, 120
poppies
  in 'Break of Day in the Trenches' (Rosenberg), 106, 148–9

poppies (cont.)
  and desert flowers in Douglas, 163
  in 'Vlamertinghe: Passing the Chateau, July 1917' (Blunden), 143–4
Postgate Cole, Margaret
  'Afterwards', 48–9
propaganda, 20
prosopopoeia
  anticipatory, 44–5
  'As Ye Have Sown' (Bannerot), 140
  'A Terre' (Owen), 44–5, 139, 142–3, 166, 201
  and ekphrasis, 181, 184
  'In Flanders Fields' (McCrae), 180–1
  poetic inscriptions on memorials, 111
  'Portrait Photograph, 1915' (Dunn), 180–3
  'Strange Meeting' (Owen), 45–6
Prost, Antoine, 11
Proust, Marcel, 14

Ramazani, Jahan, 24, 33, 193–4, 204
Rawlinson, Mark, 14–15, 189
Rickword, Edgell
  'Trench Poets', 20
Ringnalda, Donald, 128–9, 130
Roberts, Beth Ellen, 102–4
Robichaud, Paul, 87–8
Rosenberg, Isaac
  'Break of Day in the Trenches', 105, 106, 148–9, 154
  and the corpsescape, 149
  criticism of Brooke, 37
  crucifixion allusions, 100–1
  'Daughters of War', 102, 104–9, 154
  'Dead Man's Dump', 20fn.1, 37–40, 83, 99–102, 145–8, 154, 161–2, 165
  disillusionment with Judeo-Christian God, 102
  Earth mythopoeia, 99–100, 101–2
  'The Female God', 103–4
  'God', 102
  Homeric antecedents, 40–1, 146–9
  I. M. Parsons on, 151
  influence on Keith Douglas, 149–50, 154, 160–5, 167
  mythopoeia in the work of, 83–4, 108–9
  outsider status of, 41
  terrible goddess figures, 103–8
  use of Jewish folklore, 102–4
  use of Shelleyan tropes, 148–9

Sagar, Keith, 173
Sassoon, Siegfried
  'Counter-Attack', 137–8
  at Craiglockhart, 208–9
  'The Death-Bed', 71–3
  'Died of Wounds', 71
  'The Effect', 73–4
  emotional response to war memorials, 118–19, 127
  'To his Dead Body', 22
  introduction to Owen's *Poems*, 189
  'The Last Meeting', 5
  'On Passing the New Menin Gate', 116–18
  'The Redeemer', 82
  'Repression of War Experience', 74–5
  sense of the absurd, 73–4
  Sherston's Progress, 208
Scannell, Vernon, 152
Scott, Grant F., 129–30
the senses
  denial of, 63–5
  disorientation of, 84
  the haptic, 63
  phenomenological geography, 63
Shelley, Percy Bysshe
  'Adonais', 9, 44, 138–9
  Shelleyan tropes in Owen, 44, 142–3
  Shelleyan tropes in Plowman, 9, 141
  Shelleyan tropes in Rosenberg, 148–9
  Shelleyan tropes in Wilkinson, 140–1
socio-cultural memories
  and representations of death, 42–3
  term, 9
The Song of Roland, 92–3
Sontag, Susan, 168, 176
Sorley, Charles
  'All the hills and vales along', 32
  classical tradition, 31, 32, 33
  criticism of Brooke, 33–4
  'When you see millions of the mouthless dead', 31–2, 33–4, 36, 37, 44
Spenser, Edmund, 87
Spring, R. Howard
  'Hic Jacet', 138
Stallworthy, Jon, 149, 198

Tate, Trudi, 136
Thomas, Edward
  'Adlestrop', 178

Vandiver, Elizabeth, 24–5, 27, 32, 40, 45, 147, 148–9
Vietnam Veterans Memorial
  design of, 127, 128–30, 134
  'Facing It' (Komunyakaa), 128, 130–4
  inscriptions of names, 127, 129–30
  'The Invasion of Grenada' (Ehrhart), 127–8

war memorials, *see also* names/naming; Vietnam Veterans Memorial
  ambivalent responses to, 119–22, 130–4

Index

Buttermarket War Memorial, Canterbury, 110–12
Cenotaph, London, 115–16, 119–22, 134
common features of, 11
as communal response, 110
La Maison Forestière Wilfred Owen (Patterson) as meta-memorial, 191–3, 195
memorial tablet, Canterbury Cathedral, 111–13
modernist examinations of, 122–3
as national recognition of personal loss, 113–14, 115–16
New Menin Gate, Ypres, 113–14, 116–18
as official acts of closure, 114–15, 116–19, 127–8
poetic inscriptions, 110–13
Portstewart in Northern Ireland, 124–6, 134–5
prosopopoeia, 111
Shaw monument, Boston, 123–4, 134
Thiepval Memorial, 118
Vera Brittain's response to, 118
war memorial, Sorigny, 12
Wedderburn Cannan, May
'Lamplight', 22
Welland, Denis, 189
West, Arthur Graeme
attack on sentimental poetry, 59–60
Diary of a Dead Officer, 5–6, 59
'The Night Patrol', 5, 6–8, 9, 58–9, 60
Whitman, Walt
'As Toilsome I Wander'd Virginia's Woods', 1–2, 4–5, 8, 12, 110
'Drum Taps', 2–3
influence on the First World War poets, 2–3
Wilkinson, E. F.
'To "My People," before the "Great Offensive"', 140–1, 153
use of Shelleyan tropes, 140–1
Winter, Jay, 113–14
Woolf, Virginia, 23, 30–1
Wordsworth, William, 38, 44, 46, 49, 69, 146

Y Gododdin, 87, 88, 90–2

Lightning Source UK Ltd.
Milton Keynes UK
UKHW021010190819
348164UK00007B/140/P